Conserving the Oceans

Conserving the Oceans

The Politics of Large Marine Protected Areas

JUSTIN ALGER

OXFORD
UNIVERSITY PRESS

OXFORD
UNIVERSITY PRESS

Oxford University Press is a department of the University of Oxford. It furthers the University's objective of excellence in research, scholarship, and education by publishing worldwide. Oxford is a registered trade mark of Oxford University Press in the UK and certain other countries.

Published in the United States of America by Oxford University Press
198 Madison Avenue, New York, NY 10016, United States of America.

Library of Congress Cataloging-in-Publication Data
Names: Alger, Justin, author.
Title: Conserving the oceans : the politics of large marine protected areas / Justin Alger.
Description: New York, NY : Oxford University Press, 2021. |
Includes bibliographical references and index.
Identifiers: LCCN 2020041602 (print) | LCCN 2020041603 (ebook) |
ISBN 9780197540534 (hardback) | ISBN 9780197540558 (epub)
Subjects: LCSH: Marine parks and reserves—Management—Case studies. |
Marine parks and reserves—Government policy—Case studies. |
Marine resources conservation—Government policy—Case studies. |
Marine resources conservation—Political aspects. | Political ecology.
Classification: LCC QH91.75.A1 A44 2021 (print) | LCC QH91.75.A1 (ebook) |
DDC 333.91/6416—dc23
LC record available at https://lccn.loc.gov/2020041602
LC ebook record available at https://lccn.loc.gov/2020041603

DOI: 10.1093/oso/9780197540534.001.0001

1 3 5 7 9 8 6 4 2

Printed by Integrated Books International, United States of America

Contents

Figures

Figures

Tables

Acknowledgments

Thinking back, this book started while learning to scuba dive on the Great Barrier Reef in 2010. A wrenching sea sickness and anxiety about sucking air through a small tube for survival quickly turned to fascination as I descended on my first dive and witnessed the plentiful biodiversity around me. Many divers, I'm sure, can relate to this and likely hold similarly vivid memories. Having grown up and spent most of my life in the Toronto area, I will always in some way be an ocean tourist. But this experience, and others that followed, instilled in me a sense of wonder of the world's oceans that stuck. That wonder inevitably also comes with a sense of sadness. In 2016, while conducting research for this book, I revisited the Great Barrier Reef, diving those same sites again. This time, the marine life was noticeably thinner, and many of the corals were bleached white from that year's global coral bleaching event. As an environmental politics scholar, I was well read enough on the scientific studies of ocean decline, but to see it so starkly firsthand was off-putting in a way that I didn't anticipate.

This book is an effort to ask big questions about the current state of the oceans and what we are doing to protect them. I have had the support of many wonderful and talented people in this pursuit, to whom I owe thanks. Foremost, I am grateful to Peter Dauvergne—mentor, colleague, and friend—for his boundless support over the years. I have grown immeasurably as a scholar, writer, and teacher under his tutelage. Working with Peter has been the joy of my professional life, and I look forward to the co-authorship and pints still to come. I have also been lucky to have had a number of supporters at the University of British Columbia and the University of Toronto. A special thanks to both Jane Lister and Rebecca Monnerat, who have been among my biggest supporters and to whom I owe a debt of gratitude. I am also grateful to Steven Bernstein, Max Cameron, Simon Donner, Kate Neville, Taylor Owen, Rashid Sumaila, and Yves Tiberghien. I have had the pleasure of working with each one of these scholars in various capacities and have learnt a great deal from all of them.

The research for this book also benefitted immensely from a long list of incredibly welcoming and supportive people throughout my fieldwork in

Australia, Palau, and the US. It was inspiring to talk to conservationists who have devoted their lives to protecting the oceans about the fruits of their labor and their drive to do more. I also learned a great deal from those who rely on the oceans for their livelihoods, as a constant reminder that every conservation decision impacts the lives of people who are just trying to get by. And a special thank you to the people who took particular interest in my work and enabled me to succeed, namely: Tova Harel, Tarita Holm, Koebel Sakuma (including for the Muay Thai lessons), and Matt Rand.

Grants from the Social Sciences and Humanities Research Council of Canada and the Killam Trusts provided essential support for this research. I am indebted to Angela Chnapko at Oxford University Press for her support for this book. I also want to extend thanks to the anonymous reviewers who devoted their time and energy to providing such valuable feedback on this manuscript. Your insightful suggestions enhanced this book greatly, and I feel fortunate to have had your guidance.

I am also lucky to have had a wonderful support system along the way. A number of friends have been my family-away-from-home, always in my corner and providing good, old-fashioned escapism when needed. A notable shout-out to Dave Moscrop, for all of the work we've accomplished and for not missing a beat of this process. Big thanks to Jim Aitkin, Spencer McKay, Ollie McPartlin, Rebecca Monnerat, Chris Patterson, Y-Dang Troeung, and Amanda Watson for all of their support over the years. Thank you to my mother, Sandra, sister, Kristin, and stepparents, Cathy and Steve, for being there every step of the way. To Brooke, your love and support have always kept things in perspective and for that I am grateful.

My greatest debt is to my father, Brian, who has empathized with every challenge and celebrated every victory—no matter how small—along the way. This book is the culmination of a process that began with a decision made during a conversation that we had on a walk back in 2005. This is for you.

1

A New Era of Ocean Conservation

The world has turned a corner on ocean conservation. We no longer accept that the oceans are boundless—that human activity could never substantially impact such a vast space. We now know that quite the opposite is true. Human activity is at once warming and acidifying the oceans, depleting them of fish, and flooding them with plastics. But after decades of neglect as these trends accelerated, politicians, conservationists, and businesses alike are turning their attention to better protecting oceans, the life blood of the planet. Their efforts have culminated in nothing less than a paradigm shift in global marine conservation. This book documents that shift, explaining the politics of how governments were able to protect millions of square kilometers of previously unprotected ocean space.

The pace and scale of global marine conservation efforts changed dramatically in 2006. This shift began when the US designated the Papahānaumokuākea Marine National Monument—a 362,000 km^2 marine reserve that became the largest marine protected area (MPA) in the world. Within a decade, more than a dozen other marine reserves surpassed it in size, marking a new trend in how states protect marine biodiversity. This trend was toward large, pelagic (open ocean), and, when feasible, no-take MPAs. "Large" in this context means areas exceeding 200,000 km^2, nearly the size of the entire UK land mass. This new practice of designating large MPAs has led to an unprecedented rate of marine protection, with governments protecting over 15 million km^2 in the decade following Papahānaumokuākea, a total exceeding the entire area of Canada or the US. Many of these areas are fully protected marine reserves that prohibit all extractive activity from oil and gas drilling to commercial fishing. Others are mixed-use, typically permitting various types of commercial fishing that regulations often restrict to specified zones. This new practice is, for better or worse, reshaping the way that states protect marine biodiversity.

This trend toward large MPAs is a response to the growing scientific awareness that the oceans are declining at an alarming rate (Wilhelm et al. 2014). Global market forces have been having a devastating impact on the world's

Conserving the Oceans. Justin Alger, Oxford University Press (2021). © Oxford University Press.
DOI: 10.1093/oso/9780197540534.003.0001

oceans (Jacques 2006; Lobo and Jacques 2017; Jacques and Lobo 2018), with scientists dubbing our rapidly growing reliance on ocean resources the "blue acceleration" (Jouffray et al. 2020). Scientific research into ocean health ramped up in the early 2000s, showing that conditions were worse than previously thought (Roessig et al. 2004; Pauly, Watson, and Alder 2005). Over three-quarters of coral reef ecosystems worldwide are currently threatened, meaning that they are actively in decline (Burke et al. 2011). The main culprits are climate change, terrestrial run-off, and overfishing. These three environmental threats have each had a devastating impact on the health of our oceans.

In 2016, the oceans experienced the most prolonged and widespread coral bleaching event in recorded history. The 2016 bleaching was only the third ever global bleaching event, with the first in 1998 (an El Niño year) and the second in 2010. These climate change–induced events will continue to overwhelm reef ecosystems at an escalated rate, leading many to inevitable functional collapse (Donner et al. 2005; Hoegh-Guldberg et al. 2007). At the same time, terrestrial run-off from agriculture and mining—the most overlooked of these three environmental threats—is eroding water quality in coastal reef ecosystems and is a significant source of ecosystem stress in some of the world's most iconic marine habitats, such as Australia's Great Barrier Reef (Furnas 2003; Fabricius 2005).

For decades, improvements in commercial fishing technology and practice have been masking the ongoing global collapse of fish stocks (Pauly et al. 2002; Barkin and DeSombre 2013). As the global commercial fishing industry continues to deplete fish stocks at an alarming rate, advancements in the size and range of fishing vessels have allowed large outfits to remain profitable. Fisheries management solutions to overfishing have had some limited success (Webster 2009, 2015), but on a global scale have been undermined at virtually every turn. Reporting on catch is notoriously woeful, with some countries underreporting their catch by as much as 500% (Pauly and Zeller 2016). In addition to underreporting, some commercial fishers find other creative ways of avoiding regulation, such as flying "flags of convenience," further undermining fisheries management efforts (DeSombre 2005). A projected 68% of global fish stocks are below the critical biomass threshold at which they can sustain themselves, with most projected to experience further depletion due to overfishing (Mullon, Fréon, and Cury 2005; Costello et al. 2016; Worm 2016).

In 2020 there were nearly 17,000 MPAs in the world. Designating protected areas is one of the primary policy tools that states use to protect marine ecosystems, but they have had mixed success at best in protecting marine life. The median MPA is only about 5 km^2, much smaller than what most scientists agree is necessary to be effective (Edgar et al. 2014). Governments also tend to do a poor job of managing them, and they are often not much more than "paper parks" that contribute little to conservation (Kareiva 2006; West and Brockington 2006). Effective management can pose a challenge in many places in the global South, home to the majority of the most ecologically vulnerable reef ecosystems, where capacity and implementation challenges often seem inescapable (Kareiva 2006; Burke et al. 2011). But many issues transcend North and South, including key management mishaps such as poorly adapted terrestrial strategies, conservation programs that do not fit local realities, and cumbersome top-down management structures (Gaymer et al. 2014; de Morais, Schlüter, and Verweij 2015). Perhaps the most significant challenge is that states are often quick to establish MPAs, but fail to commit to active enforcement, community involvement, and no-take zoning (Rife et al. 2013). Wealthier states tend to establish more MPAs, but do not invest more resources into managing them, underscoring the weak commitments of governments in protecting marine ecosystems (Fox et al. 2012). In short, global marine conservation efforts have fallen far short of being able to adequately combat the trifecta of climate change, terrestrial run-off, and overfishing.

Large MPAs are distinct from typical MPAs in their size, of course, but also in that they protect pelagic ecosystems—the least protected ecosystem on the planet before the advent of large MPAs (Game et al. 2009). These MPAs emerged in the mid-2000s as one method for scaling up global marine conservation efforts, and government reliance on them to protect marine ecosystems has multiplied since, as depicted in Figure 1.1. But despite their promise, they are by no means a panacea for marine conservation. They are in fact quite divisive, with many scholars and environmental groups opposed to or skeptical of them. One criticism is that governments tend to establish large MPAs in areas that are too remote from commercial activity, therefore failing to address the causes of ocean decline (Toonen et al. 2013; Jones and De Santo 2016). Another is that large MPAs are incompatible with sustainable development and prioritize closures over fisheries management practices or tackling climate change. These critics argue that there is a normative preference for conservation over resource management among large

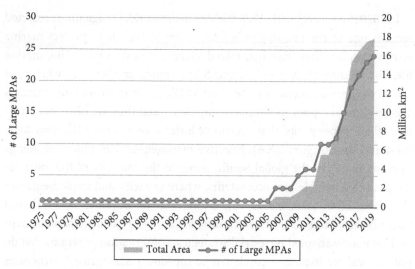

Figure 1.1 The Growth in Large MPAs

MPA advocates that prevents progress toward sustainable global fisheries (Agardy, Di Sciara, and Christie 2011; Caveen et al. 2013; Leenhardt et al. 2013). Others caution that large MPAs are a form of "fortress conservation" in which governments establish protected areas that erode the rights of local and indigenous communities (De Santo, Jones, and Miller 2011). These criticisms all have merit, but they have not deterred states from creating new large MPAs.

One shortcoming of many of these criticisms is that they tend to homogenize large MPAs, sometimes neglecting the reality that these areas can vary considerably (Gruby et al. 2017). Governments have located many large MPAs in remote areas, notably the UK and US around their territories in the Pacific Ocean. But other states do not, with large MPAs in some cases comprising nearly the entirety of a nation's exclusive economic zone (EEZ), or located in areas with a moderate amount of commercial activity. How states manage these large MPAs similarly varies, with many fully no-take, and others mixed-use and permitting a range of economic activity in various zones. And while certain large MPAs have undoubtedly eroded the rights of local and indigenous communities, in other instances these groups have been among the primary advocates for a new large MPA, often playing a prominent role in their design. Governments need to make a variety of decisions about where to locate and how to manage a large MPA, and these decisions inevitably lead to many large MPAs taking on distinct characteristics from one another.

This book is devoted to answering two questions about the emergence of large MPAs as a solution to rapid and ongoing ocean decline. First, why have large MPAs emerged as the solution of choice for so many governments? And second, what explains the variance in how those governments manage large MPAs? These questions are ultimately about how states make decisions that balance conservation with the interests of various stakeholder groups, including environmental groups, extractive and non-extractive industries, and local communities. These stakeholder groups influence the decisions that governments make about MPAs, and this book will explore precisely how the interests of these stakeholder groups amalgamate to impact conservation outcomes. It does so through an analysis of the recent trend toward larger and, in some ways, more ambitious MPAs, but there are useful insights here into the political dynamics of smaller MPA processes, and those of their terrestrial counterparts as well.

In the pages to follow, I will argue that we can better understand the politics of marine conservation by paying closer attention to the economics of marine reserves. Commercial interests influence whether or not a government creates a large MPA, where it sets its boundaries, and how it regulates it. While this may sound like a cynical starting point, the narrative to follow is as much a story about the limitations of commercial influence as it is about the ability of business interests to undermine conservation. In some cases, industry can be a positive influence, pushing governments for robust conservation. This book is an effort to explain how commercial interests and conservation have intersected in the oceans, ultimately allowing for the protection of millions of square kilometers of ocean space.

Explaining Largescale Marine Conservation

This book makes two overarching claims about the trend toward large MPAs. The first is that it is the result of a new global norm. A norm, in international relations parlance, refers to a standard of appropriate behavior shared by similar actors. By a large MPA norm, I am referring specifically to the push for MPAs that are bigger than 200,000 km^2, contiguous, pelagic, and, whenever possible, no-take. A large MPA norm refers to a shared acceptance among states and other political actors that MPAs meeting these criteria are an appropriate response to the environmental threats facing the oceans.

A select few environmental nongovernmental organizations (ENGOs) were essential to propagating the large MPA norm, most notably The Pew Charitable Trusts (Pew) and National Geographic Society (National Geographic). These environmental groups have strategically built momentum toward large MPAs by promoting them in one country at a time and targeting specific biodiversity hotspots. Many other major transnational environmental groups do not actively support large MPAs because of the criticisms cited earlier, so just a few have borne the brunt of the global campaigning for this new norm. Pew and National Geographic have been the most important and consistent drivers of new large MPAs globally through a series of domestic advocacy campaigns. These campaigns included efforts to establish partnerships with domestic environmental groups, lobbying governments, producing scientific and socioeconomic reporting on an MPA site, and conducting promotional campaigns to rally public support. Campaigners targeted MPA sites where they thought political resistance would be low, building momentum toward this global norm. Those efforts were successful, with several states now recognizing the value and feasibility of large MPAs as high-profile marine conservation initiatives.

The second claim of this book is that we can explain how states set boundaries for and manage large MPAs by examining the configuration of industry interests in a given marine area. How reliant industry is on a given marine space is critical to whether or not protecting that space is politically feasible. This connection may seem obvious, but the story that will unfold here is more complicated than it appears. Industry often does not get what it wants and, in some cases, industry is supportive of conservation. Every new large MPA involves a bargaining process with stakeholder groups, which may or may not be a formal government-initiated process. During this process, a state ultimately aligns with environmental groups, certain industries, or local communities, depending on how these groups use the marine area in question. Governments of course continue to ostensibly serve the interests of all stakeholders and constituents, but their priorities reflect this alignment above all. These various interest alignments are in effect informal "coalitions," and the kind of coalition that forms is one of the most precise predictors of just how rigorous a government regulates a large MPA.

When I refer to the rigor of MPA regulations, I am above all pointing to the distinction between MPAs that meaningfully limit or prohibit damaging

commercial activity and paper parks that allow for business-as-usual operation on the water. The preexisting stake of industries in a marine area is central to explaining this divide between meaningful MPAs and paper parks.
In instances where extractive activity is high—such as commercial fishing
or oil and gas extraction—governments face much steeper political resistance to conservation. In the cases where non-extractive activity is high—
such as ecotourism—the opposite is true, and industry is often a significant
proponent. Weighing the relative importance of an area to these commercial
interests is key to understanding what motivates government conservation
decisions.

One of the contributions of this book is to better explain the nuances of
industry influence over conservation policy decisions. That corporations are
powerful and influential global actors in environmental politics is not a particularly new insight (Cutler, Haufler, and Porter 1999; Clapp 2006; Newell
2006; Fuchs 2007; Clapp and Fuchs 2009; Dauvergne and Lister 2013). But
this book deconstructs industry influence to explain when and under what
conditions industry stakeholders shape domestic environmental policymaking. Why are industry stakeholders often influential in a conservation
decision even when commercial activity in an area is minimal? And why do
industry stakeholders fail to prevent governments from regulating an area in
other instances, even when they claim it is vital to their interests? Businesses
are privileged political actors because of their economic importance, but
there are limits to their influence (Falkner 2008). This book engages with
those limits.

These two overarching claims are the two pillars of my argument
throughout this book. They are claims about what international relations
scholars call "norm diffusion"—a broad term that refers to how global norms
initially emerge, how they spread to new states, and then what unique characteristics a norm might take on across states. More formally, diffusion involves
the two synchronous processes of "norm adoption" and "norm localization"
(see Figure 1.2).

Norm adoption refers to the spread of a norm to new jurisdictions, typically states, and the process through which those states accept it. It is in effect
about how an original idea emerges, spreads, and takes hold in the world.
Norm localization refers to the distinct characteristics that a new norm takes
on in different places to reflect local customs and practice. In the process of
"accepting" a new norm, a state does not do so wholesale. Relevant actors adjust certain aspects of the norm to make it consistent with local practice while

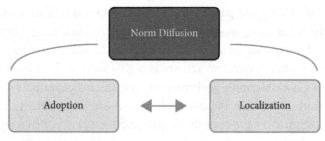

Figure 1.2 Norm Diffusion

adhering to the broader principles of the norm. A state may, for example, establish an MPA bigger than 200,000 km^2 that does not prohibit commercial fishing at all. Analyzing the trend toward large MPAs through a norm diffusion lens allows us to answer a key, somewhat paradoxical question: how is it possible that states have protected tens of millions of square kilometers of ocean space while still being highly responsive to influential commercial stakeholders?

An Economic Explanation of Norm Diffusion

The framework that I develop throughout this book reflects both of these aspects of international norm diffusion. Existing international relations scholarship provides a compelling explanation of how global norms emerge and spread in the international system. My account of the emergence and spread of the large MPA norm—detailed in chapter 2—does not stray much from what scholars have already said about other global norms. It does, however, deviate significantly from conventional explanations of the norm localization part of norm diffusion, which tend to emphasize local cultural practices (Acharya 2004). Instead, I adapt the work of prominent political economists Peter Gourevitch and James Shinn (2005), who use coalitions to explain governance structures in the corporate world. Their research is divorced from any discussion of global norms, but I nevertheless adapt it here to offer a novel approach to norm diffusion that systematically incorporates local political economy dynamics.

The norm diffusion process involves states simultaneously engaging with a new norm both internationally and domestically. Internationally, states and environmental groups in favor of a new norm work to convince other countries to adopt it as well. The target state during this process is asking the question "should we embrace this new norm?" This is not typically a bargaining process but rather works through persuasion and socialization, often over a long period of time (Finnemore and Sikkink 1998; Price 1998). Pressure mounts on hold-outs as more states adopt a given norm. A state "accepting," "embracing," or "adopting" a norm is rarely a finite decision, but rather occurs over time as relevant actors continually update their beliefs about what constitutes appropriate behavior. As a state wrestles with whether or not to embrace a new norm, it is simultaneously asking itself, "how do we make this new norm fit with our established practices?" States negotiate (explicitly or implicitly) with domestic stakeholder groups over how to make the norm work locally. It is this localization process that leads to different domestic coalitions forming and ultimately different environmental outcomes across states.

The chapters to follow present an original norm diffusion framework. My aim in developing this framework is to provide a tool for better understanding the connection between the power and influence of businesses and governments' conservation decisions. I have designed it with answering three questions in mind:

1. How can we better explain and measure industry influence over conservation decisions?
2. How do governments decide which stakeholder group to align with (i.e., environmental groups, extractive industry, non-extractive industry)?
3. How do political and legal institutions (i.e., conservation laws, law-making rules) enable or constrain conservation?

A norm diffusion framework grounded in these questions can explain differences between large MPAs. It can tell us why governments shut out businesses in some instances, yet do virtually nothing to limit them in others. This book looks to answer one of the most critical questions in the discussion about the desirability of large MPAs to combat ocean decline: are governments making meaningful conservation decisions by creating these large MPAs, or are they mere window dressing in a world in which business interests remain paramount?

A New Type of Norm Diffusion Explanation

This economic explanation of norm diffusion is aligned with international relations scholarship on norms emphasizing domestic politics, which emphasizes both ideational and rationalist factors (Checkel 1997; Risse 2016). Much of the norms literature outside of this subset focuses primarily on ideational factors. Ideational international relations scholarship is the world of identity, ideas, customs, and norms, while rationalist scholarship is the world of cost–benefit calculations. The large MPA norm is, by definition, ideational. It is a practice that states have adopted based on the idea that it is an appropriate way to combat ocean decline. But explanations of how states localize that norm do not necessarily need to be ideational as well. This book examines both the rationalist and ideational determinants of norm diffusion, with particular emphasis on advancing the theory of the former. As with previous scholars, I look to bridge the rationalist–constructivist divide (Adler 1997; Lewis 2003; Zürn and Checkel 2005; Nielson, Tierney, and Weaver 2006). States can adopt a new norm (ideational) while still being responsive to the material impacts of that norm domestically (rationalist).

The framework of norm diffusion that I propose in this book does, however, push the boundaries of what scholars would usually consider norm localization, which has so far been specific to the interaction of global norms with local custom and practice. Localization, as scholars currently think of it, is the process by which local actors reshape a global norm so that it is consistent with local "cognitive priors and identities" (Acharya 2004). Culture explains why a new norm is not homogenous across jurisdictions. Scholars have used this explanation of norm localization to explain the diffusion of human rights norms, the spread of the responsibility to protect doctrine throughout Asia, local resistance to small arms limitations, and more (Capie 2008; Prantl and Nakano 2011; Acharya 2013).

This traditional approach to norm localization could certainly apply to a marine conservation context. The characteristics of large MPAs could vary due to differences in local cultural practices across jurisdictions. It is not unreasonable to expect, for example, a Pacific island nation with a longstanding cultural attachment to oceans and subsistence fishing to localize the large MPA norm differently than a wealthy industrialized country with a large commercial fishing fleet. These cultural differences tend to influence the discourse surrounding large MPA campaigns, but it is less clear how well they explain environmental policy decisions.

The case studies to follow suggest a different explanation. They show governments that are highly responsive to commercial interests. In their policy decisions about the location and boundaries of MPAs, and the commercial activities allowed within them, states tend to neglect local custom and practice in favor of economic analysis. How well the large MPA norm fits with local custom and practice can contribute to (or hinder) public support for a large MPA. But the pages to follow show that, for better or worse, custom and practice do not have the same demonstrable impact on government decisions as cold, hard economics. An economic norm diffusion analysis can explain large MPA norm dynamics, including whether a state's large MPAs are mixed-use or no-take, and whether the intention is to enforce them strictly or run them as paper parks.

An economic explanation of norm diffusion is also necessarily asymmetrical. Business interests do the majority of the explanatory work in this framework, to the neglect of accounts that focus on the ability of environmental groups to mobilize on an issue well. Put simply, it is possible that some advocacy campaigns are just more effective than others. These campaigns often do vary in their effectiveness, which could affect government conservation decisions. There is, in fact, a rich body of international relations scholarship that examines the efficacy of various social movements and their approaches (Khagram, Riker, and Sikkink 2002; Bennett 2004; della Porta, Donatella, and Tarrow 2005; Tarrow 2005; Batliwala and Brown 2006; Seidman 2007; Weible 2007; Sabatier and Weible 2007).

The social movement literature covers a range of questions about why some movements succeed in their goals while others falter. One facet considers agenda-setting, explaining how certain issues end up on the agenda of states or other stakeholders (in contrast to all of those that do not) (Keck and Sikkink 1999; Bob 2001; Carpenter 2005; Bob 2007). Another current of thought looks at how nongovernmental organizations (NGOs) are organized and motivated internally, and how that affects their ability to shape policy (Cooley and Ron 2002; Carpenter 2007; Bloodgood 2011; Stroup and Murdie 2012; Bloodgood, Tremblay-Boire, and Prakash 2013). Another looks at how well NGOs garner public support through lobbying, pressuring industry groups, and framing an issue in an appealing way (Wapner 1995; Wapner 2002; Evenden 2004; Khagram 2004). All of these diverse currents of thought provide invaluable insight into the nuances of civil society movements and campaigns. They do not, however, explain large MPA campaigns well.

The main reason the social movement approach falls short is that many large MPA advocacy campaigns have so far been remarkably similar to one another. Either Pew or National Geographic have spearheaded most of them, and they have used the same campaign strategy for each. These campaigns have all been high-profile environmental campaigns. The size of the targeted areas and the wealth of biodiversity that they typically contain attracts a lot of public, industry, and international media attention. These select, few transnational ENGOs have needed to effectively collaborate with local ENGOs to develop a campaign strategy that works for a given constituency. In some instances, Pew or National Geographic have made costly missteps that undermined public opinion about a large MPA and further galvanized industry opposition. But these failures, as I will demonstrate throughout my case studies, had a minimal impact on government policy decisions. Civil society explanations provide insight into why transnational advocacy campaigns succeed on some issues and falter on others, but the similarity of large MPA campaigns to date and the relatively minor impact of campaign missteps warrant a more convincing explanation of variation in large MPA policy decisions.

One final distinction between the explanation I offer here and existing scholarly thinking is in how the large MPA norm emerged and spread. Usually, broad coalitions of NGOs promote a norm and pressure states to adopt it. The main arena for this advocacy is usually multilateral venues, most notably the UN (Finnemore and Sikkink 1998; Price 1998; Keck and Sikkink 1998; Khagram, Riker, and Sikkink 2002). Whether NGOs are successful in garnering support for a new norm depends on their access to these venues, which they usually obtain by offering their expertise to fill gaps in state knowledge (Betsill and Corell 2001; Böhmelt and Betzold 2013; Tallberg et al. 2018). This process accurately characterizes the initial emergence of a wide array of global norms, on issues ranging from restrictions on certain types of weapons to better human rights standards (Price 1998; Risse, Ropp, and Sikkink 1999; Seidman 2007; Acharya 2013). It has become the predominant explanation of how civil society persuades states to adopt new norms.

But this explanation does not explain the emergence of the large MPA norm. Pew and National Geographic have had to go it alone in the global push for large MPAs, for the most part. Many other ENGOs are concerned that large MPAs are too remote to address the sources of ocean decline and that they can undermine sustainable development by denying access to resources. Major transnational ENGOs such as the World Wide Fund for

Nature (WWF), Greenpeace, and The Nature Conservancy (TNC) are therefore often lukewarm at best about large MPAs as a solution to ocean decline (at least in their current form). Pew and National Geographic have also benefited from the existing area coverage targets enshrined in the Convention on Biological Diversity (CBD). These preexisting targets mean they do not need a new UN legal mechanism, and can instead focus their efforts on convincing individual state leaders of the benefits of a large MPA. In contrast to the history of most global norms, the large MPA norm has emerged in a more piecemeal way, never coalescing around discussions for a new multilateral convention.

Methods and Organization

By 2020, there were 24 large MPAs in the world. US President Barack Obama also expanded two US large MPAs in 2014 and 2016, and the Cook Islands expanded its large MPA in 2016, bringing the total number of instances in which a governing body protected more than 200,000 km^2 to 27 at the time of this writing (see Table 1.1). Of these, all but the 1.55 million km^2 multilateral MPA in the Ross Sea in Antarctica are national MPAs. There are no clear cases of failed large MPA campaigns, in part because environmental groups have done well so far to target politically feasible sites (indeed, this is one of the major criticisms of them). There are undoubtedly instances in which an environmental group assessed the possibility of a large MPA internally and decided not to pursue one. These null cases could yield useful insight into how and why governments decline (or would be likely to decline) a large MPA, but data for these cases is too sparse to include them in this research. The Ross Sea MPA is similarly a fascinating case study, but it is primarily about geopolitics, with China and Russia concerned about their influence in the region until eventually relenting in their opposition. The 26 instances

Table 1.1 Large MPA Designations to 2020

Type of Designation	Number	Included in Population
National, New MPA	23	Yes
National, Expansion of Existing MPA	3	Yes
Multilateral, New MPA	1	No

(and counting) of national large MPA designations and expansions form the population of cases for this research.

The framework that I just introduced here warrants qualitative, case-based analysis given a high number of explanatory variables and the small number of cases in the population. The main causal variables in this analysis are the extractive and non-extractive division of industry interests in an area and the salience of various industry interests (an amalgamation of four indicators), outlined in depth in chapter 3. Interest salience refers to the degree to which an industry or business would suffer tangible and significant costs in response to some new stimulus, which can include new policies or environmental changes.

Case-based process tracing is ideally suited to provide the inferential leverage needed to make an argument about cause and effect in large MPA processes. Process tracing involves finding diagnostic evidence that can provide the basis for both descriptive and causal inference (Collier 2011). Put simply, by digging deep into each individual large MPA case I can present an accurate narrative of the process leading to its creation, as well as identify the key reasons why a government made the policy choices that it did along the way (Brady and Collier 2010; Collier 2011). The first step toward identifying those reasons is an accurate characterization of how a large MPA campaign unfolded—from inception to implementation—and the roles and motives of the stakeholders involved. A process tracing methodology meets both needs.

Process tracing requires an explanatory framework—a purpose satisfied here by my economic norm diffusion framework. In-depth case study analysis will allow me to assess the explanatory power of a few, key theoretical expectations that I introduce in chapter 3, all derived from this framework. The purpose of process tracing here is to apply this set of expectations to each case to see if they accurately explain large MPA political processes and outcomes. The goal is to determine why governments make the conservation policy decisions that they do. What stimuli do they respond to? What processes do they establish or participate in? How do they define their interests relative to other stakeholder groups?

Case Selection

Purposive rather than random sampling is necessary when the number of cases is small. To that end, I use a diverse case selection technique that

Table 1.2 Case Selection

		Explanatory Variables		Outcomes	
Case	Year	Salience of Extractive Industry Interests	Salience of Non-Extractive Industry Interests	Remoteness from Economic Activity	Management Type
PRIMNM (US)	2014	Low	None	High	No-Take[a]
Coral Sea Marine Park (Australia)	2012	Moderate	Moderate	Moderate	Mixed-use
PNMS (Palau)	2015	Low	High	Moderate	No-Take

[a] The PRIMNM legislation technically permits recreational fishing, but as the name suggests it is highly remote. In practice, virtually no recreational fishing occurs within the borders of the monument and the MPA is, for the foreseeable future, a de facto no-take zone.

allows me to identify cases that take on distinct values on both explanatory variables and outcomes (Seawright and Gerring 2008). Specifically, these case studies need to vary in two key explanatory variables for a given large MPA: the distribution of extractive versus non-extractive industry interests and the salience of each industry's interests within the target MPA site. Cases need to also vary in their conservation policy outcome so that I can draw conclusions about why governments enact robust protections in some instances and not others. Selecting on the dependent variable is a pitfall of some types of qualitative research (Geddes 1990), but one that process tracing avoids because of the potentially limitless amount of evidence a researcher can gather even for just a single case (Collier, Brady, and Seawright 2010).

Table 1.2 outlines three case studies that adhere to this case selection criteria: the expansion of the Pacific Remote Islands Marine National Monument (PRIMNM) in the US; the Coral Sea Marine Park in Australia; and the Palau National Marine Sanctuary (PNMS) in Palau. These three cases reflect a range of extractive and non-extractive industry interest salience in a proposed large MPA site. None of these cases has a high salience of extractive industry interests since ENGOs (and states) have so far avoided targeting sites with high extractive commercial activity. These three large MPAs nonetheless reflect a range of industry interest configurations and MPA outcomes.

Data Collection

There is very little academic literature available about any of these three cases given how recent they are, and given that marine politics is an understudied area of global environmental politics. Data collection required an intensive interview process with MPA stakeholders. The case study research in this book draws from interviews with 74 key large MPA stakeholders and experts. Interviewees include politicians, government officials, industry representatives, ENGO employees and managers, and marine scientists. This involved in-person interviews in Washington, DC, in the US; Cairns, Canberra, and Sydney in Australia; and Koror in Palau. When in-person interviews were not feasible, phone interviews took place in their stead with individuals throughout Australia, the UK, and the US. All interviews were semi-structured and varied in length. Interview questions centered on asking for detailed descriptive accounts of large MPA campaigns and government processes, as well as the goals and roles of stakeholders involved in them. These interviewees remain confidential to protect their professional and personal interests. I sought permission for attribution in instances where I cite interviewees by name. The Appendix includes a comprehensive list of all interviewee positions, affiliations, and locations, except where doing so would reveal their identity.

In addition to these interviews, I rely on a variety of secondary sources. Government and ENGO reporting on prospective large MPA sites is often extensive, and I draw from a number of these scientific and socioeconomic reports. These three large MPAs were also high-profile conservation initiatives, so media reporting on stakeholder positions and expert views was similarly extensive, providing another useful source of data. Because these are high profile initiatives, there have also been numerous parliamentary and congressional proceedings on them across cases. Transcripts of these proceedings tend to be readily available and provide further insight into the political processes leading to the creation of new large MPAs. I was able to attend one such congressional hearing in person in Washington, DC, in September 2015. I use these additional sources to verify and support data collected from the interview process. Together, these sources provide a basis for assessing the power and influence of various stakeholder groups to explain government conservation policy decisions (Arts and Verschuren 1999).

Chapter Organization

This book has two parts. The first part documents the emergence of the large MPA norm and proposes in detail my economic norm diffusion framework. Chapter 2 draws from existing international relations literature to explain how and why the large MPA norm emerged. It more precisely defines the characteristics of this new norm and specifies its origins within the US environmental community. It then turns to explaining how and why this new norm has spread since the mid-2000s and the reasons why it is likely to continue to spread. It also briefly discusses the (rather feeble) challenge to the science of large MPAs, and why it is unlikely to impede the continued spread of the large MPA norm.

Chapter 3 introduces my economic norm diffusion framework, with particular emphasis on its political economy explanation of norm localization. Together, this framework and my application of it to the large MPA norm are the main original theoretical contribution of this work. This chapter provides an in-depth account of that framework. It also provides an overview of the four major stakeholder groups involved in large MPA bargaining processes, namely, the state, industry, environmental groups, and local communities. Applying the framework to the large MPA norm, it then proposes a set of theoretical expectations that explain government conservation policy decisions.

Part II is the empirical case study component of this book, which applies the norm diffusion framework and theoretical expectations that I develop in chapter 3 to three large MPA case studies. Chapter 4 analyzes Barack Obama's 2014 expansion of the PRIMNM. Previously established by President George W. Bush in 2011 as a 225,000 km^2 non-contiguous marine reserve; the Obama expansion increased it to 1,270,000 km^2. The minimal commercial interests in the region made the expansion a prime candidate for a coalition between the state and environmental groups, eventually yielding a large, de facto no-take marine reserve.

Chapter 5 tells a different story through an analysis of Australia's 2012 Coral Sea Marine Park. This large MPA has involved what is likely the most contested stakeholder bargaining process of any large MPA up to 2020. There is a moderate amount of commercial fishing and ecotourism activity in the Coral Sea, and the MPA is directly adjacent to the Great Barrier Reef Marine Park, itself a hub of commercial activity. This industry activity led to a protracted battle over how the area was to be regulated, a problem exacerbated by political instability as Australia had four prime ministers in just five years at the height of the bargaining process. This political instability complicated the negotiations and created a great deal of uncertainty, but ultimately did not prevent a stable coalition between the state and commercial fishing industry from emerging. This coalition produced a mixed-use MPA that facilitates business-as-usual activity in the Coral Sea.

Chapter 6 turns to an analysis of the Palau National Marine Sanctuary, a reserve that comprises 80% of Palau's EEZ. Palau's economy is critically dependent on its ecotourism industry, which contributed 54% of its GDP in 2015 (Asian Development Bank 2016a). Its commercial tuna stocks, however, were exported primarily by foreign-owned fleets with little local benefit. This reserve is an attempt to protect Palau's ecotourism sector while shifting toward building a domestic commercial fishing capacity to take place in the remaining 20% of Palau's EEZ. The idea for the sanctuary initially emerged out of the ecotourism sector. This coalition between the state looking to protect its economy and the critical ecotourism sector have been driving establishment of the reserve, with Palauan President Tommy Remengesau Jr. its primary advocate.

Finally, a concluding chapter discusses some of the insights that these case studies provide about the how the power and influence of business shapes government environmental policy. This chapter, above all, weighs in on the debate about whether large MPAs are a desirable solution to ocean decline, and what they might mean for the future of global marine conservation in the face of an ecological crisis. But first, chapter 2 lays the foundation for discussion of these bigger conservation questions. In it, I will trace the history of the large MPA norm, showing how just a few individuals committed to protecting the oceans were able to transform global marine conservation.

PART I

THE NORM OF LARGE MARINE PROTECTED AREAS

2

Rethinking Ocean Protection

The emergence of a new norm of large MPAs has led to a fundamental shift in the way that states protect marine ecosystems. Although countries continue to establish smaller, often networked MPAs, at no time in history has nearly as much ocean space been protected in so short a time. Before 2006, the only MPA exceeding 200,000 km^2 was Australia's Great Barrier Reef Marine Park (GBRMP), established in 1975. By 2020, 13 different states and one multilateral body had created 24 new MPAs that surpass this metric. For over 30 years the GBRMP was the most massive MPA on the planet; by 2020, 18 exceeded it in size. The large MPA norm has already taken hold in global marine conservation as state leaders continue to protect large swaths of ocean at an unprecedented rate (Alger and Dauvergne 2017a, 2017b).

The large MPA norm has its roots in a long intellectual tradition of protecting ecosystems from human activity. The idea that these principles could be applied to remote, pelagic marine ecosystems began to emerge in the mid-2000s as environmentalists searched for novel ways to combat rapid ocean decline. The declining cost of satellite and drone monitoring technology had made it more feasible than ever for governments to cost-effectively monitor large and remote ocean spaces. Three American environmental groups, Pew, National Geographic, and Conservation International, were the early proponents of the global push for large MPAs. That push began in 2006, with Pew and National Geographic lobbying for the creation of a large reserve around the Northwestern Hawaiian Islands, in what would later become the Papahānaumokuākea Marine National Monument. At the same time, Conservation International undertook a campaign in Kiribati that led to the creation of the Phoenix Islands Protected Area (PIPA). These two large MPAs were the first manifestations of what was to become a new norm in global marine conservation.

The large MPA norm has three defining characteristics, listed in Table 2.1. When ENGOs lobby a state for a new large MPA they tend to promote these three features.

Conserving the Oceans. Justin Alger, Oxford University Press (2021). © Oxford University Press.
DOI: 10.1093/oso/9780197540534.003.0002

Table 2.1 Characteristics of the Large MPA Norm

Characteristic	Description
Large and Contiguous	The protected area is (or contains) a contiguous area exceeding 200,000 km².
Pelagic	The area protects pelagic ecosystems, often in addition to coastal ecosystems.
No-Take	Extractive use for commercial purposes is banned in the area, or in specific zones in the area.

The 200,000 km² floor for a large MPA captures well the shift in scale that occurred from 2006 onward. There were a few MPAs that approached this size before 2006—most notably perhaps the 133,000 km² Galapagos Marine Reserve—but only the GBRMP surpassed it. That MPAs are large and contiguous as well as pelagic are the two deterministic features of this norm. The third feature—that large MPAs are designated no-take—is common to many large MPAs, but is often contested. However, the large MPA norm can still be influential and active in particular cases even absent no-take status. For example, ENGOs such as Conservation International tend to be more open to mixed-use MPAs that promote both environmental protection and sustainable development goals and will therefore not necessarily advocate for a fully no-take area. Stakeholder consultation processes can also sometimes lead to an ENGO-proposed MPA being reduced in size, being mixed-use, or ultimately having few or no new restrictions on use.

This chapter is loosely organized around what international relations scholars refer to as the "norm life cycle," summarized in Table 2.2. As Martha Finnemore and Kathryn Sikkink (1998) outline in their seminal article, norms become engrained in international politics through a three-stage process: (1) norm emergence; (2) norm cascade; and (3) norm internalization. In the norm emergence stage, "norm entrepreneurs" motivated by an ideational commitment work to persuade decision makers about an appropriate course of action. Once these norm entrepreneurs have convinced a critical mass of states to accept a given norm, it reaches a tipping point. After a norm reaches this tipping point, it moves on to the norm cascade stage, at which point it becomes widely adopted in the international system. In the norm cascade stage, states that have not already adopted the norm become socialized into it as they seek legitimacy, often responding to social pressure from influential states. Some norms become so deeply ingrained in

Table 2.2 The Norm Life Cycle

	Stage 1 Norm Emergence	Stage 2 Norm Cascade	Stage 3 Norm Internalization
Actors	Norm entrepreneurs with organizational platforms	States, international organizations, networks	Law, professions, bureaucracy
Motives	Altruism, empathy, ideational commitment	Legitimacy, reputation, esteem	Conformity
Dominant Mechanisms	Persuasion	Socialization, institutionalization, demonstration	Habit, institutionalization

international politics that they reach the final internalization stage. A norm is internalized when it has become institutionalized across most, if not all, states, and conformance with the norm is virtually automatic. This pattern of norm adoption is evident across a wide range of issues in international relations (Meyer 1979; Finnemore 1993; Price 1998; Sunstein 1999; Kelley 2008). Some scholars have criticized this life cycle model as being too static or linear to accurately capture the dynamism of various international norms (Krook and True 2012), but it nonetheless remains the dominant model in international relations norms scholarship and is well suited to explaining the rise of the large MPA norm.

The pages to follow document the origin, emergence, and spread of the large MPA norm, discussing the various actors, motives, and mechanisms of the norm life cycle throughout. They provide an account of the intellectual roots of the norm in early US environmentalism and of the ENGO strategy to frame ocean decline as a problem requiring large MPAs as the appropriate solution. The two parallel campaigns in the US and Kiribati in 2006 became the template for large MPA advocacy that ENGOs used to launch additional large MPA campaigns around the world. The proliferation of large MPAs has not gone uncontested, with some skeptics sowing seeds of doubt about their efficacy. Nonetheless, the large MPA norm has flourished. I will make the case by the end of this chapter that, as of 2020, it had reached the cascade stage of the norm life cycle, becoming increasingly institutionalized in the international system. As a whole, this chapter will argue that a new large MPA norm has emerged, that it came out of civil society advocacy, and that it will continue to shape global marine conservation. But before recounting the origin and emergence of the large MPA norm, it is worth exploring why it was so well positioned to prevail.

Why Large MPAs?

Why did the international community "select" the large MPA norm instead of other ideas for strengthening marine conservation? The answer, I argue, is that large MPAs had a high degree of social fitness with the extant social structure (Bernstein 2000). The norm was promoted by reputable environmental organizations, it coincided well with existing biodiversity governance institutions, and it fit well with what states already viewed as their role in protecting marine environments. The concluding chapter of this book will discuss why this social fitness is, in some ways, problematic for conservation. For now, though, I make the case that international conditions were ripe for the large MPA norm to spread as quickly as it did.

For a new norm to spread beyond its early proponents, it needs to be institutionalized in a set of international rules and organizations (Goldstein and Keohane 1993; Katzenstein 1996; Finnemore and Sikkink 1998). Many new global norms challenge existing standards of appropriateness, often leading to contested, or even combative, efforts to promote and institutionalize them (March and Olsen 1998). This was not the case with the large MPA norm, which was already consistent with existing rules and practice for biodiversity conservation. It was, in a sense, a "privileged" emerging norm because it did not challenge the existing institutional order (Collier and Collier 2002), and was instead an incremental and complementary change to it (North 1990).

The current global environmental regime—the structures and institutions that organize how states agree on collective environmental commitments—has two core tenets. The first is that it is grounded in rational, scientific authority that manifests through agreements such as the 1992 CBD. The second is the normative imperative that environmental policies should not impede economic growth and development. These two tenets of the global environmental regime explain why states tend to focus on MPAs as their marine conservation tool of choice.

In the international system, states are socialized into converging around particular sets of standards and practices for pursuing shared goals. States are remarkably similar in that they are of the same structure at a fundamental level, which can partly explain why they establish MPAs at all (Meyer,

Boli et al. 1997). They tend to conform to a standard world culture because global networks of competition, exchange, and association condition specific behaviors and institutions (Bull 1977; Meyer 1980; Buzan 2004). These global processes of interaction lead to isomorphism among states not just in state structure, but in the way that they pursue their shared goals (Scott and Meyer 1994; Finnemore 1996b; Meyer, Boli et al. 1997). Their standards and practices tend to be similar because states are socialized through their interaction in a world society. This convergence through socialization applies to the types of environmental policies that states tend to adopt as well (Dimitrov 2005). The rationalized scientific interpretation tenet of the global environmental regime leads countries to pursue environmental policies that are measurable and negotiated through an international body (Meyer, Frank et al. 1997). For the large MPA norm, clearly defined, measurable targets were already embodied in existing international agreements.

Prior to the emergence of the large MPA norm, states had already agreed to formal protected area targets on two separate occasions. The first—Article 8 of the 1992 CBD—obliges states to establish a system of protected areas to conserve biodiversity. Protected areas are (comparatively) easy to define and easy to measure, so they have become perhaps the key metric for how states track their conservation progress (a problematic metric on its own, of course). Wanting concrete biodiversity targets, states further institutionalized protected areas as a central conservation tool with the creation of the 2010 Aichi Biodiversity Targets, which included protecting 10% of their respective marine areas by 2020. The Aichi Targets also call for the effective management and ecological representation of protected area networks. To that end, policymakers have adopted concepts such as "biomes" to rationalize biodiversity conservation further, allowing them to measure not just the extent of the area covered but also the diversity of ecosystems covered. States' marine conservation strategies are shaped by this highly rationalized global conservation regime as they work to meet their international protected area targets.

Large MPAs can also be highly compatible with the second tenet of the global environmental regime: that environmental policies need to be consistent with economic growth and development. Global processes of interaction lead to convergence toward "marketization"—the reduction of government constraints on economic behavior (Simmons, Dobbin, and Garrett 2008). In the environmental arena, this convergence to marketization is what gives rise to the second tenet, what environmental politics scholar Steven Bernstein (2001, 2002) called the compromise of liberal environmentalism. The policies that states tend to agree on in the international arena are those that either promote some form of economic growth, or at the very least do not hinder it. This is certainly true of the world ocean regime, as Peter Jacques and Rafaella Lobo (2017, 2018) have demonstrated in the context of the Food and Agricultural Organization's (FAO) cooptation of sustainability norms. By definition, though, protected areas are meant to limit or prevent economic activity in a given space, so on the surface they appear to be contrary to this compromise. But states make decisions about where to locate them and how to manage them based on a thorough analysis of their economic impact. The framework that I present in chapter 3 and the case studies to follow will analyze the political economy of large MPAs in depth. For now, it is enough to note that states can create MPAs in ways that are compatible with domestic economic interests, making the norm palatable.

Compliance with the biodiversity regime is mixed. Once norms are codified into an international agreement, they do often have high levels of compliance (Chayes and Chayes 1993). This compliance is usually a by-product of states agreeing to treaties with few substantive commitments that would require them to change their behavior (Downs et al. 1996). Agreements that do have more ambitious commitments, like the Kyoto Protocol for example, tend to have reduced compliance rates as a result (Cass 2012). But decision-making is costly for states, so it is more efficient for them to adhere to already agreed upon arrangements than to devise their own independently. Even the process of negotiating and agreeing to a treaty is a learning process through which states can and do internalize new conceptions of national interest (Checkel 2001), in this case protecting vast swaths of ocean space. The CBD and the Aichi Targets pressure states to create protected areas by binding them to do so through international law. Whether or not states meet these targets is secondary to the fact that the commitments themselves condition state behavior, socializing them to take action that they otherwise might not. Well-structured environmental agreements can and do generate substantive social change (Schofer and Hironaka 2005). Even states that are not party to a given convention are often more inclined to work toward its objectives. To cite a fitting example, the US is not a CBD state party but well exceeds the 10% marine area protected target with 33% of its EEZ protected because of a few remote, large MPAs.

Finally, large MPAs were an attractive policy option because they are consistent with an international system that provides nations with sovereign control over their surrounding waters. Article 57 of the UN Convention on the Law of the Sea (UNCLOS) established a 200-nm limit for states' EEZs, within which they have the sovereign right to control all resources and govern as they see fit. This international convention afforded former colonial powers huge EEZs due to their overseas territories, most notably France, the UK, and the US. A small military outpost on a remote Pacific island was sufficient to give these former colonial powers sovereign control over large, remote swaths of ocean. These international rules coupled with colonial legacies have afforded certain states opportunities for large-scale marine conservation that would not otherwise be possible.

The large MPA norm prevailed because it is consistent with the well-established social structure of environmental governance. ENGO strategies, discussed later, have worked because they are advocating for policies with which states are already comfortable. They are not trying to alter state behavior radically, but are instead helping countries to identify opportunities to take policy action that most have already agreed to take through international agreements. In sum, the large MPA norm was a win-win for conservationists wanting more ambitious protections and for states already socially invested in a liberal technocratic environmental regime.

Origin, –2006

The idea of protecting large ocean spaces is rooted in a long intellectual history of conservation, but it was with the rise of the modern environmental movement in the 1960s that momentum toward protected areas began to pick up. These early calls for conservation were primarily for terrestrial ecosystems, where ecosystem degradation was most visible (Chape et al. 2005). The first international commitment to protecting ecologically representative areas was made at the 1972 United Nations Conference on the Human Environment. States reiterated this commitment at several other environmental conferences, later enshrining it in the 1992 CBD. These responsibilities applied equally to terrestrial and marine ecosystems, but states tended to neglect marine ecosystem protections (Wood et al. 2008). The oceans seemed too massive and bountiful for anthropogenic decline. In the 1990s, prominent marine biologists and explorers such as Sylvia Earle and Jean-Michel Cousteau increasingly devoted their efforts to raising awareness about the finite limits of the ocean.

The work of these early ocean conservation pioneers foreshadowed growing interest among scientists to document the extent and severity of ocean decline. As our understanding of the human threat to marine ecosystems gradually improved in the 1990s and 2000s, environmentalists increasingly voiced their support for protecting our oceans in the same way that we protect land (Alpine and Hobday 2007). In response, MPAs began to proliferate rapidly from the 1990s onward. In 2000, MPAs covered roughly 0.7% of the ocean, whereas by 2020 that number had risen to over 7.9%, including over 17% of national waters. This staggering increase in quantity has not always been matched by an increase in quality, with less than 2.5% of the global ocean fully protected by no-take areas. Nonetheless, these numbers show that ocean protection was becoming a new and important frontier for conservation. Recognizing that even this sizable growth was inadequate to protect the oceans from human activity, many marine scientists and environmental groups began calling for a more ambitious 30% global ocean protection target in the 2010s.

Of the nearly 27 million km^2 of global ocean protected, nearly 18 million km^2 (66%) is covered by MPAs exceeding 200,000 km^2. Initially, large area protections were reserved for iconic biodiversity hotspots, most notably the 345,000 km^2 Australian GBRMP, established in 1975. The Great Barrier Reef is one of the seven wonders of the natural world, so it was always an exception due to its uniqueness. Ecuador similarly established the 133,000 km^2 Galapagos Marine Reserve over 20 years later in 1998. Like the Great Barrier Reef, the Galapagos is a globally iconic biodiversity hotspot, in no small part because it is often cited as the inspiration for Charles Darwin's *Origin of Species*. It was not until the mid-2000s that the idea emerged that large-scale marine protections did not need to be restricted to just these iconic areas.

When states were not protecting iconic biodiversity hotpots, their efforts were devoted to protecting inland and coastal marine ecosystems rather than pelagic ecosystems. Part of the reason states prioritized inland and coastal waters was that they tend to have higher concentrations of biodiversity (Gray 1997). Protecting pelagic waters also, however, seemed like a daunting task. The enormity of the pelagic ocean led skeptics to claim that area protections were ecologically, logistically, and economically infeasible (Alpine and Hobday 2007; Game et al. 2009), but it is also part of what makes protecting it essential for healthy oceans (Angel 1993). Luckily, by the mid-2000s remote monitoring of marine spaces via satellites and drones was becoming technically and economically viable. With the private sector increasingly using remote monitoring technologies for commercial purposes, MPA proponents were quick to argue that they were viable pelagic conservation tools as well.

Throughout the 2000s, a growing movement advocating pelagic MPAs was emerging. Declining oceans, the neglect of pelagic ecosystems, and technological advancements had all coalesced at this moment in time. Within the environmental community, the perception of pelagic seas was shifting from bountiful to threatened, and from infeasible to manage to viable conservation targets.[1] This recognition among many marine biologists and conservationists was the intellectual origin of the large MPA norm, evidenced in part by the emergence of scientific papers demonstrating the importance of large, pristine areas for biodiversity (i.e., DeMartini et al. 2008; Sandin et al. 2008).

In response to the growing consensus about the need for pelagic ecosystem protections, Pew, National Geographic, and Conservation International began expanding their marine conservation advocacy efforts to include large MPAs. These organizations were norm entrepreneurs, motivated to do more to protect marine ecosystems in the face of growing scientific knowledge about the rapidity and severity of ocean decline. To make progress, they needed to convince states that large MPAs were the appropriate policy response to the poor state of marine protection. In the first, emergence stage of the norm life cycle, the dominant mechanism for the growth of a norm is persuasion (in contrast to the socialization and institutionalization that come later). To promote the large MPA norm, then, environmental groups needed a strategy for persuading governments.

Framing the Large MPA Norm

For a new norm to emerge, norm entrepreneurs need to construct a "cognitive frame" for the issue (Snow et al. 1986; Finnemore and Sikkink 1998). The goal of this frame is to present the new norm in a way that will convince others to support it (Payne 2001). Generally, norm entrepreneurs' strategies for promoting a new norm involve either "persuasion" or "strategic manipulation" (Payne 2001). Persuasion is the attempt to alter the preferences of the target audience, or put differently, to convince the audience that a certain course of action is desirable, whereas strategic manipulation refers to norm entrepreneurs' use of material levers to distort frames and convince a target audience to adopt a norm that might not be in its interests. ENGOs tend to lack material leverage over states, so strategic manipulation was not a viable option. ENGOs needed a persuasive frame to get states on board.

In the emergence of most norms, norm entrepreneurs need to try to alter the preexisting preferences of states (and other stakeholders), as was the case with the anti-landmine campaign in the 1990s or the spread of human rights norms throughout the latter half of the 20th century (Price 1998; Risse, Ropp, and Sikkink 1999). But states had not already settled the matter of whether or not they should protect remote, large swaths of ocean—they had not really considered it before 2006. Because state preferences had not yet formed, ENGOs had a decidedly easier task in convincing them. These environmental groups were not advocating for large MPAs to replace the existing practice of designating networks of smaller MPAs, but rather were proposing an additional marine conservation tool that complemented current practice. Advocating for large MPAs in the mid-2000s was an exercise in preference formation rather than preference alteration, which explains why state opposition to the norm was rather muted. The goal was not to overthrow the existing paradigm of marine conservation but to expand on it.

When actors form new preferences, they are influenced by both ideational and instrumental factors (Fearon and Wendt 2002). They form their preferences according to what international relations scholars refer to as either a "logic of appropriateness" or a "logic of consequences," respectively (March and Olsen 1998). That is, they form preferences based on both what they should do and on what is beneficial to them. The spread of a new global norm involves a complex combination of ideational and instrumental causes and constraints (Kelley 2008). ENGOs wove together elements of both to convince states to establish large MPAs. They persuaded state leaders that large MPAs were the appropriate policy response to ocean decline, but also that there were political benefits to creating large MPAs. In practice there was a lot of cohesion between the ideational and instrumental frames ENGOs used, but I address each type in turn here for clarity.

Ideational Persuasion

The main objective of environmental groups' ideational persuasion efforts was to convince states that protecting pelagic waters was worthwhile. They needed to highlight the impacts that such stressors as overfishing and climate change were having on marine ecosystems, and they needed to convince governments that pelagic ecosystems were both biodiversity-rich and essential to protect. Whereas in the past pelagic spaces were the policy realm of fisheries management programs and climate change mitigation efforts, ENGOs needed to persuade decision makers that they should also be the realm of traditional conservation policy, and that large MPAs were the right tool for the job.

Advocates of the norm presented two kinds of arguments about why large MPAs were essential. First, they provided scientific evidence that even a small amount of human activity can drastically alter the composition of a marine ecosystem. Studies of both the Line Islands and the Pitcairn Islands have shown that there is significantly less top predator biomass in areas where even a small amount of commercial fishing occurs (DeMartini et al. 2008; Sandin et al. 2008; Friedlander et al. 2014). Marine ecosystems, unlike their terrestrial counterparts, are healthiest when top predator biomass is most abundant (the reverse pyramid ecosystem structure). Top predators are generally migratory, so protecting them meant protecting entire ecosystems to the greatest extent possible. In short, scientific evidence was mounting that larger MPAs were more effective. Environmental groups used this evidence to advocate for large, and usually no-take, MPAs. Second, environmental groups emphasized the connection between climate mitigation policy and conservation policy. Area protections are an essential part of strategies to make ecosystems more resilient to the impacts of climate change (Hughes et al. 2003; Bellwood et al. 2004; McLeod et al. 2008).

MPAs were already well established as a marine conservation tool by the mid-2000s, so ENGOs emphasized the urgency of the ocean decline problem as a way to convince states to increase the scale and pace of area protections. Historically, states used MPAs for the small-scale conservation of local reefs and marine habitats rather than more comprehensive ecosystem protection. MPAs were formally included in the International Union for the Conservation of Nature's (IUCN) protected areas network in 1982, contributing to the rapid increase in the number of MPAs in the latter half of the 20th century. In 2020, there were nearly 17,000 MPAs in the world, but their median size was only about 5 km^2. With growing evidence in the mid-2000s that the size of MPAs was an important factor in their efficacy, environmental groups began putting a premium on scale. Pointing to this disconnect between historical practice and contemporary science was one way that they positioned large MPAs as essential for addressing ocean decline.

Another part of environmental groups' framing strategy was to attach the large MPA norm to preexisting norms—what international relations scholars call "grafting" (Price 1998). Grafting a new norm involves rooting it in existing practices and ideological frameworks. The goal is to frame a new norm in a way that will resonate with how the broader public and policymakers already understand a given issue and solutions to it (Payne 2001). Environmental groups grafted the large MPA norm onto states' pre-existing practice of establishing smaller MPAs, but also the more common and prominent practice of conserving terrestrial ecosystems. By 2020, 15% of the earth's terrestrial area was under some protection compared to only 7.9% of the global ocean (a figure that had recently risen dramatically from 0.7% in 2000) (Protected Planet 2020). Because of the advent of large MPAs, the world made considerable progress toward meeting the 10% Aichi biodiversity target. This advent happened in part because states were already well practiced in using spatial management conservation tools by the mid-2000s. Environmental groups just needed to convince states that the practices they had been using on land for generations were equally as viable for conserving pelagic marine areas.

Throughout their advocacy efforts, environmental groups also framed the need for stronger ocean protections as consistent with a precautionary approach to conservation. This framing served two purposes. First, it allowed them to undermine arguments that large pelagic MPAs would be ineffective. Marine conservation science is complicated, and the appropriate conservation tool for a given area can vary based on what needs protecting and what threatens it. For example, the scientific basis for using MPAs to protect localized coral reef ecosystems is well established (albeit not against climate change), whereas the notion that MPAs can also be useful in protecting pelagic ecosystems with migratory species such as tuna is newer, and therefore less deeply engrained. I will elaborate on challenges to the science of large MPAs later in this chapter, but the point here is that by advocating a precautionary approach to environmentalism, ENGOs put the onus on those opposed to large MPAs to demonstrate that they do not, in fact, protect migratory species. In the face of any scientific uncertainty, these advocates argued, the government should err on the side of greater protections.

The second reason ENGOs advocated for a precautionary approach was to bolster their arguments that large MPAs in remote areas were necessary. Many large MPA sites are remote from the commercial activity that causes ocean degradation, so industry groups and even some ENGOs claim that they do not address the real root of the problem anyway. Large MPA advocates argued that remote MPAs acted as an insurance policy, guaranteeing that they are forever protected from commercial activity.

Increasing technological sophistication and overcapitalization of the fishing industry has increased the geographical reach of fishing fleets over the past few decades, putting intense pressure on fish stocks (DeSombre and Barkin 2011; Barkin and DeSombre 2013). Locating MPAs in remote areas insulates them from this ongoing trend. And as noted earlier, even a minimal amount of human activity can have wide-ranging ecosystem impacts (DeMartini et al. 2008), so environmental groups argued that remote areas with little commercial activity needed protection too.

Finally, environmental groups made emotional appeals directly to state leaders.[2] Affect, empathy, and moral belief are vital to spreading a new norm (Fearon 1999; Clark 2010). Strategies for promoting a new norm therefore often involve a more personal, emotional appeal to someone with decision-making authority. Environmental groups do not want to rely solely on communicating complex scientific concepts and reasoning to state leaders to convince them of the merits of a new large MPA, so they work to romanticize the marine life that a new MPA would protect.[3] The first step for an ENGO is often to conduct an expedition to gather scientific information about the richness of biodiversity in a given space.[4] They then communicate this information to a state leader or high-level officials through a combination of reports and documentaries and, when possible, even bringing them on one of their expeditions.

Instrumental Persuasion

Large MPAs are also, it turns out, a good political bargain. Environmental groups communicated this bargain to state leaders and policymakers. They highlighted the low cost of large MPAs, the relative ease of establishing them, and the minimum industry stake in the regions that they have targeted so far. The most substantial cost of maintaining a large MPA is monitoring the area for any illegal activity, but with cheaper satellite monitoring technology now available to replace patrol boats, remote monitoring was feasible. Environmental groups could make the case that large MPAs were cost effective, especially per km^2 protected.[5] Pew was so confident of the effectiveness and affordability of satellite monitoring in the UK's Pitcairn Islands Marine Reserve that it committed to paying for it for the first five years.[6] Large MPAs also require little initial investment to establish. The first step for a government to create a large MPA can sometimes be as simple as setting its boundaries by drawing lines on a map, followed by the decidedly more challenging process of deciding on the restrictions for the area, and then monitoring and enforcing them. The government resources required for a large MPA are reasonably modest given the amount of space protected, making them an attractive, high-profile environmental policy initiative to state leaders.[7] For politicians looking for environmental policy wins, large MPAs were an attractive option.

Environmental groups also deliberately targeted areas remote from commercial activity to limit industry backlash. They do this in part to further romanticize intact ecosystems that warrant protection, but it also serves a strategic purpose. In these remote areas, state leaders can pursue a high-profile conservation initiative that will receive less corporate backlash than many alternatives (i.e., protected areas closer to commercial activity). They appear to be an "easy win" for state leaders looking to bolster their environmental credentials, and in many instances, they are. For example, the public and conservation groups alike praised British Prime Minister David Cameron for creating the Pitcairn reserve in the middle of the Pacific, but the announcement also partly masked the government's failure to deliver on its marine conservation promises for the UK continental shelf at the time. The caveat here is that even in these remote areas, industry can still be highly influential. The chapters to follow will analyze industry influence in depth, but for now it is enough to note that these remote areas provided politically attractive conservation options for states compared to the alternatives.

There was also a long-term strategic goal in environmental groups' decisions to target remote areas. Convincing governments to conserve remote areas now would, in their view, make it more likely that ocean conservation would become a greater priority, leading to protection of less remote areas in the future. There is certainly some evidence to suggest this view is correct. The US established its three large MPAs in 2006 and 2009, all in remote areas far from the continental US. The Obama administration not only expanded two of these large MPAs, but also pursued another large MPA (albeit less than 200,000 km^2) at Cashes Ledge off the coast of New England, an area with a higher level of commercial activity. Although Obama decided that the Cashes Ledge MPA was too politically difficult, that it was even on the table suggests that less remote protections were becoming a possibility. It is hard to say how a future president might attempt to ramp up US marine conservation efforts further. President Trump was a lost cause, but the precedent for large-scale marine conservation is set for his successors.

Finally, large MPAs are attractive environmental policy options to leaders because they tend to bring with them the rewards of political capital and favorability. The enormity of large MPAs means they will likely receive high-profile announcements and promotional campaigns. The prospect of high-profile announcements and promotional campaigns attracts high-level attention, so senior politicians generally attach themselves to large MPAs early to reap the rewards, often in the form of a major environmental policy victory and generally positive public sentiment. In the US, President Bush received praise from otherwise hostile environmental groups for establishing Papahānaumokuākea. After he created PIPA, President Anote Tong of Kiribati became a high-profile spokesperson for Pacific Island states on climate change, joined the board of Conservation International, won several environmental awards, and an international committee was formed devoted to awarding him a Nobel Peace Prize.

Protected areas are also a legacy initiative for state leaders. Teddy Roosevelt will forever be associated with the creation of Yellowstone National Park—the world's first national park. President Bush—for all of his environmental shortcomings (to put it mildly)—will forever be associated with the creation of the Papahānaumokuākea, Pacific Remote Islands, and Mariana's Trench protected areas. These three large MPAs were the genesis of US leadership on large-scale ocean conservation in the 2000s. In persuading state leaders to establish large MPAs, environmental groups entice them with the idea of leaving behind a "blue legacy."[8] Unlike much of what a leader will accomplish while in office, large MPAs are a lasting, physical manifestation of that time.

Through ideational and instrumental frames working in tandem, large MPA advocacy campaigns have been highly successful to date. Environmental groups have done well to frame ocean decline as an increasingly urgent problem that calls for an ambitious response, advocating large MPAs as the appropriate one. By also appealing to state leaders' instrumental interests these ENGOs provide a compelling rationale for establishing large MPAs. This framing strategy was remarkably effective in putting large MPAs on the agendas of states. The initial victories of the Papahānaumokuākea and PIPA campaigns, both in 2006, were quickly replicated in several other coastal nations in the following decade. Many international norms begin as domestic norms and later spread internationally (DuBois 1994). The large MPA norm is such a norm, with its beginnings in the two campaigns to designate Papahānaumokuākea in the US and PIPA in Kiribati.

Papahānaumokuākea

In 2005, Pew executives Josh Reichert and Steve Gainey—motivated by growing evidence of ocean decline and the poor state of marine protections in the US—decided that they wanted to identify a significant marine conservation initiative in the Pacific.[9] They quickly selected the Northwestern Hawaiian Islands as a prospective site and put eventual Global Ocean Legacy program founder Jay Nelson in charge of the campaign. Global Ocean Legacy is Pew's precursor to the Pew Bertarelli Ocean Legacy program, as of 2020 the most extensive global advocacy initiative for large MPAs. The Northwestern Hawaiian Islands were already partly protected but had been bogged down in the National Oceanic and Atmospheric Administration's (NOAA) marine sanctuary designation process since 2001. Pew saw the opportunity to increase both the pace and the scale of protections for the area through an executive order, so started immediately lobbying the Bush administration to take action.[10] This lobbying represents the first efforts to frame the large MPA norm.

Pew, along with the like-minded National Geographic, Environmental Defense Fund, and Marine Conservation Institute, needed to convince the Bush administration of the value of protecting the remote Northwestern Hawaiian Islands. The strategy was to use a combination of scientific information and emotional appeals made directly to President Bush to convince him of the area's importance, in what would later become the template for large MPA advocacy. The Bush White House never released the scientific report that these environmental groups compiled on Papahānaumokuākea to the public, but it detailed the richness of biodiversity in the area.[11] The Northwestern Hawaiian Islands contain more than 11,500 km^2 of coral reefs, are home to over 14 million seabirds, and support one of the highest ever recorded top predator biomasses in a coral reef ecosystem (Morgan 2013). The area had also received various environmental protections in 1903, 1940, 1967, and again in 2000, so previous US presidents had already acknowledged the area's importance by the time ENGOs were lobbying the Bush administration in 2006. All that was left was for environmental groups to convince President Bush that the area warranted more ambitious protections than those already in place.

Environmental groups made their initial appeal to the Council on Environmental Quality (CEQ)—the environmental arm of the Executive Branch—holding several meetings with them.[12] The CEQ agreed that the government should close the area, but wanted an indication of the potential political response to creating a reserve.[13] It wanted the support of the governor of Hawaii and reassurance that the Hawaiian congressional delegation would not oppose the measure.[14] Representatives from Pew, the Environmental Defense Fund, and the Marine Conservation Institute lobbied Hawaiian politicians for their support, including meeting with the governor.[15] These lobbying efforts worked, and the CEQ received the assurances it required.[16] It helped considerably that commercial activity in the region was small. Only nine fishers had permits for the area, one of which happened to be in jail at the time, so there was virtually no industry resistance.[17] A strong political or industry backlash seemed unlikely.

The next step was for environmental groups to appeal directly to President Bush, which they were able to do at a White House event in 2006 with CEQ support. ENGO executives along with other prominent marine conservation luminaries, such as Jean-Michel Cousteau and Sylvia Earle, made an emotional appeal to President Bush during a documentary screening at the event (Revkin 2016). The documentary was Cousteau's *Voyage to Kure* (Cousteau 2005). It depicts his team's trip to the Kure Atoll in the Northwestern Hawaiian Islands and catalogs the vast array of marine species over the course of several dives. Like many documentaries of its kind, *Voyage to Kure* romanticizes the marine biodiversity of the region while simultaneously calling for action to protect it. National Geographic's 2005 book of photographs taken in the Northwestern Hawaiian Islands, *Archipelago*, complemented this screening to provide a visual overview of flora and fauna on and around the islands (Liittschwager and Middleton 2005). The dinner following the White House screening provided a more intimate setting for the conservationists present to further educate the president on the importance of the area. It was at this dinner that legendary marine biologist Sylvia Earle (in her early 70s at the time) gave President Bush what he playfully refers to as a "pretty good lecture about life" (Revkin 2016). The documentary moved both President Bush and First Lady Laura Bush, and President Bush committed to establishing the 362,000 km^2 region the night of the screening.[18]

The political response to Papahānaumokuākea was resoundingly positive. The praise that President Bush received for the monument had such a substantial effect on him that it encouraged him to establish two more large MPAs during his remaining time in office.[19] The short-term impact on US marine conservation was directly evident in Bush's expressed desire to leave a blue legacy.[20] The positive reaction from the public and environmental groups provided the first clear evidence that large MPAs could be politically rewarding for the leaders that establish them. In 2016, President Obama expanded Papahānaumokuākea to the full 200 nm limits of the US EEZ, and it now protects 1,508,870 km^2 of ocean.

The campaign for the protected area became a practical model that ENGOs could replicate elsewhere. Papahānaumokuākea reflects all three characteristics of the large MPA norm: it is large and contiguous, protects pelagic waters, and is no-take. The rapidity and severity of ocean decline was the preamble to the advocacy campaign for Papahānaumokuākea, but environmental groups focused their messaging on the biodiversity and legacy benefits of protecting the area.[21] Their message was that a large MPA was scientifically crucial to the region's biodiversity. Moreover, they instilled a sense of stewardship over this pristine area in President Bush.[22] Environmental groups had so effectively presented the case for Papahānaumokuākea that they convinced a conservative US president with an otherwise poor environmental record to create what was, at the time, the world's largest MPA.

Phoenix Islands Protected Area

Meanwhile, Conservation International was engaged in a similar process in Kiribati under the leadership of marine biologist Gregory Stone. A New England Aquarium expedition in 2000, led by Stone, was among the first attempts to document the marine life of the Phoenix Islands.[23] In what would become a fairly common story for large MPA campaigns, these first dives revealed a richness of previously undocumented biodiversity.[24] Stone reported the findings of this and subsequent expeditions to Kiribati government officials and President Anote Tong himself, convincing them that protecting the area should be a priority.[25]

It was, however, the government that expressed a desire to create a more ambitious reserve. The government wanted to include pelagic waters in the reserve in response to evidence of white caps spotted along the borders of Kiribati's EEZ.[26] These white caps imply a shallow reef ecosystem further inshore, which means biodiversity richness. Stone's tacit strategy in Kiribati mirrored the concurrent advocacy campaign for Papahānaumokuākea: he provided evidence of a thriving, lush ecosystem directly to state leaders, instilling the sense of stewardship that has become essential to large MPA designations. In Kiribati, though, Stone was working with a president that was already predisposed to ambitious conservation policy.[27] President Tong announced PIPA in 2006 and formally established it in 2008 after a government process. PIPA, like Papahānaumokuākea, is large and contiguous, no-take as of 2015, and was the result of an entrepreneurial state leader taking advice from conservationists.

The one major obstacle to protection that was not present around Papahānaumokuākea was that the waters surrounding the Phoenix Islands were essential to the Kiribati economy. A no-take MPA was not, at first, politically attractive to President Tong because of the potential lost commercial fishing revenue in the area.[28] Kiribati is primarily known for its profitable skipjack tuna, the most common species of tuna for canning. Kiribati is also one of the least-developed Pacific Island states, with the government relying on fishing licenses for nearly half of its revenue (Central Intelligence Agency 2019b). The potential revenue loss from banning fishing in such a significant portion of its EEZ made it difficult for Tong to protect the area.[29] Stone proposed having an ENGO set up a trust to offset this revenue loss.[30] These types of arrangements are common on land, but this had not been done in the ocean, with one exception around Iceland.[31] Conservation International was willing to attempt to raise the funds for the trust: the group has what it calls a more humanist philosophy toward conservation, favoring an approach that combines sustainable development and conservation goals, so the trust idea resonated with this core philosophy.

The Conservation International trust was not immediately available in 2008, so Kiribati did not ban commercial fishing in PIPA until January 2015 and used the time to increase revenue from fishing licenses substantially. A modest income of $23 million in 2011 skyrocketed to $100 million in 2014, through an increase in the number and fishing allowances of its licenses (Korauaba 2015). The delay in the PIPA fishing ban and the increased revenues in the waters just outside of PIPA demonstrated how challenging large-scale marine conservation could be in areas with higher commercial activity. Large-scale ocean conservation and economic growth were potentially at odds in Kiribati, so the lesson for environmental groups was that they needed to be sensitive to the economic impact of a given MPA if they wanted to be successful. Conservation International demonstrated that a trust was one possible way to convince states to create a large MPA. Kiribati, for its part, showed that closing off one area to fishing did not necessarily mean an overall revenue loss. Many conservationists criticize PIPA for not effectively reducing the total biomass taken from Kiribati waters, as the reduction in the protected zone was more than offset by increases elsewhere.[32] This increase led to some scathing critiques of PIPA as an undelivered promise (Pala 2013).

Criticism aside, PIPA set a precedent for developing countries to establish large MPAs. In 2008, PIPA was the biggest MPA in the world at 408,250 km^2 until it was surpassed two years later by the UK's Chagos Marine Protected Area. Global environmental politics literature often (rightly) treats environmental problems and solutions as distinct for developed and developing countries (Miller 1995; Najam 2005; Williams 2005; Newell 2005; Pattberg 2006). International norms tend to have a North to South trajectory, with a few exceptions that demonstrate the reverse (Clapp and Swanston 2009). The large MPA norm owed its intellectual origins primarily to US conservationists, but its diffusion happened concurrently in the global North and South. Though the US designated Papahānaumokuākea before PIPA, Kiribati actually announced PIPA two months before the US announced Papahānaumokuākea, demonstrating that a small developing country could take the lead on largescale ocean conservation alongside the US. The PIPA decision further challenges the notion that developing countries are too limited in their capacity to exhibit environmental leadership (Steinberg 2001). Chile, the Cook Islands, New Caledonia, Mexico, and Palau would all later follow Kiribati's example, all establishing large MPAs of their own by 2020.

The announcements of Papahānaumokuākea and PIPA in 2006 marked a turning point in how states protect marine biodiversity. Lance Morgan, President of the Marine Conservation Institute, credits these two MPAs with "setting a new standard" for marine conservation.[33] They were an example to the rest of the world that large MPAs could be an essential tool for protecting marine ecosystems—one that was also politically attractive to state leaders. These two conservation success stories led these norm entrepreneurs to ask an important question: if large MPAs worked here, why not pursue them in other places as well?

Emergence, 2006–2014

With two demonstrated large MPA successes as their foundation, conservationists began in earnest the process of promoting large MPAs as a new standard for global marine conservation. The norm emerged quickly after 2006 in large part because of the efforts of a few individuals at prominent environmental groups to capitalize on these successes. Jay Nelson of

Pew and Enric Sala of National Geographic—who had both advocated for Papahānaumokuākea—led the efforts to turn this initial success into what would become long-term campaigns to promote large MPAs. Bolstered by the broader support of a strong intellectual and scientific push for large MPAs, they were among the foremost "transnational moral entrepreneurs" and "meaning architects" (Finnemore and Sikkink 1998). Empathy, altruism, and ideational commitments tend to motivate norm entrepreneurs such as those at Pew and National Geographic (Keohane 1990; Mansbridge 1990; Keohane 2005). To better protect ocean ecosystems, both organizations worked tirelessly to convince others of the moral imperative of the norm and to frame it in terms that would make it accessible to decision makers and the public (Nadelmann 1990; Lessig 1995; Clark 2010). Pew and National Geographic benefitted immensely from the support, insight, and hard work of local environmental groups in promoting the large MPA norm, to whom they give considerable credit. In many large MPA advocacy campaigns, these local environmental groups were more influential and more important than their transnational counterparts. But ultimately it was through the dedicated programs created by these transnational ENGOs that efforts coalesced into a coherent commitment to expand the large MPA norm globally (Park and Vetterlein 2010).

These norm entrepreneurs are also quick to give due credit to political leaders as the individuals who ultimately decide to establish a large MPA.[34] Despite his poor overall environmental record, George W. Bush was a particularly important "political entrepreneur" in large-scale marine conservation. In international relations scholarship, a political entrepreneur is a politician that takes up the cause of a new norm and works to promote it domestically (Tiberghien 2007). Bush had nothing to do with the inception of the idea to protect the Northwestern Hawaiian Islands, nor the idea to protect large ocean spaces more generally. But his willingness to listen to environmental groups and ultimately establish the monument set the tone for future large MPAs. As noted, Bush went on to create two more large MPAs toward the end of his second term, again at the urging of environmental groups. Bush's support for large MPAs cemented the large MPA norm in US politics at the time, and it positioned the US as a global leader in marine conservation. President Anote Tong similarly demonstrated in Kiribati that developing countries could also take leadership on large MPAs.

The programs that Nelson and Sala would go on to launch nonetheless ensured that large MPAs would extend beyond these early successes in

Kiribati and the US. Nelson and Sala independently worked to create more coherent "organizational platforms" for pursuing large MPAs elsewhere—the institutional basis from which norm entrepreneurs promote a norm (Finnemore and Sikkink 1998). These platforms are often explicitly created to support a given norm (Sikkink 1993; Klotz 1995; Keck and Sikkink 1998; Price 1998). In this case, however, both Pew and National Geographic were well-established institutions dedicated to advancing a broader normative agenda. These organizations took on a leadership role because promoting the large MPA norm was already consistent with their internal values and objectives (Dashwood 2012). Although both took on leadership roles, their preexisting agendas shaped precisely how they promoted the large MPA norm (Adler 1992; Strang and Chang 1993; Finnemore 1996a). Pew focused on using its substantial financial resources to lobby for large MPAs globally, often remaining involved in large MPA processes from identifying sites through to implementation. National Geographic, on the other hand, focused on scientific expeditions and produced high-quality media to gain the support of decision makers and broader audiences.

In 2006, Papahānaumokuākea project leader Nelson founded the Global Ocean Legacy program at Pew—now the Pew Bertarelli Ocean Legacy program—with the support of other foundations. It was the success of both the strategy for and the outcome of Papahānaumokuākea that inspired Nelson to explore the potential for new large MPAs abroad and create this program.[35] Initial funding constraints meant that Pew needed to look at projects that could be completed within a five-year window, so feasibility was a high priority.[36] To attain the kind of scale that Pew wanted for these MPAs they needed to target remote areas, which would be the most expedient.[37] Pew also made the decision early on to focus on areas within EEZs so that it could target its lobbying efforts at a single decision maker.[38] Pew identified four initial projects at Chagos (UK), the Coral Sea (Australia), Kermadec (New Zealand), and Marianas Trench (US). All four of these projects have led to the creation of a new large MPA. All told, Pew was involved in roughly half of the large MPAs states established from 2006 to 2020, summarized in Table 2.3.

National Geographic's Pristine Seas initiative has been similarly ambitious, although with a more specific focus. As the name suggests, the Pristine Seas initiative targets only the most remote, untouched ecosystems on the planet for protection. Launched by Explorer-in-Residence Enric Sala in 2008, this project had a finite goal of protecting 20 pristine marine environments

Table 2.3 Large MPAs and NGO Participation

Year[a]	State	MPA Name	Size (km^2)	Pew[b]	NGS[b]	CI[b]
1975	Australia	Great Barrier Reef	345,000			
2006	United States	Papahānaumokuākea Marine National Monument (expanded in 2016)	1,508,870	Yes	Yes	
	Kiribati	Phoenix Islands Protected Area	408,000			Yes
2009	US	Marianas Trench Marine National Monument	247,000	Yes		
	US	Pacific Remote Islands Marine National Monument (expanded in 2014)	1,270,000	Yes	Yes	
2010	UK	Chagos Marine Protected Area	640,000	Yes		
2012	Australia	Coral Sea Marine Park	990,000	Yes		
	Australia	South-West Corner Marine Park	272,000			
	UK	South Georgia & South Sandwich Islands Marine Protected Area	1,000,700	Yes		
	Cook Islands	Marae Moana (expanded in 2016)	1,900,000			Yes
2014	France (New Caledonia)	Natural Park of the Coral Sea	1,369,000	Yes	Yes	Yes
2015	Palau	Palau National Marine Sanctuary	500,238	Yes	Yes	
	UK	Pitcairn Islands Marine Reserve	834,300	Yes	Yes	
	Chile	Nazca-Desventuradas Marine Park	297,500		Yes	
	New Zealand	Kermadec Ocean Sanctuary	620,000	Yes		
2016	UK	Ascension Island Marine Reserve	234,000	Yes		
	UK	St. Helena Marine Reserve	444,916			
	UK	Tristan da Cunha Marine Reserve	750,510			
	CCAMLR[c]	Ross Sea Marine Protected Area	1,550,000			

Continued

Table 2.3 *Continued*

Year[a]	State	MPA Name	Size (km²)	Pew[b]	NGS[b]	CI[b]
2017	Chile	Easter Island Marine Park	740,000	Yes		
	Chile	Juan Fernández Islands Marine Park	484,000		Yes	
2018	Brazil	São Pedro and São Paulo Archipelago	449,550			
	Brazil	Trindade and Martim Vaz Archipelago	471,532			
2019	Canada	Tuvaijuittuq Marine Protected Area	320,000			

[a] Represents the year that the MPA was formally announced, but not necessarily fully implemented.
[b] Pew = Pew Charitable Trusts; NGS = National Geographic Society; CI = Conservation International.
[c] CCAMLR = Convention for the Conservation of Antarctic Marine Living Resources.

over its 10-year duration, which it exceeded. Like Pew, National Geographic was involved in several large MPAs (see Table 2.3), but the program's accomplishments also include many MPAs smaller than 200,000 km². National Geographic has a uniquely high capacity to conduct scientific expeditions and produce high-quality media to document their findings, most notably documentaries. Using their respective strengths, Pew and National Geographic often collaborated in their advocacy campaigns for a given large MPA. Their combined efforts contributed to what was at the time the world's largest contiguous MPA, as well as both the world's largest contiguous and non-contiguous no-take marine reserves.

The expansion and future potential of the large MPA norm is also naturally tied to geography. The overwhelming majority of large MPAs in 2020 were in the Pacific Ocean, and the vast majority were located far from major continental shelves. Countries that did establish a large MPA all had relatively large EEZs. The US and the UK, because of their colonial legacies, boast overseas territories that vastly increase their EEZs, as does Chile, while small island nations such as Kiribati and Palau have relatively large EEZs given their small land masses. Which countries adopt the large MPA norm depends on geographical features, which environmental groups considered as they identified prospective large MPA sites.

Through the Global Ocean Legacy and Pristine Seas initiatives, Pew and National Geographic were the predominant environmental groups behind the global spread of the large MPA norm. They were involved in campaigning for the majority of the large MPAs states created between 2006 and 2020, with Conservation International involved in a handful of others. Smaller domestic or local environmental groups supported these efforts on a variety of campaigns. For example, the Marine Conservation Institute is influential in the US, providing its research and lobbying capacity to bolster advocacy efforts there. The Marine Reserve Coalition in the UK emerged during Pew and National Geographic's lobbying efforts for the Pitcairn Islands Marine Reserve and has since taken on a domestic leadership role in advocating for more—successfully, with the UK announcing or establishing three new large MPAs in 2016 alone. It was, for example, the leading organization in the campaign to convince the British government to designate a reserve around Ascension Island.

There was an initial lag time before the large MPA really took hold and began spreading rapidly to new states. In the five years following Papahānaumokuākea and PIPA, states only established three more large MPAs—one in the UK and two in the US. Campaigns for a new large MPA often take years since they usually involve the time-consuming process of a scientific expedition, local outreach, political lobbying, and a government approval process. So the Global Ocean Legacy and Pristine Seas programs needed time to expand their efforts, which began in earnest in 2006 and 2007 respectively. Once those efforts came to fruition, large MPA coverage began to expand dramatically, seemingly overnight. In just 15 years, from 2006 to 2021, global large MPA coverage expanded more than fifty-fold from just 345,000 km^2 to roughly 18 million km^2 of protection.

Pushback: Sowing Scientific Uncertainty

As large MPAs have become more prominent in global conservation, industry-friendly scientists have attempted to sow seeds of doubt about the level of consensus on the science of large-scale marine protection. Their strategy mainly capitalizes on a longstanding—though increasingly outmoded—normative division over whether governments should prioritize conservation or marine resource management. It highlights the distinction between the purpose of conservation as strictly biodiversity protection and the purpose of management approaches as promoting sustainable resource use. The challenge is partly to MPAs generally, but much of the most vocal criticism is specific to the conservation potential of large MPAs in pelagic waters, especially for protecting migratory species. Despite this vocal push-back, the scientific consensus in favor of large MPAs has, in fact, been growing.

Scientific research has repeatedly demonstrated that MPAs can be highly effective for conserving marine biodiversity (Jameson, Tupper, and Ridley 2002; Halpern 2003; Lubchenco et al. 2003; Chape et al. 2005; Pomeroy, Parks, and Watson 2004; Selig and Bruno 2010; Edgar et al. 2014; Emslie et al. 2015; Lamb et al. 2015). Whether or not a given MPA is effective depends mainly on how well managed it is. The vast majority of the world's protected areas are, unfortunately, poorly maintained. According to one prominent study—commonly referred to as the NEOLI study[*]—effective MPAs need to be no-take, adequately enforced, old (> 10 years), large (> 100 km^2), and isolated by deep water or sand (Edgar et al. 2014). For an MPA to be statisti-cally different from a fished area regarding richness of species and biomass it needs to meet at least three of these five criteria. This study used 87 MPAs as case studies, and 59% of them met less than three of these requirements. Numerous other studies have confirmed the poor state of MPA management globally (Kareiva 2006; Jentoft, van Son, and Bjørkan 2007; Burke et al. 2011; de Morais, Schlüter, and Verweij 2015). All of these studies nonetheless rec-ognize that well-managed MPAs are a useful marine conservation tool. Some go even further to recommend that community managed networks of small MPAs need to be supplemented with large no-take areas to make meaningful progress toward conservation targets (Weeks et al. 2010).

Critics of large MPAs tend to acknowledge the conservation potential of MPAs generally, but claim that they are not a panacea for marine conserva-tion. Whether or not an MPA is effective, they argue, depends on its specific conservation goals and whether a static marine reserve is the best tool for achieving them. Scientists that are critical of MPAs call for a case-by-case analysis of the structure of an ecosystem and of the human impacts on it to de-termine if an MPA is the appropriate conservation tool (Hilborn et al. 2004). These critics argue that other fishery management tools like equipment regulations, catch limits, and vessel limits may be more appropriate. They say that MPAs do not address most of the major threats to ocean ecosystems, namely warming temperatures, ocean acidification, pollution, illegal fishing, land-based run-off, and plastics (Hilborn 2015). They also contend that the one issue that MPAs do address—legal fishing—is already well regulated

---

[*] NEOLI is an acronym for the five criteria listed in the study.

(Hilborn and Ovando 2014). Further, they note that scientific research citing the benefits of MPAs tends to partly reflect a normative preference for conservation over management (Agardy, Di Sciara, and Christie 2011; Caveen et al. 2013; Leenhardt et al. 2013). Detractors use these criticisms to challenge the idea that MPAs can protect migratory species.

Despite the size of large MPAs, they are not nearly large enough to encompass the entire habitats of highly migratory species like tuna. Whether or not a large MPA is useful depends on whether protecting a partial habitat has conservation benefits. As one prominent marine biologist argues, there are two criteria that scientists should evaluate to determine the potential benefit of a large MPA (Costello et al. 2016).[39] The first is whether or not it will reduce the total mortality of species. Even large no-take areas may not necessarily do this because of activity outside of them. When Kiribati closed PIPA to fishing, it did not likely decrease the mortality of species due to increases in commercial fishing just outside of the zone. The second criterion is whether the large MPA protects a bottleneck habitat that is disproportionately important to a given species, like a nursery or spawning area. Opponents disparage many of the world's large MPAs based on these criteria. In response, MPA advocates have been arguing that protecting partial habitats does have conservation benefits.

The existing literature on the conservation benefits of large MPAs does not necessarily apply to pelagic reserves over 200,000 km^2. The studies that do address MPA size tend to use a much lower benchmark that reflects the small size of MPAs, such as the 100 km^2 figure used in the NEOLI study (Aswani and Hamilton 2004; Edgar et al. 2014). Since large MPAs are still relatively new, studies are just recently starting to emerge that provide direct evidence of their benefits (i.e., White et al. 2017). Otherwise, scientists rely on research into intact ecosystems and research about the more general benefits of MPAs for conservation writ large. For example, the DeMartini et al. (2008) study of the Line Islands was among the first to note the abundance of top predators in intact ecosystems, which marine scientists now use as one of the leading indicators of marine ecosystem health. Another study of the Pitcairn Islands supported the same conclusion (Friedlander et al. 2014). The only large MPA more than 10 years old that can provide a direct baseline is the GBRMP, which is a mixed-use MPA with a dynamic management system. Studies of the reef have shown that marine life has fared better in the more strictly regulated areas (Emslie et al. 2015; Lamb et al. 2015). There is also an overwhelming scientific consensus that no-take areas are far more effective than their mixed-use counterparts (Sala and Giakoumi 2017). These studies of pristine areas and the GBRMP provided the initial scientific basis for large MPAs, but will soon be presumably bolstered by direct studies of the conservation potential of large MPAs. With several large MPAs now at least 10 years old, it is only a matter of time before marine scientists begin to release results of longitudinal studies that can further cement the scientific consensus on the importance of large, no-take areas.

Advocates also claim that large MPAs provide a haven for migratory species such as tuna so that they can reproduce and grow in specific zones untouched by human activity. They support this haven claim with studies demonstrating that large predatory fish stocks have dramatically declined globally, by 74% to 90% (Baum et al. 2003; Myers and Worm 2003; Lotze et al. 2006). The message is that current fishery management efforts are failing miserably and that large MPAs are one crucial option for trying to reverse the trend. As I discussed earlier in this chapter, advocates argue in favor of a precautionary approach. Faced with rapidly declining fish stocks, they argue that the burden is on detractors to prove that large MPAs would not be useful. Moreover, claims that large no-take areas are unnecessary and lock out human use neglect the pervasive problems of catch underreporting and shifting baselines (Pauly 1995; Pauly and Zeller 2016; Sala and Giakoumi 2018).

The scientific challenge to large MPAs is in some ways analogous to climate denialism. Greenpeace even went so far as to label Ray Hilborn—one of the most prominent sceptics—an "overfishing denier," uncovering millions of dollars of his undisclosed funding from the fishing industry in the process (Hocevar 2016). Industry stakeholders that stand to lose access to marine resources due to an MPA tend to latch on to the claims of sceptics—a tendency that I saw firsthand during the fieldwork for this book. The attempt to sow scientific uncertainty has largely fallen on deaf ears, however, and is not likely to have much of an impact on the future of large MPAs for a few reasons. First, there is an extensive body of evidence documenting the benefits of well-managed MPAs. Second, studies of pristine seas reveal the impact that even a small amount of human activity has on marine ecosystems, justifying large no-take marine reserves. Third, global fisheries have undeniably declined rapidly and are in crisis despite many fisheries management efforts, with large MPAs positioned as a relatively politically expedient way to combat the issue. And fourth, this crisis provides a compelling case for a precautionary approach to marine conservation. The scientific consensus supporting large

MPAs has overwhelmed the attempts to undermine them. As I will demonstrate in the case studies, though, denialism about the benefits of large-scale marine conservation has shaped the politics of many large MPA campaigns.

Cascade, 2014–

The large MPA norm's fit with extant social structure, environmental groups' success in framing and promoting it, and the scientific consensus on the benefits of large, no-take areas suggest a bright future for large MPAs. It is difficult to identify precisely when a new norm reaches its tipping point in the norm life cycle—the point at which it begins to cascade—and the large MPA norm is no exception. Finnemore and Sikkink (1998) suggest two criteria for identifying when a new norm has reached it. The first is that it has the support of about one-third of the states in the international system, but the large MPA norm's threshold to reach a tipping point is lower than that of most global norms. Only 77 of 196 countries have EEZs that exceed 200,000 km^2. As of 2020, only 13 states and one multilateral body to date have adopted the norm by establishing a large MPA, but others are poised to do so. The second criterion is that a norm has the support of critical or influential states, as is the case with the large MPA norm. France, the US, Australia, and the UK have the first, second, third, and fifth largest EEZs in the world respectively, and have been among the most proactive countries in establishing large MPAs so far. In 2015, France appointed the world's first Ambassador to the Oceans to promote ocean conservation worldwide. The US still has substantial normative influence in setting the global agenda, so its early embrace of and advocacy for large MPAs made it more likely that the norm would emerge and spread. US leadership on large MPAs was put on hold with the election of Donald Trump. But by that point, the US had already played a significant role in creating the initial momentum for the norm, President Trump's petulant attempts to undermine it aside.

Despite the difficulty of identifying a precise moment, it is reasonable to claim that the large MPA norm has reached a tipping point, with evidence mounting that states are now working to embed it further in the international system. As a norm cascades, we can expect to see its spread driven more and more by socialization and institutionalization rather than ENGO persuasion (Katzenstein 1996; Fearon 1999; Risse, Ropp, and Sikkink 1999). States' need for legitimacy, conformity, and esteem will become more prominent drivers of the large MPA norm as they look to emulate influential states (Axelrod 1986; Barnett 1997; Barnett and Finnemore 1999; Hyde 2011). As the norm reaches this point environmental groups will continue their advocacy, but will also increasingly benefit from the complementary advocacy efforts of like-minded states. There was already clear evidence of this shift to more state-driven initiatives as early as 2013. In a reversal of the typical large MPA process to that point, it was the Palauan government that reached out to transnational environmental groups to request their support in making the 2015 Palau National Marine Sanctuary happen—the subject of chapter 6.

What is more telling of the large MPA norm's growth is its ongoing institutionalization. The annual *Our Ocean* conference has become a focal point for domestic marine protection announcements. An initiative of then US Secretary of State John Kerry, the US hosted the inaugural *Our Ocean* conference in 2014 as a way for states to coordinate their marine conservation initiatives. At the conference, the US announced a large MPA, only for Chile and New Zealand to follow suit at the 2015 conference. The 2016 conference included the UK's announcement of three new large MPAs and the announcement of the US expansion of Papahānaumokuākea. Each year sees a slew of new conservation announcements from a growing number of states, suggesting a shift in the motives and mechanisms driving the norm. Rather than ENGO persuasion, conferences such as *Our Ocean* socialize states into a set of appropriate behaviors around ocean protection, encouraging faster and broader adoption of the large MPA norm.

As of this writing, states are also in the process of negotiating a legally binding mechanism through UNCLOS that will allow them to establish MPAs on the high seas. Such an instrument dramatically increases the population of prospective large MPA sites since the high seas represent 64% of the ocean's surface. The jury is still out on how robust this instrument will be and early signs point to fairly weak measures steeped in compromise. Specifically, it looks as if fully no-take areas without an opt-out provision are off the table, though time will tell. These negotiations nonetheless reflect the further institutionalization of the large MPA norm. As early adopters of the norm have exhausted some of their domestic waters for designations, they are looking to open up new possibilities for protections through multilateral cooperation on the high seas.

This chapter has traced the history of the large MPA norm from its intellectual origin to current efforts to institutionalize it. It did so through the lens of the norm life cycle, analyzing the primarily international components of norm diffusion. So far, I have glossed over questions of how states navigate often competing domestic stakeholder interests to create a large MPA. The next chapter addresses those questions directly. It presents an economic framework of norm diffusion, with emphasis on the relationship between business interests and government conservation policy. This framework provides an analytical tool for explaining the politics and economics of large MPA stakeholder battles.

3

The Political Economy of Conservation

Chapter 2 explains why and how the large MPA norm emerged, but it does not explain differences across large MPAs. As I have described, large MPAs vary. Many are no-take, others mixed-use, and some have no new restrictions. Some of them were no-take immediately, whereas in others states introduced regulations gradually. Some management plans are fixed and permanent, and others deliberately more dynamic. Some are remote from a state's economic activity, often in its overseas territories, while others encompass the majority of a state's EEZ. The mere existence of a large MPA does not necessarily tell us much about how or even if a given marine space is better protected. It also does not tell us how various industry and local community stakeholders influence and are impacted by a large MPA. This chapter expands on the politics of the emergence of the large MPA norm to discuss its localization.

One of the driving questions of this work is how it is possible that states protected millions of square kilometers of ocean space while still being highly responsive to industry interests. This chapter lays the foundation for answering that question. It presents a strategic actor framework of environmental norm diffusion—one that advocates an economic understanding of norm localization. This framework explains how stakeholder coalitions form around a given MPA based on the salience of various industry interests in a given region. Interest salience, along with an extractive–non-extractive industry dichotomy, are the key explanatory variables in this framework.

Interest salience, as defined in chapter 1, refers to the degree to which an industry or business would suffer tangible and significant costs in response to some new stimulus. That stimulus can be a new regulation, such as losing access to a fishing ground, or it can be environmental, such as a coral reef dying. The salience of industry interests can be deconstructed into parts, allowing for a more nuanced understanding of why and under what conditions industry succeeds or fails in achieving its policy objectives. Those four parts are: intensity of activity, factor specificity, asset specificity, and exogenous stressors. These components of industry interests determine the level of influence that industry has over government policy in a given space.

Conserving the Oceans. Justin Alger, Oxford University Press (2021). © Oxford University Press.
DOI: 10.1093/oso/9780197540534.003.0003

Industry interests therefore intersect closely with those of the state. The challenge, then, is to determine the limits of that connection. States are the ultimate MPA decision makers, so how their interests align with other relevant stakeholders is central to explaining MPA outcomes.

The goal of this chapter is nothing short of providing a way of better measuring and understanding industry influence over how and why global norms diffuse in different ways in different places. Industry is influential, but that influence is not ubiquitous. This framework provides the tools for distinguishing between a strong industry position on an environmental issue and a vapid one that falls on deaf ears. It explains how business power and domestic political economies interact with new global norms as they spread. As chapter 2 argued, global activists and states can and do drive the emergence and spread of global norms. But their success is contingent on the materiality of a norm—on the ability of potential adopters to reconcile it with powerful economic interests. The central argument of this chapter is that a more thorough incorporation of domestic material interests into norm diffusion theory can better explain: (1) why certain environmental norms gain traction in a liberal environmental regime; and (2) why there is considerable variation in how environmental norms are localized.

The stakeholder norm diffusion framework that follows draws some insight from Peter Gourevitch and James Shinn's (2005) political economy work on corporate governance structures. In their framework, the interaction of stakeholder preferences is central. Preferences predict the formation of powerful, informal coalitions that shape governance outcomes. Their process of coalition formation, goal pursuit moderated by intervening institutions, and eventual regulatory outcome are also central to my framework. The goal of the framework that I present here is, however, distinct from and broader than Gourevitch and Shinn's work on corporate governance. My goal is to explain environmental norm diffusion through a political economy lens, at once emphasizing the international and domestic, the ideational and material.

The pages to follow will present this framework while simultaneously applying it to the politics of large MPAs. The result is a theory that explains governments' large MPA policy decisions, taking the form of four theoretical expectations that that I apply to three large MPA case studies in the second part of this book. In this framework, industry groups and political institutions predict the likelihood and comprehensiveness of environmental protections. How much industry depends on a given area has a significant influence on the probability that a government will enact policies to protect it, as well as the extent of that protection. Whether the industry is extractive or non-extractive is a significant component of this. For example, an area that is essential to the commercial fishing industry is less likely to receive stringent protections, but the reverse is true for an area crucial to the eco-tourism industry. In some cases, even extractive sectors may prefer some protection. For example, recreational fishers may want commercial fishing banned in their preferred fishing areas. These dynamics are at play whether an area comprises a few square kilometers or is bigger than Alaska, and whether stakeholders debate it in a local town hall or a national capital.

This chapter will work toward the parallel goals of presenting my framework and outlining a theory of the politics of large MPAs concurrently. The next section introduces the framework while positioning it within the norm diffusion literature.

A Strategic Actor Framework of Environmental Norm Diffusion

In constructivist thought, agents and structures are mutually constituted. The actions of agents contribute to the formation of institutions, and those institutions shape and condition the actions of agents (Wendt 1987). The development of new social norms and institutions is therefore the result of a process by which actors are continually updating their beliefs in response to their environment while at the same time shaping that environment with their actions. A norm emerges when enough relevant actors update their beliefs about what constitutes appropriate behavior in the international system. When enough actors' updated beliefs coalesce, the emergence of the new norm leads to the formation of new institutions to codify and internalize it. Scholars have documented this process of norm diffusion across a wide range of security, human rights, and environmental norms in international relations (Keck and Sikkink 1998; Price 1998; Rucht, Kriesi, and della Porta 1999; Bernstein 2002; Khagram, Riker, and Sikkink 2002; Tilly 2005; Clapp and Swanston 2009).

Chapter 2 examined the formation of the large MPA norm through this traditional constructivist lens, with transnational environmental activists pushing for better ocean protections. As is common with many global norms, the idea of large MPAs started small with concurrent campaigns in

Kiribati and the US, followed by activists quickly looking to take the idea global. Seeking to better protect marine biodiversity, activists changed their beliefs about what was possible for large-scale marine conservation. They then acted as norm entrepreneurs to alter the beliefs of others, most notably policymakers and politicians responsible for conservation policy. Throughout the process, they benefited from the CBD's codification of area targets. Over time, large MPAs came to represent a new norm in global environmental governance, with new institutions such as the *Our Ocean* conferences to propagate it. This narrative focuses largely on the international dimensions of norm emergence: transnational activists, international institutions, and the global adoption of the norm. It similarly focuses on causal mechanisms associated with this international lens: persuasion, socialization, and institutionalization.

But the construction of a new norm over time involves a domestic component as well. Why and how actors update their beliefs is not only about transnational activists or international agreements and institutions but is deeply rooted in local cultural, social, and economic factors. Existing constructivist literature theorizes cultural and social factors well (Cortell and Davis 2000; Acharya 2004, 2013; Capie 2008; Prantl and Nakano 2011; Betts and Orchard 2014). The large MPA case studies to follow will touch on some of the cultural and social factors that shaped each case, but what is largely underdeveloped in constructivist thought is an understanding of how domestic economic forces shape global norms. At the structural level, it seems clear that norms are selected to be compatible with a decidedly liberal environmental regime (Bernstein 2000, 2001; Jacques and Lobo 2018). The success of an environmental norm depends on it not hindering economic growth and development. But this insight alone does not necessarily tell us much about how economic forces shape norm localization. It does not fully answer two of the central questions of this book: (1) why is there considerable variation in how environmental norms are localized; and (2) what are the limits to business power and influence in shaping a new norm?

A norm diffusion framework centered on domestic political economies can better answer these two questions. Environmental norms are particularly responsive to domestic political economies because of how central processes of exchange and wealth creation are to their core tenets. Put simply, new environmental ideas tend to focus on limiting or reshaping various commercial activities to minimize environmental harm. They almost always face pushback from powerful economic elites and industries who stand to lose as a result of their adoption. Shifting the analytical lens to strategic actors in the domestic arena allows for deeper engagement with the political contestation that occurs between economic stakeholders and norm entrepreneurs in an environmental norm diffusion process.

Figure 3.1 depicts the norm diffusion process for an individual state operating in both the international and domestic arenas. The two arenas are connected, with the adoption and localization of a new norm the result of actors updating their beliefs in response to both international and domestic stimuli. While the international arena is one of persuasion, socialization, and institutionalization (Finnemore and Sikkink 1998), in this framework the domestic arena is one of stakeholder bargaining. The case studies to follow will argue that a stakeholder bargaining lens is a more powerful predictor of environmental norm localization than the interaction of a norm with local custom and practice—the traditional constructivist explanation of localization.

The international and domestic arenas involve a different subset of stakeholders. In the international arena, ENGOs and states are the primary actors. In the domestic, ENGOs are joined by extractive industry, nonextractive industry, and local communities as the primary actors. ENGOs operate prominently and simultaneously in both arenas in a norm diffusion process. Internationally, they persuade states to adopt the norm and lobby for its institutionalization. Domestically, they lead advocacy campaigns and contribute to the policy process and implementation. In practice, these actions are often one and the same: for example, a domestic advocacy campaign for a new large MPA is a form of persuasion, as Finnemore and Sikkink (1998) conceptualize it. Including ENGOs in both arenas accurately reflects their role in practice, but it also speaks to the synchronicity of norm adoption and localization.

I do not include industry as an international actor because this framework addresses norm diffusion from the perspective of an individual state. Businesses shape individual states' behavior because they generate revenue for the economy and the state, employ citizens, and can venue shop if regulations become too strict. While ENGOs rely on persuasion to influence states, businesses also have the leverage to bargain with the state because of their importance to the domestic economy. That is not to say that businesses do not powerfully influence global environmental norms or engage in the international arena. Businesses are the central proponents of norms that have evolved around corporate social responsibility and eco-labeling, for example

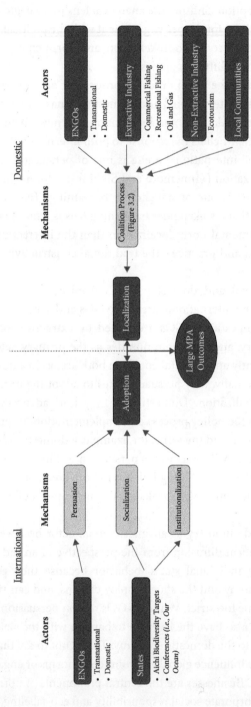

Figure 3.1 Strategic Actor Norm Diffusion Framework

(Dauvergne and Lister 2013; Alger and Dauvergne 2020). They also regularly lobby in multilateral venues to shape environmental treaties and codes of conduct (Clapp 2006; Newell 2006; Falkner 2008; Clapp and Fuchs 2009). But for an individual state engaging with a new environmental norm, the power and influence of those businesses is rooted in domestic political economies.

Finally, there are two practical implications specific to applying this framework to explain the diffusion of large MPAs. The first is that local communities tend to be less prominent as distinct stakeholders: their interests often aggregate over such large spaces through either an environmental campaign or industry associations. The line between local community and environmental groups or industry becomes blurred in these cases. The exception to this is when a local community affected by a large MPA comprises the majority or entirety of a country or overseas territory's population, as in Palau and Pitcairn Island. The large scale nonetheless means that environmental group and industry interests tend to be more prominent in the absence of discrete, cohesive local community interests. The second implication is that large MPA decisions are made at a higher level than their smaller counterparts. It is typically the head of state or a high-level minister who decides to establish a large MPA. Subnational governments, or often the civil service itself, generally make smaller protected area decisions.

Applying this framework to the large MPA norm yields a political economy–driven theory of why and how states establish large MPAs. This approach integrates a combination of rationalist and ideational factors to explain various aspects of the emergence of the large MPA norm, its spread, and its localization in different domestic constituencies. By problematizing strategic actors in the domestic arena, this work follows mainly in the tradition of rationalist accounts of international norm diffusion (Akerlof 1980; Jones 1984; Axelrod 1986; Elster 1989; Morrow 1994; Fearon and Laitin 1996). The rest of this chapter develops the key theoretical contribution of this book: explaining how domestic material interests shape environmental norm diffusion. The first step to doing so is to examine the preferences of the domestic stakeholders involved.

Stakeholder Preferences

The domestic context for norm diffusion depends on the preferences of four stakeholder groups: the state, industry, ENGOs, and local communities.

There is a distinction between a stakeholder's preferences and their interests. Preferences refer to a general set of assumptions about what a given actor desires to maximize its utility. They tend to be static, but new ideas can alter stakeholder beliefs about how best to pursue those preferences. For example, in an environmental bargaining process industry prefers outcomes that maximize their profits and their autonomy from regulation, usually followed by the belief that minimal environmental protections are desirable. But industry groups may alter this belief if they come to see environmental degradation as a threat to the longevity of their business (i.e., their long-term profits). Interests refer to the specific application of an actor's preferences in a given political or economic context. A commercial fishing operator may have a keen interest in a specific area remaining open to fishing because it relies heavily on it for its take, for example. This section will outline the preferences of MPA stakeholders, while the following section will pay particular attention to the salience of industry interests in a large MPA context.

State

Broadly speaking, states in the domestic arena have a preference for appeasing constituents. But states have multiple constituencies, so their beliefs about how to pursue their preferences tend to be less parsimonious than other stakeholders. This general assertion therefore tells us little about state behavior. It is states' beliefs about how to appease constituents that determine their interests, which can vary considerably. States are concerned about growing their economies and therefore facilitating industry interests. But they also care about meeting their international obligations and appeasing often influential environmental groups. Similarly, they must satisfy the interests of the local communities that form the electorate. State preferences surrounding conservation policy are therefore not independent of the interests of other stakeholders. A state's beliefs about how to pursue its preferences—and by extension how to formulate its interests—depends on a given domestic context.

One key commonality is that states are exceptionally responsive to domestic industry preferences. As the driver of economic growth and exchange among nations, industry tends to maintain a privileged position in politics (Nye and Keohane 1971; Cutler, Haufler, and Porter 1999). Policy changes that threaten investment or resource yield are likely to trigger automatic recoil against the government, so industry interests permeate most environmental policy decisions (Lindblom 1982). When industry presents a unified front in environmental negotiations—international and domestic—it can have a strong influence on the outcome (Clapp 2006; Newell 2006). This privileged position is further bolstered by ongoing and rapid global economic integration, as globalization makes it costly for states to exercise policy autonomy over decisions that impact their national economy (Frieden and Rogowski 1996; Milner and Keohane 1996; Rodrik 1997; Rodrik 2011).

Industry influence over the state has limits, though. How responsive a state is to a particular industry on a given issue depends, I argue, on the industry's interest salience and on whether it is extractive or non-extractive—the two key explanatory variables in this framework. The weight of an industry's influence depends on how salient industry interests are in a specific geographic space. Industry influence over the state wanes if it cannot convincingly make the case that it relies on an area. States also tend to privilege extractive industry interests over non-extractive interests. I will elaborate on these two explanatory variables in the next section. For now, it is enough to note that these two elements mean that states do have choices to make about how they want to align their interests in various contexts.

States are of course not unitary actors, so synthesizing state preferences can be complicated. Different branches of government have different priorities. Politicians and political parties similarly have different policy priorities depending on their constituencies and supporters. Disambiguating the state in this framework would, however, come at high cost to its parsimony without significantly improving its accuracy. Put simply, doing so adds layers of complexity that would not enhance the framework's ability to explain conservation outcomes, so I treat the state as a unitary actor.

Industry

Industry has a preference for profitability above all, followed by autonomy (Cutler, Haufler, and Porter 1999). Autonomy refers to the ability to operate free from government control or regulation. Industry groups prefer that government not interfere with their activities, but there are exceptions to this when profitability is at stake. Industry operators may prefer government involvement in instances where a commons resource is depleting. They typically want another industry competing for a given commons resource further regulated, but in some cases even prefer regulation of their own industry. Ecotourism outfits may wish to see commercial fishers banned from surrounding reefs, for example. Or commercial fishers may want limits on the number of vessels allowed to operate in a given region to limit competition for resources from their competitors. Industry preferences for profit and autonomy do not necessarily mean they will be opposed to new protected areas.

Industry beliefs about whether protected areas are good for business depend on whether it is an extractive or a non-extractive industry. Extractive and non-extractive industries have different interests that tend to pit them against one another in a new MPA process. The dichotomy between these two types of industry and the relative influence that each can exert over the policy process has a profound impact on where states locate and how they choose to manage a large MPA. The main extractive industries involved in MPA processes are commercial fishing, recreational fishing, and oil and gas, while non-extractive refers to the ecotourism industry.

Not all tourism is eco-friendly, but so far ongoing or proposed tourism activity in large MPAs appears (and claims) to be ecotourism. Even ecotourism can, however, lead to ecological degradation over time (Fennell 2014). The tourism sector nonetheless has an interest in regulations that enhance non-extractive industry access while limiting extractive industry access, so tends to support large MPAs. This support for new rules is especially apparent in areas where both extractive and non-extractive industries are competing. Extractive industries tend to be the primary local threat to a marine ecosystem, so the purpose of an MPA is usually to limit or prohibit extractive activity. Extractive industries are concerned about the location and restrictions of MPAs that could limit their ability to extract resources. They tend to be opposed to new MPAs as a result.

In some scenarios, a particular extractive industry may have an interest in supporting a protected area, contrary to other extractive industries' preferences. This division happens when different sectors are competing for the same resource. The most likely instance of this competition is between recreational and commercial fishers (Campling, Havice, and Howard 2012). Recreational fishers may well be in favor of a new MPA if it is to remain open to recreational fishing, but not commercial. The relative interests of the recreational and commercial fishing lobbies can influence which regulations a state decides to implement for a new MPA. This kind of division of extractive industry interests is rare, however. Large-scale commercial fishing tends to occur further out to sea, often in pelagic waters, while recreational fishers tend to stay closer to shore. Their interests are therefore often aligned on large MPAs that cover coastal and pelagic waters, with both usually preferring no regulation.

Non-extractive industry, on the other hand, tends to benefit from new conservation initiatives. This is especially true of high-profile efforts such as large MPAs that attract a lot of publicity, and by extension potential customers. Ecotourism and conservation therefore often go hand in hand, providing an opportunity for economic growth and development that is relatively eco-friendly (Campbell, Gray, and Meletis 2007). It is a way for nature to pay its own way, potentially increasing the appeal of conservation beyond just environmentalists (Duffy 2006). But publicity is only one of the benefits protected areas provide non-extractive industry. MPAs lead to healthier ecosystems, thereby improving the resource that the ecotourism industry depends on to attract tourists, with resort operators being the greatest benefactors (Oracion, Miller, and Christie 2005). MPA benefits such as publicity are quick and direct for ecotourism operators, whereas to fishers all of the benefits tend to be long-term, diffuse, and distributed unevenly.

Industry beliefs about how to pursue its preferences can also change in response to environmental change over time. Rapidly declining marine ecosystems, and therefore depleted marine resources, can alter an industry's beliefs about a potential trade-off between its autonomy and its long-term profitability, and even long-term survival. Sometimes, certain industry actors may see a reduction in their autonomy as a way to improve their profitability, be it through regulations that decrease the amount of competition or through better management of resources.

One final point to note is the distinction between transnational and domestic industry. These groups share the same set of preferences, with the primary difference being that transnational industry operates in multiple arenas. This transnationalism is especially common in the commercial fishing sector, with the fishing fleets operating in a nation's EEZ often coming from other countries. That these fleets are foreign, however, does not significantly alter the domestic bargaining process for a given large MPA. When transnational industry groups engage in this domestic bargaining process, they try to frame their interests within the context of a local economy. Similarly, when governments assess the salience of an industry's interest in a region, they do so to understand its domestic economic impacts. This impact tends to be higher for domestic companies integrated into the local economy. Transnational businesses with minimal integration into the local economy, and whose primary interests lie elsewhere, are therefore often at a disadvantage in a domestic bargaining context since they lack the leverage that their domestic counterparts might have.

Environmental Groups

The preferences of environmental groups are foremost for environmental protection and long-term financial stability. Balancing these two preferences can be a challenge for ENGOs. Ideally, successful campaigns for better environmental protections yield more financial backing, with an ENGO's environmental achievements closely correlated to its financial stability. In practice, however, operating within a liberal environmental regime tends to mean greater financial incentives for initiatives that push for incremental change rather than the more drastic actions that the planet needs. Funders and corporate or government partners want to see "wins" rather than sustained activism that targets complex, structural problems. The result can be the corporatization of activism, in which ENGOs tend to pursue coalition-building initiatives with modest goals that involve a range of corporate and government stakeholders (Dauvergne and LeBaron 2014).

Many conservation campaigns are nonetheless hotly contested between activists and industry. Industry groups often criticize ENGO involvement in a given region on the basis that the environmental group has no stake in it. This criticism overlooks the fact that environmental groups represent the environment as a stakeholder that would otherwise go unrepresented. Industry groups reserve this criticism primarily for large transnational ENGOs that often lack local roots. These transnational ENGOs act as stewards of the planet more generally, and in doing so often bring substantial resources to bear in various local contexts. They seek out regional allies, including local environmental groups, but their power and influence often breeds local resentment, especially from industry. This resource disparity can sometimes give large, transnational ENGOs the ability to resist corporate influence to pursue more ambitious protections. Similarly, smaller ENGOs with low overhead that do not rely on corporate partnerships or government funding at all often have the independence to pursue ambitious protections—though often without the same degree of power and influence.

The ability of ENGOs to achieve their environmental protection goals depends on financial stability. They need to engage in activities that will ensure the continued support of their backers. Those backers vary considerably from one environmental group to another and may include governments, a few wealthy donors, or smaller scale fundraising. Some environmental groups raise funds in part through their publications and museums, as National Geographic does. Regardless of how they achieve their financial stability, environmental groups tend to like high-profile initiatives that will attract a lot of attention. These efforts help them garner public and donor interest in their work, allowing them to ensure the continuation of their environmental advocacy work in the long run.

Environmental groups are not a monolith, though, and often have competing beliefs about how to best pursue a particular environmental objective. Competing ideas often lead to competing proposals about the best way to protect the environment in a given area. With MPAs this usually means different views about how to reconcile conservation with human use. ENGOs such as Pew, National Geographic, and Greenpeace tend to advocate stricter conservation measures, whereas Conservation International, TNC, and the World Wide Fund for Nature (WWF) tend to work to integrate human use into a broader management scheme. This type of tension is present in many large MPA cases, including the Coral Sea and Palau case studies to follow. Once a government decides on a given proposal or direction, however, these environmental groups tend to form ranks and support it.

Large MPAs are attractive and desirable initiatives for environmental groups that are concerned foremost about environmental protection and long-term financial stability. Protecting hundreds of thousands of kilometers of ocean space generates a lot of international attention. High-profile marine conservationists such as Jean-Michel Cousteau and Sylvia Earle, and celebrities such as James Cameron and Leonardo DiCaprio, are frequently involved in large-scale marine protection campaigns, further enhancing their stature. ENGOs tend to be especially proactive in the advocacy phase for new MPAs, because it is the most essential for achieving a positive conservation outcome, consequently attracting the most attention from backers (Benson-Wahlén 2013). Large MPAs therefore tend to be win-win for environmental groups looking to protect the environment and raise funds. It is not surprising that many prominent transnational ENGOs have shifted their marine conservation priorities toward large MPAs since 2006, nor that domestic coalitions have emerged to further advocate for them. Environmental groups' support for large MPAs stems directly from their core preferences.

Local Communities

Above all, local communities have a preference for protecting the resources they depend on for their subsistence and livelihoods. In many communities, this means ocean resources, particularly in developing countries where much higher numbers of people depend on coral reefs—while often contributing little to reef degradation (Donner and Potere 2007). When governments intervene in local economies by establishing MPAs and imposing regulations, they change the distribution of benefits from the resources contained within. Such intervention without local community involvement can lead to local resistance from segments of the population that see their access to resources diminished (Oracion, Miller, and Christie 2005). A state's failure to account for local interests when it establishes and regulates an MPA can threaten the MPA's viability, since compliance with regulations tends to be low in these scenarios (Peterson and Stead 2011). A state's capacity to credibly enforce MPA regulations is an issue not only of capacity, but also of distributive conflict and local opposition.

Local communities can also be influential voices in favor of a new MPA. They can be essential both for the creation of a new MPA and for its long-term effectiveness. MPAs in which local communities retain their resource access while commercial resource exploitation is prohibited will likely serve local interests. In these scenarios, local communities are often involved with ENGO campaigns to put political pressure on governments to establish an MPA. And when states integrate local needs into an MPA management plan there is also better compliance with regulations (Persha et al. 2010). Integrating local dependencies usually means zoning an MPA to allow local access to specific regions, or more commonly making an exception for subsistence and livelihood use. Ultimately, when states decide to establish an MPA and determine who has rights to the resources it contains, they are involved in a negotiation (tacit or otherwise) with local stakeholders. The process may include those stakeholders from the beginning, or it may exclude them and lead to resistance after the fact. Either way, they represent an often-influential interest group that has a bearing on the choices that states make.

Despite the sway of local stakeholders in many MPA decision-making processes, they tend to be less influential in the politics of large MPAs. There are some exceptions, but even in those cases local communities are not usually the driving force. In the Pitcairn Islands, the entire population of fewer than 50 islanders was supportive of the Pitcairn Islands Marine Reserve (Alger and Dauvergne 2017a). Their role was primarily to add their voice to environmental group lobbying efforts in the UK. Pitcairn is, however, an exception because of its small population and is not representative of other large MPA processes, where such comprehensive community consultation is infeasible. For MPAs over 200,000 km^2, local communities are often dispersed (and sometimes not present at all) and therefore less unified in their interests and more limited in their ability to collectively organize. As noted earlier, environmental groups or industry associations tend to represent the interests of subsets of local communities over such broad areas. I include local communities in this framework because they are often influential in environmental norm diffusion, but their interests are represented in the large MPA case studies to follow primarily through other stakeholder groups.

In the politics of many large MPAs, however, local communities are a distinct and prominent stakeholder group in their own right. There are in fact cases in which a clear and unified local resistance to a large MPA emerged that is quite distinct from that of industry. The 2010 Chagos Marine Protected Area (UK) and 2017 Easter Island Marine Park (Chile) are two such cases. Other scholars have noted the troubling human rights issues that the Chagos MPA raises (De Santo, Jones, and Miller 2011). In designating the Chagos reserve, the UK continued a longstanding colonial history of undermining the rights of displaced native Chagossians, who, along with and many others, viewed the reserve as a form of ocean grabbing intended to prevent their return to the islands (Bennett, Govan, and Satterfield 2015). The UK lost a court case at the European Court of Human Rights on the issue, but as of this writing seems poised to ignore the ruling.

The more recent Easter Island MPA raised similar concerns, with the government not adequately consulting local islanders in the early stages of the process. The fear was that the Chilean government would use the MPA as a way of exerting greater control over local islanders. But the Chilean government and ENGO advocates seemed to learn from the Chagos experience. The Chilean government held a referendum, with local islanders voting in favor of establishing the MPA. Moreover, the Chilean government will prohibit commercial fishing in the MPA while guaranteeing continued local access. Whereas the Chagos MPA clearly undermined indigenous rights, the Easter Island MPA seems poised to strengthen indigenous access to and control over local marine resources. Although I do not include the Chagos and Easter Island cases in this research, they demonstrate how local community interests can at times be unified and salient, even in the context of massive marine areas.

The Coalition Process

The preferences and interests of states, industry, environmental groups, and local communities form the political landscape for large MPAs. The interaction of these stakeholder groups determines whether a new large MPA is a conservation achievement or merely greenwashing. In most large MPA cases to date, the interests of environmental groups tend to be fairly consistent—support for large, no-take protected areas. The critical distinction between cases, then, lies in the salience of various industry interests and how the state relates to those interests. The coalition process that I present here provides a systematic way of measuring that salience, offering a predictive framework for explaining conservation policy choices.

The coalition process step of this norm diffusion framework (see Figure 3.1) unfolds in five steps. Figure 3.2 depicts those steps, once again providing large MPA-specific examples. In step 1, the state and various industries determine their interests in a given environmental policy outcome based on beliefs about how to pursue their core preferences. In step 2, the state forms an informal coalition with one of the stakeholder groups: extractive industry, non-extractive industry, environmental groups, or local communities. The type of coalition that forms is a function of the salience of industry interests in a given context. In this coalition formation step, the state also determines its preferred policy outcomes—how to locate and manage an MPA. In step 3, institutions intervene between coalitions and policy outcomes. States face various checks and balances on new legislation or regulation, so institutions play an essential role in determining if a state can achieve its preferred policy outcome. In step 4, the type of coalition and institutional setup combined

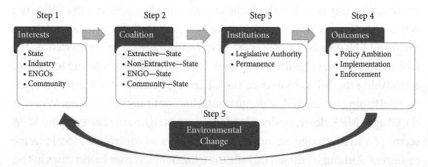

Figure 3.2 Coalition Process

predict an environmental policy outcome, which here refers to the policy choices a state makes about locating and regulating a large MPA. The final step incorporates environmental change into the framework.

Salience of Industry Interests (Step 1)

How coalitions form for a given MPA process depends on the salience of various industry interests in a region. When industries do have a strong interest in a particular area, it tends to overshadow the interests of other stakeholder groups. Large areas tend to have more significant industry interests because they encapsulate more marine resources. In other words, industry is more likely to be invested in MPA decisions about larger areas because they are more likely to have a bigger stake in them. Organized industry groups also tend to have more influence over the state than more diffuse non-industry groups due to the asymmetry of motivation, resources, and mobilization between them (March and Olsen 1983). Simply put, industry groups tend to have a more significant impact over policy outcomes because they are better organized and have more precise goals.

Table 3.1 describes the four indicators that measure the salience of industry interests in a given geographical space. Combined, they specify how dependent a particular industry is on a given region for its operations. When it is highly dependent on the area, then the salience of industry interests is high, and vice versa. The case studies to follow use a low-medium-high ordinal scale to assign values to each indicator for each industry involved.

The domestic political economy of each case determines the values that these variables take for each industry. There are two general trends worth noting across all large MPA cases. First, the factor specificity of the fishing industry relates to the size of the EEZ that it can operate in and its ability to attain licenses elsewhere. If a large MPA is only a small portion of the EEZ it is licensed to fish in, fishing fleets are much less likely to depend on it. The reverse is true in cases where a large MPA comprises most or all of a country's EEZ. And second, ecotourism operators almost always have high factor and asset specificity. They exist in the locations that they do because of the surrounding natural habitat (Hazari 1983). While fishing vessels can often travel to new waters, resorts and dive sites are not easy to relocate or substitute.

Table 3.1 Salience of Industry Interest Indicators

Indicator	Description	Guiding Questions
Intensity of Activity	The total economic output of a region for an industry, including relative to that industry's overall output and its contribution to the national economy.	• How much revenue does an industry generate in a given region? • What is the relative contribution of that revenue to the industry, the region, and the national economy?
Factor Specificity	The ability of industry to substitute land, labor, and capital resources elsewhere (i.e., coral reefs, fish stocks, oil deposits).	• Can the industry easily move its operations to other fishing grounds, dive sites, etc.?
Asset Specificity	The ability of industry to move assets from one activity to another (i.e., equipment suitability, vessel range).	• Are the industry's assets (i.e., facilities, vessels) easy to move to a new location?
Exogenous Stressors	The pressure an industry faces from factors outside of the specified region that limits its ability to absorb area restrictions.	• What is the industry's pre-existing regulatory burden? • What other external conditions affect profitability?

Of these four indicators, I place less weight on exogenous stressors to measure the overall salience of industry interests. The reduced weight is because a high value on the exogenous stressors indicator absent high values on the other three suggests that the industry is still not dependent on the area in question. If it were, some combination of its intensity of activity, factor specificity, and asset specificity would be high as well. Exogenous stressors include threats to an industry that exist outside of the proposed MPA area, such as the unexpected denial of fishing permits in other fishing grounds, minimum wage hikes, or a global decline in fish stocks. These stressors can strengthen an industry's resolve around its interests in a particular area, and they can sway governments to adopt a potentially more industry-friendly policy. But an industry still needs to convince the government that a specific area matters to its profitability, which exogenous stressors alone do not do.

When combined, these four indicators give us a sense for how much an industry depends on a given region. In the case studies to follow, I aggregate these indicators to provide one overall measure of each industry's salience of interests in the proposed MPA area. Like the individual indicators themselves, I assign an overall value on a low-moderate-high ordinal scale. These values predict the coalitions that form in an MPA process.

Coalition Formation (Step 2)

The salience of industry interests predicts which stakeholder group the state will align itself with in a large MPA process. Two theoretical expectations predict what type of coalition will emerge based on industry interests:

> Expectation 1. The state is more likely to form an informal coalition with an industry partner if that industry can demonstrate salient interests in a prospective large MPA site.

> Expectation 2. Holding interest salience equal, governments are more likely to privilege extractive industry interests over non-extractive industry interests.

The null of expectation 1 is that, absent salient industry interests, we can expect the state to form an informal coalition with environmental groups or a local community instead. In this framework, the state prioritizes industry over other stakeholder types if industry can demonstrate salient interests. These two expectations are consistent with scholarship on the neoliberal paradigm of environmentalism, discussed in chapter 2.

It is more accurate to think of these coalitions as representing a particular type of MPA politics rather than exclusive arrangements. For example, environmental groups may support a non-extractive–state coalition and even operate in ways similar to how they would in an ENGO–state coalition. The distinction lies in the underlying material interests and arguments used to support a given MPA policy outcome. When a state establishes a large MPA because it is expected to yield substantial benefits to the ecotourism industry, it relies on a different set of supporting arguments than it would for a strictly conservation-motivated MPA. The predicted outcomes for these two coalition types are often similar, but the process of arriving at them is different. A non-extractive–state coalition is also better suited to overcoming moderate extractive industry interests than an ENGO–state coalition because the state can claim to be bolstering rather than hindering the economy.

Institutional Factors (Step 3)

In this framework, institutions are an intervening step between coalitions and outcomes that can influence whether a state coalition can achieve its preferred policy outcome. The ability of the state—whether the main actor is a state leader or a branch of the civil service—to enact new MPA policy therefore depends on its ability to circumvent potential veto points. States face domestic checks and balances, so political opposition can prove insurmountable to a preferred result. Institutions that circumvent those checks and balances are therefore vital for new MPA legislation:

> Expectation 3. Political and legal institutions that allow a government to circumvent veto points make it more likely a coalition will achieve its policy goals.

These political and legal institutions are typically exogenous to a large MPA process, relying on preexisting political institutions or laws.

This expectation is deliberately broad because there are a few potential mechanisms through which it can work. In parliamentary systems, a state leader with a majority government can push through any legislation consistent with the law. There are virtually no veto points between executive preference and legislation. In a presidential system, on the other hand, it is usually difficult for an executive to enact legislation that needs congressional approval. The ability of the executive to achieve its preferred policy outcome may depend on the degree of authority that the executive has over protected area designations. In other instances, a new designation may not require legislative approval at all. Instead, a civil service organization may have a mandate with legal authority to identify and establish protected areas. When environmental groups initially lobby a state to create a new MPA, they tend to target the branch of government that has the highest likelihood of being able to legislate a new area.

Institutions are also crucial for determining the permanence of protected areas. The initial designation of an MPA is often not enough to ensure its longevity. Future governments can theoretically abolish them or alter their management plans. The permanence of an MPA and its management plan exists on a spectrum. Technically any piece of legislation can be overturned with the right level of support. How high the threshold to overturn an MPA is determines its degree of permanence. If that threshold is unfeasibly high, an MPA has a high degree of permanence. If MPA managers or politicians can easily alter a management plan unilaterally rather than through legislation, then that management plan has a low degree of permanence. Permanence is ultimately a measure of how likely it is that a government can alter an existing MPA, which again comes down to its ability to circumvent veto points. In some cases, it is actually easier to designate a new MPA than it is to alter an existing one. US president Donald Trump experienced that difficulty first-hand, as his administration faced a series of court challenges and law suits after attempting to reduce protections in a number of terrestrial and marine protected areas in the US.

Permanence is an especially important consideration because of the long-term importance of environmental change in this framework. As environmental conditions change, stakeholder beliefs about how best to pursue their preferences, and their interests, may shift. This shift can lead to a new coalition forming that may want to alter the existing management arrangement of an MPA. Whether the new coalition strengthens or weakens the restrictions within an area depends on the reasons it formed. Replenished fish stocks, for example, may motivate a government to loosen regulations. Conversely, the collapse of an ecosystem or species might provide a wake-up call that leads to stricter rules. Either way, the permanence of MPA legislation has a bearing on how dynamic the management of an MPA is.

Policy Outcomes (Step 4)

The state's coalition partner determines its level of policy ambition to protect an area, as well as its commitment to implementation and enforcement. Those policy decisions ultimately determine whether an MPA is rigorously protected, protected in name only, or somewhere in between. The following two-part expectation predicts the relationship between coalition type and MPA policy outcomes:

Expectation 4. a) An extractive industry coalition is more likely to yield weak or ineffective environmental policies.

b) A non-extractive industry, environmental group, or local community coalition is more likely to yield more robust environmental policies.

Determining the effectiveness of environmental policies can be challenging and, as noted, there is no one-size-fits-all approach to MPA management (see Claudet 2011). There is nonetheless a strong scientific basis for large-scale, no-take protections. The majority of the world's MPAs are paper parks that lack meaningful regulation, so despite the challenge of evaluating management effectiveness, we can still distinguish between no-take reserves, mixed-use MPAs with some conservation potential, and paper parks.

Assessing both the location of MPAs and their management is important for evaluating the level of policy ambition a given MPA represents. Location refers to the geographical site selected for a proposed large MPA as well as its boundaries. Is that site a biodiversity hotspot? Does the site contain damaging commercial activity? Why are the boundaries where they are? Will activity just outside the boundaries undermine its conservation potential? All of these questions, among others, speak to the conservation value of a prospective site. Sites that protect biodiversity hotspots, prevent damaging activity, or ideally both, represent more robust policies.

Comprehensive management plans are those that have explicit restrictions on use that the government then actively tries to enforce. The most comprehensive type of management plan is to create an entirely no-take reserve, in which the state bans all extractive uses. When a state sees a no-take reserve as impractical, there are a range of other planning techniques it can use. It may ban only specific extractive industries, impose stricter limits on vessels or catch, or designate specific zones within which industry can still operate. These mixed-use MPAs have fewer conservation benefits than no-take MPAs but may represent an important compromise between conservation and human use.

Often, a state will establish an MPA with little intention of effectively managing it. There are several reasons why a state would bother to do this, including social pressure from other states, meeting treaty commitments, or succumbing to pressure from environmental or local community groups. Once a state has committed to establishing an MPA in principle, it is more politically expedient to create the MPA with a weak management plan than it is to cancel or relocate it. The outcome in these scenarios is a paper park with few conservation benefits. These poorly managed MPAs are quite common, and states establish them in part to appease interest groups with little intention of adequately investing in them (Fox et al. 2012; Rife et al. 2013). Put simply, the state may feel it is politically prudent to establish an MPA and not manage it well than to be seen as ignoring marine conservation entirely.

One final point worth noting is that these expectations refer specifically to management plans, rather than actual conservation results. Many smaller countries lack the resources to adequately implement these strategies, despite the motivation to do so. The policy outcome of interest is therefore whether a management plan is comprehensive relative to the capacity of a given country. It would distort any global assessment of MPAs to compare implementation without controlling for capacity. My analysis of the US and Palau case studies to follow, for example, takes into account their wildly different financial and technical resources.

Environmental Change (Step 5)

The final stage of this process incorporates environmental change. A large MPA and its management plan are not necessarily permanent; states can respond to changing environmental conditions. Environmental change refers to changes in the underlying ecosystems an MPA protects and can take several forms. For example, it can indicate increasingly declining fish stocks or coral bleaching, but it can also indicate species recovery or ecosystem restoration. Canada's decades-old moratorium on the Northwest Atlantic cod fishery in response to a total collapse of fish stocks in the 1990s is one (extreme) example of environmental change leading to a revised management plan (Walters and Maguire 1996). D. G. Webster has documented these processes of environmental change and governance response in the oceans, demonstrating an ongoing iterative process of fisheries management (Webster 2009, 2015). Her action cycle/structural context (AC/SC) framework provides a sophisticated model of these processes (Webster 2015).

This process is iterative because the underlying ecological and economic incentive structures in an area shift. Economic incentives contribute to the environmental policy decisions that states make, but those decisions also lead to environmental change that can, in turn, reshape economic incentives. The fishing industry does not usually like restrictions on take, but it cares about its long-term survivability (Webster 2009). Healthy marine ecosystems are similarly the cornerstone of the ecotourism industry. The political economy of an area and environmental change within it are interconnected. A decline in marine resources can, sometimes, be a precursor to better management over time. The commercial fishing industry in some fisheries has been more open to area management strategies in recent years as it realizes that business-as-usual management practices are failing to ensure sustainable fish stocks (DeSombre and Barkin 2011; Campling, Havice, and Howard 2012). When their preferred less costly and less effective schemes fail to preserve fish, many fisheries management groups have over time adopted stricter and more efficient management strategies (Webster 2009). MPA management is therefore not static but is an iterative process that must take into account dynamic underlying incentive structures.

On balance, fisheries management is failing to prevent the severe overexploitation of global fish stocks. As previously noted, the increasing technological sophistication and overcapitalization of the fishing industry have rapidly devastated fish stocks over the past several decades (DeSombre and Barkin 2011; Barkin and DeSombre 2013). This depletion is leading to subsequent changes in how governments and the industry itself are managing fisheries, albeit often on too small a scale and too late (Campling, Havice, and Howard 2012). The increasing scarcity of fish stocks is leading to the use of MPAs as fisheries management tools to ensure the long-term sustainability of the industry. Increasing shortage is also leading to conflict between recreational fishing, commercial fishing, and non-fishing sectors such as ecotourism over how and for whom governments should manage MPAs (Campling, Havice, and Howard 2012). What all of these trends point to is that threats to the long-term viability of their businesses could potentially shift fishing industry interests toward stricter government regulation of marine resources in some regions, including through MPAs.

Environmental change is the reason that the coalition process outlined here is an iterative one. No group has such rigid interests for a given MPA that rapid environmental decline would not give it pause for thought. The industry profit-motive is not strictly a short-term one, and businesses care about their longevity. As resource scarcity threatens long-term viability, many companies will prefer outcomes that may reduce their short-term profits. Though environmental change is an important theoretical component of this framework for the reasons just given, I neglect it in the case studies to follow. The reason for the neglect is that large MPAs are still too new—my earliest case study is from 2012—for long-term policy shifts due to environmental change to be observed. Webster (2009, 2015), however, develops the theory and empirics of environmental change in fisheries in her work, citing many examples that, I would argue, foreshadow the future of large MPA politics and policy.

A Theory of Large Marine Protected Area Politics

This chapter proposed a domestic political economy driven environmental norm diffusion framework to explain the adoption and localization of the large MPA norm. Chapter 2 explored the emergence of the norm, from its early proponents in the US environmental community to its global spread, with a focus on international actors and mechanisms of norm diffusion. This chapter provides the conceptual framework for looking more closely at the role of domestic actors pursuing their strategic interests in a norm diffusion process. Domestic political economies are what explain norm localization in this framework. This approach suggests that norm localization is a process through which the state amalgamates and integrates the interests of domestic stakeholders with its own, ultimately forming an informal coalition with a specific group. Whether that coalition is with extractive industry, non-extractive industry, environmental groups, or local communities predicts environmental policy outcomes.

In this framework, the salience of industry interests does most of the explanatory work. There are a few reasons why this is both justifiable and important. First, it accurately reflects that state-based environmentalism is decidedly neoliberal. Industry interests are privileged because, simply, states privilege them. Second, by breaking down interest salience into its component parts, we can move further, beyond the more generic understanding that industry is powerful to better understand the source and the limits of that power. And third, as the case studies to follow demonstrate, an industry-focused theoretical framework captures the political dynamics of large MPA campaigns and policymaking well.

I will turn now to those large MPA case studies. The politics of large MPA campaigns have been incredibly dynamic, ranging from straightforward conservation wins to hotly contested battles. They have directly involved presidents, prime ministers, high-level officials, and marine conservation luminaries. They also reveal much about the reach and the limitations of industry influence over conservation. The campaigns for PRIMNM in the US, the Coral Sea Marine Park in Australia, and the Palau National Marine Sanctuary in Palau tell a varied story. They all led to hundreds of thousands of square kilometers of protections. But how they got there and whether they represent conservation "wins" are decidedly more difficult questions to answer—questions that the following chapters will take up.

PART II
THE POLITICS
OF CONSERVATION CAMPAIGNS

4
Presidents Bush and Obama in the Pacific Remote Islands

The Pacific Remote Islands comprise seven islands, atolls, and reefs located southwest of Hawaii. President Bush established a national monument, the PRIMNM, there in 2009. Five years later, in 2014, President Obama expanded it six fold from its original 225,000 km^2 to 1,270,000 km^2. This chapter documents the politics of that expansion. The expanded monument covers an area that is entirely uninhabited and—aside from occasional military personnel or conservation workers—the islands themselves receive no visitors. The Pacific Remote Islands monument is what many marine conservationists would consider low-hanging fruit: it is remote, has no indigenous population, and commercial activity there is minimal.[1] A small amount of commercial fishing did, however, occur within the boundaries of the monument before its creation. The fishing industry took up arms in response to both the monument's initial designation and its expansion, seeing it as an infringement on their autonomy. The efforts to expand the monument led to a highly politicized battle between congressional Republicans and President Obama, and between the fishing industry and ENGOs. Expansion of the Pacific Remote Islands monument was a victory for marine conservation, but as of this writing the main industry body in the region was still fighting to regain its lost access to these waters, albeit so far without much luck.

The commercial fishing industry's inability to mount a coherent, convincing challenge to protections characterizes the politics of conserving the Pacific Remote Islands. Despite clear opposition to the monument, aggressive lobbying in Washington, and efforts to rally community support, the fishing industry had relatively limited impact on conservation policy in the area. Presidents Bush and Obama opted for ambitious protections that represented a victory for conservation groups at the expense of industry, though there were some concessions. The central argument of this chapter is that the commercial fishing industry failed to substantially impact policy because its bargaining position was weak, and that position was weak because

Conserving the Oceans. Justin Alger, Oxford University Press (2021). © Oxford University Press.
DOI: 10.1093/oso/9780197540534.003.0004

the industry was unable to demonstrate high interest salience in the Pacific Remote Islands. The 2014 expansion of the monument reflected a pattern of diffusion of the large MPA norm in the US that by then was becoming well established: the designation of robust, predominantly no-take large MPAs surrounding overseas territories with minimal commercial activity. The designation and expansion of the Papahānaumokuākea and Marianas Trench monuments followed this pattern, as did the designation and expansion of the Pacific Remote Islands.

The Western Pacific commercial fishing industry and Republicans opposed the Pacific Remote Islands monument because they saw it as a threat to the long-term viability of the fishing sector, but also on the grounds that the protections represented an overreach of executive authority—granted to the president by the 1906 Antiquities Act. Executive action to create large marine monuments was unprecedented in the first 100-year history of the act, but became common practice under President Bush. President Bush's multiple uses of the act to establish marine monuments paved the way for President Obama to pursue even more ambitious marine conservation initiatives, like the Pacific Remote Islands monument expansion. Congressional Republicans now openly refer to Bush's use of the Antiquities Act as an "unfortunate mistake," but blithely contend that Obama was "on steroids" with the monument expansions (*Committee on Natural Resources* 2015). The industry and congressional Republicans eventually found an ally in President Trump, whose administration unprecedently scaled back protections for national monuments in Utah and the Atlantic. Trump was poised to attempt the same in the Pacific Remote Islands toward the end of his presidency, but, as of this writing, was running out of time after losing the 2020 election.

This chapter will explore the diffusion of the large MPA norm in the US through an in-depth case study of the 2014 expansion of the Pacific Remote Islands monument. The political economy of the Pacific Remote Islands was conducive to large-scale, robust environmental protections. This chapter will examine that political economy to show how and why the fishing industry failed to achieve its goals in the environmental policy bargaining process leading up to the expansion. Vehement opposition and strong rhetoric were not enough to counteract a lack of bargaining leverage—the result of having a minimal demonstrable commercial stake in the area. Recognizing the favorable political economy of the area, environmental groups acted to persuade Bush and Obama that the benefits of large-scale, remote protections far outweighed minor industry interests. Pew, National Geographic, and the Marine Conservation Institute, among others, wielded considerable influence with the White House, paving the way for what was at the time the world's largest non-contiguous MPA.

Establishing the Precedent for Marine Monuments

President Bush's dissatisfaction with the pace and effectiveness of federal marine conservation measures led to his use of the Antiquities Act to establish Papahānaumokuākea in 2006, the first marine national monument in the US.[2] The obstacles to quicker and more ambitious federal designations were both bureaucratic and political. At the root of both types of obstruction is a relatively convoluted legal structure around MPA designation. This convoluted legal structure leads to competing processes at different government departments, and occasional jurisdictional battles. It also provides a source of political discontent when one type of designation is used to circumvent the preferred process of a given stakeholder group, such as when conservation measures impinge on fisheries management areas. This inexorably upsets the fishing industry, as it did in the Pacific Remote Islands. At the federal level alone, there are five distinct marine area management designations: refuges, marine sanctuaries, national parks, sanctuaries, fisheries management areas, and monuments. Table 4.1 summarizes the five types of designation and the agencies and authorities associated with them.

Refuges can only extend up to 12 nautical miles from shore, so they are necessarily small scale. They are created and administered by the Fish and Wildlife Service (FWS) for various reasons, including responses to crises, the personal preferences of officials and legislators, funding, social program priorities, donations, and wildlife needs (Fischman 2005). These refuges are all designed with specific conservation and sustainability goals in mind, with management practices intended to reflect those goals.[3] As of 2020, the refuge system included 568 refuges, with more than 180 of those protecting marine habitats.[4] Marine areas beyond 12 miles from shore are federal waters and typically fall under NOAA jurisdiction.[5] In addition, there are 61 National Parks in the US, some of which contain ocean areas. National Parks are created through congressional legislation and are administered by the National Park Service.

A federal MPA under NOAA jurisdiction can refer to either a sanctuary or a fisheries management area, depending on which division of NOAA

Table 4.1 US Federal MPA Designations

Designation	Legal Basis	Administered By	Parent Agency
Refuge	1966 Refuge Administration Act	Fish and Wildlife Service	Department of the Interior
National Park	Act of Congress	National Park Service	Department of the Interior
Sanctuary	1972 Marine Protection, Research, and Sanctuaries Act/1992 National Marine Sanctuaries Act	National Oceanic and Atmospheric Administration	Department of Commerce
Fisheries Management Area	1976 Magnuson-Stevens Fishery Conservation and Management Act	Regional Fishery Management Councils, NOAA	Department of Commerce
Monument	1906 Antiquities Act	Determined by Proclamation	Determined by Proclamation

oversees it. There is a bureaucratic and philosophical divide within NOAA between its Office of National Marine Sanctuaries (NOAA Sanctuaries) and its National Marine Fisheries Service (NOAA Fisheries).[6] The 1972 Marine Protection, Research, and Sanctuaries Act (MPRSA)—later amended and now formally known as the 1992 National Marine Sanctuaries Act (NMSA)—gave NOAA the authority to identify and designate national marine sanctuaries that are of national significance following a public review process (Studds 1992). The 1976 Magnuson-Stevens Act, on the other hand, established eight regional fisheries management councils that are mandated to manage fisheries to achieve maximum sustainable yield (Magnuson and Stevens 1976). One such council—the Western Pacific Regional Fishery Management Council (Wespac)—was the primary opposition to the Pacific Remote Islands monument.

NOAA Sanctuaries runs the sanctuaries program, while NOAA Fisheries in conjunction with the eight fisheries councils are responsible for fisheries management areas. Both NOAA Sanctuaries and NOAA Fisheries operate in the same ocean space, with the former having a strict conservation mandate and the latter a sustainable extraction mandate. There is a provision within NOAA's statute for Sanctuaries to take over if Fisheries fails to achieve sustainability goals for a given area, but its use is uncommon.[7] The fisheries councils had established 182 fishery management areas with various levels of protection as of 2013 (NOAA 2015), while NOAA Sanctuaries has established 14 sanctuaries as of 2020 (NOAA 2020).

The eight fisheries management councils established by the Magnuson-Stevens Act feature prominently in the politics of marine conservation in the US. They tend to be opposed to executive action on MPAs, seeing it as an infringement on their efforts to manage their respective areas. These councils and the local fishing industry are closely affiliated, with council members often drawn directly from industry. The councils, while each a government body under NOAA, are de facto industry organizations with a government mandate to ensure sustainable fisheries. This industry-friendly composition has led to mixed results. The North Pacific Fishery Management Council (NPFMC) has arguably performed well in pursuing maximum sustainable yield, for example, whereas the Northwest Atlantic Fisheries Organization (NAFO) failed to prevent the collapse of cod stocks in the region (*Committee on Natural Resources* 2015). Wespac oversees the area where all three marine national monuments exceeding 200,000 km^2 are located.

In addition to these federal MPA designations through the FWS, NOAA, and its affiliated fisheries councils, there are also hundreds of state-level MPAs. All told, the US has nearly 1,800 MPAs of various federal- and state-level designations (NOAA 2020). The vast majority of these, however, have relatively weak management provisions. According to the National Marine Protected Areas Center—the MPA research arm of NOAA—86% of US MPAs allow some form of extractive activity (NOAA 2020). As of 2020, the US had designated only 3% of its continental waters as no-take (NOAA 2020). Many of these refuges, sanctuaries, and fisheries management areas may be achieving crucial local conservation and sustainability goals, but they are not leading to a comprehensive MPA network that is ecologically representative of the marine life of the US. The lack of cohesion is not surprising given the distinct processes in place at multiple levels of government, and is certainly not unique to the US (Kareiva 2006).

The history of the Northwestern Hawaiian Islands—now home to the Papahānaumokuākea Marine National Monument—reveals the complexity of this system of overlapping jurisdictions at work. The first protections for the region date back to President Teddy Roosevelt's protection of seabirds from poachers in 1903. President Franklin Roosevelt followed suit by establishing a wildlife refuge in 1940. Lyndon Johnson, Ronald Reagan, and Bill Clinton would also add their own protections during their presidencies. When Bush took an interest in the area in 2006 it had been undergoing the NOAA sanctuaries process for five years, which had been initiated by President Clinton in 2001.[8] The sanctuaries process was at a standstill because of a developing turf war between NOAA Sanctuaries and NOAA Fisheries over the region.[9] The CEQ—the environmental arm of the executive branch—repeatedly set deadlines for NOAA that it always missed.[10] Frustrated with the slow process, Bush asked his advisors how he could expedite it.[11] After consulting with Department of the Interior legal counsel, they proposed using the Antiquities Act to establish a marine monument.[12] Bush agreed, and his use of the act to create Papahānaumokuākea in 2006 was its first ever use to establish a marine national monument, setting a precedent for the creation of large MPAs in the US.

Bush's creation of Papahānaumokuākea had a direct and immediate impact on further marine conservation efforts in the US. President Bush was so pleased with the positive response to Papahānaumokuākea from the environmental community and the public that he became committed to the idea of leaving a blue legacy—an idea encouraged by the environmental groups lobbying Bush for more designations.[13] The Marianas Trench and Pacific Remote Islands designations were the byproducts of Bush's newfound commitment.[14] One environmental group executive refers to Papahānaumokuākea as one of the MPAs that marked a "turning point in marine conservation that set a new global standard."[15]

Following Papahānaumokuākea, decision makers began to view MPAs in the Marianas Trench, the Pacific Remote Islands, and even the more commercially active northeast coast as likely possibilities.[16] It was the Antiquities Act that made these large-scale designations possible. The Antiquities Act expedites the creation of large MPAs for a few reasons. First, a president can unilaterally invoke it, bypassing any potential congressional opposition to a given monument. Second, a president can also invoke it rather easily, as the only major stipulation for the creation of a nature monument is that there be a scientific basis for it.[17] Third, the act does not require any public consultation, including with industry groups, although despite this not being a legal requirement, every marine national monument created to date has nonetheless included some form of civic engagement (*Committee on Natural Resources* 2015). And fourth, the Antiquities Act allows a president to bypass the civil service. Avoiding the civil service is beneficial because NOAA is required to engage in public consultation, and as noted, is internally divided. According to prominent environmental activists, the civil service also often forms the most significant opposition to large-scale conservation because it tends to be slow moving, and large marine national monuments tend to realign authorities within the bureaucracy, leading to some pushback.[18]

But invoking the Antiquities Act involves a trade-off between expedience and public engagement. The lack of public engagement is one of the major criticisms stemming from the fishing industry about the designation and expansion of the Pacific Remote Islands monument. There was broad public support for the monument at the time, but industry stakeholders argue that the process excludes them, and furthermore that the Antiquities Act is an illegitimate way of avoiding the regional fisheries councils. Industry heavily influences these councils, so it is no surprise they are its preferred regulatory body. This tension between executive action and traditional, more industry-friendly mechanisms was central to the politics of coalition formation surrounding the designation and expansion of the Pacific Remote Islands monument.

Conserving the Pacific Remote Islands

Conserving the Pacific Remote Islands was a two-phase process, depicted in Figure 4.1, with both phases involving a similar set of industry and ENGO stakeholders. In the first phase, President Bush created the monument in five distinct zones around seven islands, atolls, and reefs southwest of Hawaii. The announcement was made on January 6, 2009, alongside a similar announcement creating the Marianas Trench Marine National Monument.[19] The Pacific Remote Islands monument extended 50 nautical miles from the shores of the seven fixtures—a limit that Bush felt was sufficient to achieve conservation goals and one that would not overly antagonize the fishing industry.[20] It would also appease the US Navy, which pushed back initially because it was worried the monument might impede its operations.[21] The process involved direct collaboration between environmental groups and the executive branch.[22] Leaders from Pew, National Geographic, and the Marine Conservation Institute, among others, collaborated directly with the CEQ, Vice President Dick Cheney, First Lady Laura Bush, and President Bush himself.[23] Although both Bush and Cheney expressed concern about the impact of the monument on commercial fishing in the Western Pacific, the industry had little direct involvement in the decision-making process.[24]

The second phase was Obama's expansion of the monument around three of the five zones created by Bush at Jarvis Island, the Johnston Atoll,

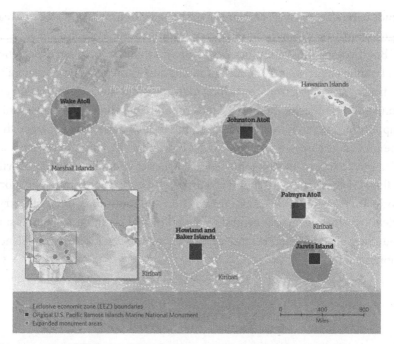

Figure 4.1 Pacific Remote Islands Marine National Monument Map

Source: The Pew Charitable Trusts (2014). Copyright © 2014–2015 The Pew Charitable Trusts. All Rights Reserved. Reproduced with permission.

and Wake Island (see Figure 4.1). The process leading up to the expansion was undertaken primarily by the CEQ in consultation with Obama and a handful of ENGO leaders. The White House kept the expansion so quiet that senior employees of some of the environmental groups involved in the 2009 designation did not know about it until the official announcement, leaving them scrambling to piece together last minute promotional campaigns to rally public support.[25] As with the Bush White House, environmental group leaders were the chief advisors to the Obama White House on the expansion of the monument, while also taking on the task of garnering political and public support.[26]

With the precedent for large MPAs established during the Bush presidency, the task of rallying support was relatively straightforward the second time around. Environmental groups had hoped for the fully expanded monument in 2009, so they had already made the case for it. In 2014 all they needed to do was provide updated scientific information about the benefits of large MPAs to migratory species (Sala et al. 2014). Bush limited the monument to

50 nautical miles from shore because he was worried about potential losses to the Western Pacific tuna fleet and hindering the US Navy.[27] Obama, as one insider put it, was "more predisposed toward [environmental] precaution and less predisposed toward minor industry interests."[28] On June 17, 2014, Secretary of State John Kerry announced that the Obama administration would expand the Pacific Remote Islands monument around all five of the existing zones—a commitment that would later be scaled back to just the three zones around Jarvis, Johnston, and Wake.

Environmental groups both lobbied the executive branch and provided the scientific reporting needed to justify the increase. Their goal was to provide Obama and the CEQ with a strong scientific justification for the expansion—a requirement for invoking the Antiquities Act—and to further make the case that it would be politically popular. The relative secrecy of the process and quick implementation suggest that Obama, like Bush, was intent on pushing the monument through. By 2014, the norm of establishing large MPAs in the US was deeply ingrained enough that environmental groups assumed that Obama would follow Bush's lead.[29] The prevailing view was that if Bush did it, Obama undoubtedly would too.[30] The question was not whether Obama would designate a large MPA, but rather when and where. So rather than convincing the Obama administration of the merits of large MPAs, environmental groups shifted some of their focus to scientific study and public outreach. They wanted to make a strong case so that Obama would pursue the most ambitious protections possible.

Following Kerry's sooner-than-expected announcement of the Pacific Remote Islands expansion, environmental groups and industry lobbyists quickly began to mobilize support for their respective positions. Environmental groups rallied support from high-profile elites, politicians, and the public, particularly in Hawaii and the US territories in the Pacific. Interest groups supporting the expansion flooded Obama with letters of support. A small group of high-profile ocean conservation luminaries including the likes of Sylvia Earle and James Cameron touted the conservation benefits of the monument (Ocean Elders 2014). A similar letter signed by over 200 cultural leaders in the Pacific Islands stated the importance of the monument to protect the ancestral and cultural heritage of the area. Another letter from a group of over 50 marine scientists from environmental groups and academia reaffirmed the science behind large MPAs, particularly their importance for protecting species at risk. Another representing six marine research institutes in the region echoed the scientific case. A letter similarly touting the monument's conservation potential from virtually all of the world's major marine conservation NGOs lauded the announcement. The message included the signatures of Conservation International, Environmental Defense Fund, Greenpeace, National Geographic, Oceana, Pew, Sierra Club, and the World Wide Fund for Nature (WWF), among others. There was certainly widespread support for the expansion, but the commercial fishing industry was intent on putting up a fight.

The Western Pacific Fleet

Opposition to the monument was led by a subset of the US Western Pacific commercial fishing industry. Neither the recreational fishing industry nor the ecotourism industry factored into the politics of the monument. The recreational fishing lobby is particularly influential in the US and is often a significant obstacle to marine conservation, so its absence was a boon for conservationists.[31] Closing an area to fishing is difficult when recreational fishing interests are salient in a region, and even basic protections for small regions have been hard fought and painfully slow to come to fruition.[32] Recreational fishing in the Pacific Remote Islands was so insignificant that the Bush and Obama administrations did not see a need to ban it, so the monument officially remains open to sport fishing (and therefore is not technically a fully no-take reserve, albeit a de facto one).[33] The monument is similarly too remote to sustain an ecotourism industry. As a consequence, environmental groups and the government could not make the case that the designation would boost ecotourism revenues.

The commercial fishing industry stake in the Pacific Remote Islands was limited to the presence of fleets based primarily out of American Samoa and Hawaii. The modest 37-boat Western Pacific industry contributes less than 2% of total US landings revenues, but it has a substantial regional presence as the biggest industry in American Samoa. Between 2014 and 2016, the US Western Pacific fishing industry came under several pressures: the Kiribati government pushed it out of its traditional fishing grounds in Kiribati; there was a global decline in tuna prices in 2015 due to oversupply; and the federal minimum wage was extended to American Samoa, increasing costs for boat operators and the two canneries on the island, one of which shut down in 2016. Given these pressures, the industry tends to be opposed to any additional fishing restrictions, no matter how minimal their impact, including the Pacific Remote Islands monument. Industry advocates see the monument as just another form of limitation imposed by authorities far removed from both the region and the industry.[34]

The primary challenge the Western Pacific fishing fleet faced was that it depended on increasingly competitive fishing licenses in the Pacific. Those licenses are coordinated by the Western and Central Pacific Fisheries Commission (WCPFC), whose membership includes all of the countries with a stake in commercial fisheries in the area. To enhance their bargaining power within the commission, Pacific island states formed the 17-member Pacific Island Forum Fisheries Association (FFA) to serve as an advisory group to and coordinating body for its member states. In 1988 the US and the FFA negotiated the South Pacific Tuna Treaty, which allots the US Western Pacific fishing fleet a specific number of aggregate fishing days across the EEZs of its member states. This agreement does not specify which countries would provide the fishing days, however, which became a problem for the US industry in 2014 following a major policy realignment in Kiribati.

In 2014, Kiribati declared that it would reduce the number of fishing days permitted to US vessels from its 2014 allotment of 4,313 to just 300 in 2015 (Annesley 2015). This reduction was in part an effort to develop its domestic fishing industry, but also to sell more lucrative permits to China and Taiwan instead. Fishing the high seas was not an option for the US fleet because the WCPFC's Tropical Tuna Measure limits the number of days its member states can fish there, reflecting historical uses of the high seas that did not account for the US fleet's sudden de facto exile from Kiribati waters.[35] The reduction in fishing days in Kiribati combined with the typically low high seas allotment forced the US fleet to the EEZs of other FFA members, which are much further away from American Samoa than Kiribati, resulting in dramatically increased operating costs.[36] The decline in fishing days in Kiribati combined with preexisting high seas limits created significant challenges for the commercial fishing industry in the region.[37]

Tuna prices also fell in 2015, further complicating regional fishery politics at the time. Parties renegotiate the South Pacific Tuna Treaty on a five-year basis, but in recent years members have had to settle for one-year interim agreements. In August 2015, the US agreed to pay $67 million for 8,250 days of fishing access in 2016. When the price of skipjack tuna plummeted in the latter half of the year, the agreement was no longer tenable. US industry operators claimed they could not afford to pay their respective fees to the island nations given the sudden price drop, instead asking to renegotiate the number of fishing days down to 3,700.[38]

In January 2016, the FFA stopped granting licenses to US operators in response to their failure to pay fees owed, and the National Marine Fisheries Service (NMFS)—the US fishing regulator—grounded the US fleet. For their part, many FFA countries rely on the region's $3 billion tuna industry for nearly 10% of their GDP (Pacific Islands Forum Fisheries Agency 2014), so they could not afford to renegotiate down to a lesser value. The US fleet faced challenges because its fee was fixed but its revenue was variable, contingent on fluctuating catch value. In poor years, such as 2015, an industry with already low profit margins suffers. The State Department eventually announced that it would intervene to prevent the potential collapse of the Western Pacific fleet, though a long-term solution to the problem seems elusive as of this writing. At the time, some industry representatives called the future of the South Pacific Tuna Treaty into question since its value to US operators is greatly diminished if Kiribati remains effectively closed.[39] They were right.

On January 18, 2016, the US formally withdrew from the South Pacific Tuna Treaty on the grounds that it was no longer viable, reneging on its previous commitment to purchase fishing days for 2016. One of the central issues was that the cost of purchasing fishing days had become prohibitively high, reportedly raising overall costs to $600 to $700 per ton (White 2019a). The problem, according to the industry, is that US operators cannot compete with heavily subsidized Chinese and Korean fleets that can absorb these costs. The US was effectively outbid. For their part, Pacific island nations were in no position to turn away increased revenue from these subsidized fleets, so the balance of power in the Pacific shifted away from the US. To compound the issue, US operators also tend to face stricter domestic regulatory standards surrounding worker safety and pay. Faced with higher operating costs and less government support than Chinese and Korean competitors, many operators were beginning to see the writing on the wall. Although parties renegotiated the treaty in December 2016 with better terms for the US, the Trump administration refused to ratify it.

Without a lifeline, the industry is poised to decline. As of 2020 that decline was seemingly underway. Federal regulations limit the Western Pacific fleet to 40 boats, ensuring that the total biomass removed the ocean remains relatively constant.[40] In the three years from 2016 to 2019, the fleet shrunk from this historical limit of 40 to just 24 vessels. One major operator—South

Pacific Tuna Corporation—slashed its fleet from 14 vessels to just 6, with plans to find buyers for the remaining boats. Tellingly, the buyers of the first 8 vessels included companies from China, the Philippines, South Korea, and Pacific island nations (White 2019b).

The decline also has consequences for American Samoa, as its economy is highly dependent on tuna, with canned tuna being the territory's primary export. In 2015, the fish processing business accounted for 15.5% of its labor force (Central Intelligence Agency 2019a). If US boats are forced to fish further away from US processing facilities, they are likely to take their catch to places like Thailand instead.[41] Adding to this industry malaise, American Samoa also lost its minimum wage waiver in 2015.[42] American Samoa is classified as a Small Island Developing State (SIDS), exempting it from some federal regulations. These exemptions included the federal minimum wage until it was rolled out across the US territories. American Samoa repeatedly delayed the rollout through Congress, citing the negative impact it would have on the territory's tuna industry.[43] Its October 2015 attempt to delay failed to pass, however, pushing the minimum wage hike through after previous successful efforts to avoid it. In addition to losing its traditional fishing grounds, the industry was also facing cost increases through this wage hike.

In 2014—when President Obama expanded the Pacific Remote Islands monument—it was not yet clear just how grim the industry outlook would become. It was nonetheless clear that the industry faced fairly severe economic pressures. In part because of these economic pressures, Wespac took an aggressive stance against the designation of marine monuments in the Western Pacific as a matter of principle. It sees executive action on marine monuments as undemocratic and a threat to the long-term viability of the Western Pacific fishing industry.[44] When a president uses the Antiquities Act and establishes a monument, Wespac no longer has the authority to manage the space within it. Wespac claimed that this threatened regional autonomy because it excludes the local fishing industry from decisions that can have significant impact on it.[45] Wespac acknowledged that these monuments have widespread public support, despite its claims of executive overreach.[46] But that support, Wespac argued, was primarily the result of well-funded advocacy campaigns with which it could not compete.[47] Despite the pressures facing the industry, Wespac had little political influence over the designation of marine monuments within its fishery management jurisdiction. This lack of control led Wespac to take a firm stance against any and all uses of the Antiquities Act in the Western Pacific.

Wespac communicated these concerns to the CEQ through a report submitted on September 9, 2014—just two weeks before the expansion was formally signed into law (Western Pacific Regional Fishery Management Council 2014). This report included testimony from a handful of local politicians and industry groups opposing the monument. Wespac argued that the monument did not have any conservation value because turtles and seabirds were already highly protected in the region, and the monument would not contribute in a meaningful way to reducing overfishing of highly migratory tuna stocks. The claim was, however, inconsistent with the growing scientific consensus that large MPAs can contribute to protecting highly migratory large predatory fish like tuna.[48] Wespac argued that, despite being the largest MPA in the world at the time, the Pacific Remote Islands monument was too small to have a meaningful impact on tuna overfishing.

The basis of Wespac's argument was that where fishers catch tuna is dynamic, varying considerably from year to year. For example, the share of the US purse seine fleet catch in the Pacific Remote Islands was 21% in 1997, 10% in 1998, and just 6% in 1999. Wespac's point was that the area might be more important for the Western Pacific fleet in certain years. The two-decade-old figures supported Wespac's point, but its reliance on them also revealed that the fleet's dependence on the region had been relatively low since then. The annual variance argument was also somewhat contradictory to the claim that large MPAs cannot protect migratory species. Large MPAs allow species such as tuna a reprieve from commercial fishing in a given ocean area, so years in which they are in the monument area in higher concentration increases the potential conservation value of the monument.

The Wespac report raised some important questions about the conservation potential and economic impact of massive closures, but it reflected a broader strategy of opposing large MPAs on any and all grounds, many of which proved to be incorrect or contradictory. Conservationists often argue that the creation of a large MPA in one place can encourage other states to follow suit. In a critique of this argument, the Wespac report claimed that "Kiribati has no intention of closing all fishing in its EEZ around the Phoenix Islands" and that "No country this dependent on fishing will close off entirely a major part of its EEZ to fishing. Not even Palau, where fishing is [the] second biggest earner after tourism" (Western Pacific Regional Fishery Management Council 2014). Since the release of the report, Kiribati did, in fact, close the Phoenix Islands to all commercial fishing and Palau closed 80% of its EEZ to fishing. These statements amount to little more than failed predictions, but they reflected a willful blindness to the growing importance of large MPAs as a tool for global marine conservation.

Similarly, in questioning the science of large MPAs, one Wespac representative claimed that Papahānaumokuākea was failing to achieve its goals because the endangered monk seal population was doing better outside of the monument than within.[49] The reason for this was that the monk seal was struggling to compete with the resurgent top predator biomass within the monument. This point certainly raises questions about how best to protect endangered monk seals, but it is also a tacit acknowledgment that large MPAs do have clear conservation benefits. Top predator biomass is one of the most important indicators of ecosystem health (DeMartini et al. 2008), so an increase in Papahānaumokuākea suggests that the then 10-year-old monument was contributing to a healthier, more resilient ecosystem. Wespac's hard-line opposition to large MPAs likely only serves to prevent it having a more influential role in marine conservation discussions, and this hard-line strategy has led many politicians, environmental groups, and often the media to perceive Wespac as being dogmatic in its opposition to large MPAs, rather than reasoned and balanced. This perception unfortunately detracts from Wespac's more valid claims about the dynamism of fisheries and the minimal stakeholder engagement in the establishment of marine monuments.

The Limits of Industry Influence in the Pacific

Advocates for the monument anticipated the arguments of the commercial fishing industry well in advance, so they were well prepared to counter them. By the time that Wespac had submitted its report to the CEQ, environmental groups and marine scientists had already submitted scientific and economic reports to the White House that addressed nearly all of Wespac's points. Establishing the biodiversity importance of the region was easy, having already successfully made the case to the Bush White House (in a still-unreleased report). More challenging was addressing Wespac's economic case. Wespac was representing a vulnerable industry with low profit margins that was critical to many people in American Samoa and Hawaii, so the White House could not dismiss it. The Western Pacific commercial fishing industry was under a great deal of strain, but advocates successfully argued that the monument had little to do with that.

Table 4.2 Industry Interests in the Pacific Remote Islands Monument

Industry	Intensity of Activity	Factor Specificity	Asset Specificity	Exogenous Stressors	Overall
Commercial Fishing	Low	Low	Low	High	Low

Commercial fishers' dependence on the area now protected by the monument was minimal, so the political economy of the region favored environmental groups. Table 4.2 summarizes the factors that determine the salience of the commercial fishing industry's interests in the area now protected by the expanded Pacific Remote Islands monument. The Western Pacific fleet did not rely on the monument area for the vast majority of its catch (low intensity), its traditional and prospective fishing grounds were elsewhere (low factor specificity), and its trawlers and gear were not in any way specific to the site of the monument (low asset specificity). The challenges the industry faced in the region revolved almost entirely around reduced access to the EEZs of Pacific Island nations, the decreasing profitability of its operations, declining tuna prices, and the wage increase discussed earlier (high exogenous stressors). While the price of tuna is only a short-term stressor, reduced access and the wage increase are potentially permanent.

The entirety of the Western Pacific fleet's annual catch is a modest portion of the entire US fishing industry's annual catch. In 2012, the total landings revenue of the US fishing industry was just shy of $5.1 billion (US Department of Commerce 2014). The Western Pacific fleet's total landings revenue for the same year was over $91.5 million—just 1.8% of the national total (US Department of Commerce 2014). There was not a large amount of revenue at stake in the region. A 2014 environmental group report strengthened the case further by noting that "tuna fishing occurs episodically in the proposed area" (Sala et al. 2014). The report used data from the Hawaii-based *Longline Logbook Summary Report* to produce figures representing the industry's reliance on the area. The landings revenue for the area now covered by the Pacific Remote Islands monument was less than $4.6 million in 2012, amounting to just 5% of the fleet's revenue and 0.09% of the national total. The intensity of fishing activity in the area was therefore quite low from both a regional and a national perspective.

Moreover, the figures in the Sala et al. (2014) report were for the expansion of the monument to the 200 nautical mile limit around all five of the zones Bush established. President Obama ultimately decided to only expand the monument around three of those zones. The $4.6 million figure was specific to a 1.8 million km² full expansion of the monument, rather than for the 1.2 million km² monument that Obama ultimately designated. It therefore overstated industry revenue in the region that was ultimately protected, especially considering that the two zones Obama did not expand were the most productive fishing areas of the five. The actual displacement figure for the final version of the monument was therefore far less than 5% of the fleet's revenue. For decision makers in Washington, it was clear that establishing the monument would have a relatively minor impact on both the national and local fishing industry, despite Wespac's protests.[50]

The industry's factor specificity was similarly low. The Hawaii- and American Samoa-based fleets were not at all confined to fishing within the specified boundaries of the monument before its expansion. In 2012, the Honolulu-based longline fleet set only 4% of its hooks in the monument area, while the mostly American Samoa-based purse seine fleet caught only 5% of its annual catch there (Sala et al. 2014). The seamounts surrounding the Pacific Remote Islands do not harbor especially productive tuna fisheries (Sala et al. 2014). Figure 4.2 depicts seamounts with high catch rates of tuna in the South Pacific, clearly indicating that tuna was far more abundant

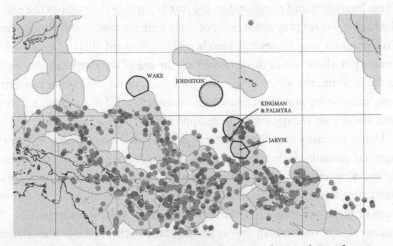

Figure 4.2 Seamounts with High Tuna Catch Rate in the South Pacific

The initially proposed PRI expansion is outlined in black. President Obama only expanded the three zones around Jarvis Island, the Johnston Atoll, and Wake Island. Circles depict seamounts with the relative catch of yellowfin (lightest), albacore (medium), and bigeye (darkest) tuna.

Source: Morato et al. (2010); Sala et al. (2014).

outside the monument. It was clear that the Western Pacific fleet was not dependent on tuna within the monument since, historically, it had already been securing 95% of its catch elsewhere anyway.

Industry representatives counter that the area could become essential fishing grounds in the future.[51] Climate modeling of tuna habitats predicts that as ocean temperatures rise tuna will migrate further eastward into the waters now protected by the monument.[52] The future value of these waters for the Western Pacific fleet is therefore not necessarily well represented by historical catch figures. Tuna also migrate eastward during El Niño events, increasing the importance of these waters in certain years.[53] Of course, rapidly depleting tuna stocks due to overfishing are another reason the area might become more commercially valuable, but the industry downplays this. The industry argument about its dependence on the monument waters tends to revolve around its hypothetical worth in the future, or in particular years. The case is not without merit, but weighed against historical catch figures, along with the conservation potential of the monument, it mostly fell on deaf ears in Washington.

The industry also did not have a case to make regarding many of its assets. Although the two canneries in American Samoa were non-transferable, the fishing fleets themselves were. The boats and gear used in the waters now occupied by the monument were not explicitly designed for use there. These longliners and purse seiners are just as capable throughout the rest of the Pacific, where they spent most of their time anyway. South Pacific Tuna Corporation's sale of several vessels only reinforced their transferability. Simply put, there was nothing restricting the use of standard industry assets to the monuments waters. There was no issue around whether or not assets were suitable for operation elsewhere, so industry did not express any concern about asset redeployment in its opposition.

Unlike intensity of activity, factor specificity, and asset specificity, the exogenous stressors facing the industry discussed earlier did lend credence to industry opposition to the monument. Reduced fishing days, price fluctuations, wage hikes, and rising fees make for a hostile business climate. Each of these challenges individually had a more significant impact on the industry in the region than the expansion of the Pacific Remote Islands monument would. For many of these exogenous issues, there is currently no apparent long-term solution, so the future looks rather bleak. A rebound in tuna prices will potentially assuage much of the distress facing the fleet, but US boats in the region depend on regional cooperation to maximize their profitability, and it is currently strained. Combined, these challenges amount to an existential threat to the industry and partly explain the dogmatic opposition of Wespac to new regulations, however minimal their projected impact. The political economy of the monument is less about the economics of the monument itself and more embedded deeply in the political dynamics of fishing in the Western Pacific. Later economic modeling would confirm this, demonstrating few, if any, negative impacts on the fishing industry due to the closure, with catch and catch-per-unit-effort in fact higher after the designation (Lynham et al. 2020). The monument itself was largely tangential to these problems, and Wespac struggled to convince the CEQ otherwise.

Wespac's report and lobbying efforts did have partial success, however. The hardline opposition to any and all protections failed to convince, but the CEQ did acknowledge that Wespac had some valid concerns about the current state of the Western Pacific fleet.[54] Some Democrats in the region also expressed concern that the expansion might affect their re-electability. Senator Schatz of Hawaii was among them, and he spoke with the CEQ at a White House meeting to articulate his concerns about the potential political backlash if the full expansion plans were formally approved.[55] In the end, a fragile industry and some mild political pressure from within the Democratic party encouraged Obama's decision to only expand three of the five zones. Like Bush, Obama was not ambivalent about the potential impact of the monument on the tuna industry, however minimal it was likely to be.

Secretary of State Kerry's June announcement of the plan to expand the Pacific Remote Islands monument also came with the promise of public engagement, the main form of which was a town hall held in Honolulu on August 11, 2014. The lead up to this town hall meeting became an arms race between environmental groups and Wespac, as both tried to rally their supporters to attend the meeting in numbers. Wespac reportedly brought out roughly 50–70 detractors, compared to the much higher number of advocates for the monument that environmental advocates rallied.[56] According to Wespac the meeting was poorly organized, and organizers relegated many of their supporters to the hallways due to the small size of the meeting space.[57] Wespac nonetheless provided testimony at the town hall stating its case in opposition to the monument. Although Wespac had the support of some local politicians and industry groups, it was unable to compete with a better financed advocacy campaign that also benefitted from presidential backing.[58] The public was widely supportive of the monument, not just in the mainland US, but in Hawaii and the Pacific territories as well.[59]

With public support, a strong scientific basis, and most importantly a favorable political economy, the path was clear for President Obama to move forward with the expansion. Following in his predecessor's footsteps, Obama invoked the Antiquities Act to expand the monument around the three zones from 50 nautical miles from shore to the maximum 200 nautical mile limit. Kerry formally announced the finalized expansion at the inaugural *Our Ocean* conference on September 25, 2014. Environmental groups widely praised the expansion, even though it fell short of their goal to expand all five zones (Howard 2014). According to industry officials, President Obama was concerned about overly antagonizing commercial fishers.[60] Despite the remoteness of the monument and minimal economic interests in the region, a conservation-friendly president still felt constrained by the need to balance environmental protection and minor economic interests. This balancing act demonstrates just how important industry interest salience is to environmental policy. Environmental groups were influential in this case in large part because the political economy of the region allowed for it: they successfully advocated for ambitious protections because they were able to demonstrate that the commercial impact of those protections would be small.

Will it Last?

The management plan for the expanded monument was a continuation of the plan for the initial monument, co-managed by the Departments of Commerce and the Interior. Presidential Proclamation 9173 to expand the monument extended the same restrictions to the new boundaries, including a prohibition on commercial fishing and managed non-commercial fishing. The challenges of interagency cooperation and the relatively vague 2009 secretariat order for management of the monument created some bureaucratic headaches for government officials. According to the FWS, those headaches have not had much impact on conservation outcomes in the Pacific Remote Islands.[61]

As with other large MPAs, the primary challenge with managing the monument is ensuring compliance given its sheer size and remoteness. The scope of the area can make it difficult, for example, to determine the status of various species in the area.[62] Its remoteness means that most monitoring effort goes into tracking illegal, unregulated, and unreported (IUU) fishing.[63] Environmental groups and government officials are less concerned about enforcement of the monument because of the rapidly declining costs of satellite and drone technology for monitoring MPAs, coupled with the US's substantial financial and technological capacity.[64] The issues facing the long-term conservation potential of the monument are less about monitoring and enforcement and more about the political backlash that it generated in Washington.

After the expansion, congressional Republicans took up arms against Obama's use of the Antiquities Act. Their opposition coalesced during the Obama presidency at an oversight hearing on marine national monument designations in September 2015, at which they voiced their condemnation for the lack of transparency in monument designations. The purpose of the hearing was both to raise opposition to future uses of the Antiquities Act and to criticize Obama's use of it for the 2014 expansion. At this hearing, Republican members of Congress referred to "extremist environmental groups" and the "creeping cancer of federal government overreach" (*Committee on Natural Resources* 2015). For many Republicans, Obama's use of the Antiquities Act was just one instance among many of what they considered executive overreach. At the time, the Republican opposition was never likely to amount to any substantial changes to the law or Obama's actions, evidenced by his expansion of Papahānaumokuākea the following year.

The Trump administration's willingness to gut US environmental regulations made this political noise suddenly very real. Never in the history of the Antiquities Act had a US president attempted to undermine the designations of her or his predecessors. But in 2017, President Trump issued an executive order calling for the review of a number of US terrestrial and marine monuments, including the Papahānaumokuākea and Pacific Remote Islands monuments. A leaked memo from the Department of the Interior suggested that the initial targets were likely to be terrestrial monuments, with the Bears Ears and Grand Staircase-Escalante monuments in Utah the main targets. The memo was correct, with Trump ordering cuts of 85% and 45% to each respectively. In the memo, then Secretary of the Interior Ryan Zinke also recommended scaling back protections for the Pacific Remote Islands.

As of this writing, President Trump had not attempted to alter the Pacific Remote Islands, but he had instead begun testing the limits of his authority in the Atlantic. In June 2020, Trump turned his attention to the Northeast Canyons and Seamounts Marine National Monument—a 12,700 km^2 monument off the coast of New England. Trump signed an executive order removing all commercial fishing restrictions in the area, claiming that he was "reversing that injustice," in reference to President Obama's designation of the monument in 2016 (Buckle 2020). As they did with Bears Ears and Grand Staircase-Escalante, environmental groups immediately sued the Trump administration for illegally revoking the protections.

In 2020, legal challenges from indigenous groups and environmental groups were still making their way through the court system. In February 2019, law makers also introduced a bill to reaffirm that only Congress can change monument designations (Udall and Haaland 2019). So whether Trump had the legal authority to alter these monuments remains an open question. It will be for the courts to decide whether the Antiquities Act grants a president the power to undo previous uses without congressional approval. There is currently no legal precedent for a current or future president to overturn a prior use of the act (Rutzick 2010). As of 2020, the Trump administration had undermined protections for these three monuments, but only time will tell if those decisions were legal. If the courts side with Trump, they will have substantially undermined over one hundred years of bipartisan conservation achievements.

All of the hopes for detractors of these monuments lie with this court battle over the limits of presidential authority to overturn previous designations. The only other route to overturning monument restrictions almost undoubtedly requires bipartisan support in Congress. Congress can overturn a monument designation, but both Republicans and Democrats acknowledge that the threshold is too high to do so without bipartisan support (*Committee on Natural Resources* 2015). Numerous bills have been introduced in Congress to overturn monuments in the 110-year history of the Antiquities Act, but they rarely succeed, and when they do it is only in response to highly controversial designations (Hartman 2011). Industry attempts to challenge monument designations in court have never been successful (Rutzick 2010). This includes a 2017 suit from five industry groups challenging the Northeast Canyons and Seamount monument. The suit did not go far, and was shot down for good by the DC Circuit Court of Appeals in 2019. Industry opposition also tends to wane over time as operators shift their activity elsewhere and politicians move on to newer issues (Hartman 2011).

In the case of these remote, mostly uncontentious monuments, the difficulty of having them overturned likely exceeds the willingness of most presidents to do so. President Trump's unscientific and dogmatic crusade against environmental regulation was, one would hope, a short-term abnormality.

Based on current legal precedent and practice, once a president establishes a monument it is effectively permanent, with rare exception.

The US Large MPA Legacy

The US not only embraced the large MPA norm, but was an influential early adopter and a central driver of it globally. In 2020, it boasted three MPAs exceeding 200,000 km^2, which combined amounted to 3 million km^2 of protected US waters. The 2014 *Our Ocean* conference—initiated and hosted by the US—would become a platform for other states to announce major marine conservation initiatives of their own, including numerous large MPAs. A separate program, *Big Ocean*, was also initiated by US officials as a peer-learning network for MPA managers to share and coordinate on best ocean management practices, with managers from every large MPA in the world participating at its inception. The original managers of the Papahānaumokuākea monument were instrumental to its founding and initial design.[65] These two institutions have persevered after the Obama presidency, despite the antagonism of the Trump administration to environmental protection.

The emergence of a large MPA norm originating in the US made the expansion of the Pacific Remote Islands monument possible. Bush's designation of Papahānaumokuākea, Marianas Trench, and PRIMNM paved the way for Obama's subsequent expansion of two of them. These successes helped to rally environmental groups around the cause of promoting large MPAs and established a legal precedent for their creation. By 2014, the only issue Obama faced was deciding just how ambitious an expansion he wanted. A minimal commercial stake in the Pacific Remote Islands coupled with a clear legal precedent facilitated a coalition between environmental groups and the state that drove the expansion. Environmental groups—armed with detailed economic reporting—were able to capitalize on a favorable political economy in the Pacific Remote Islands to partner with the White House in its creation of a robust, large MPA.

To summarize, the PRIMNM expansion case study demonstrates how the domestic political economy of the region shaped the diffusion of the large MPA norm in the US. Like earlier large MPA designations, the remoteness of the targeted area meant that commercial stakes were low. Environmental groups therefore had substantial influence with the White House not only in pushing for large MPAs but successfully pushing for outright bans on extractive commercial activity within them. There is undoubtedly a neocolonial element to large-scale US marine conservation. These protections were only viable because of overseas territories remote from more entrenched and politically powerful commercial actors. In 2015, President Obama also considered protecting Cashes Ledge—a biodiversity hotspot about 130 km off the coast of Maine—but industry pushback in the more commercially active area dissuaded him. The Cashes Ledge decision was telling. An optimistic reading might suggest that, because of large MPA successes elsewhere, the US continental shelf was now part of the conversation for marine monument protections. But the eventual decision reveals just how powerful a predictor of conservation policy the domestic political economy of a region is. When extractive industry stakeholders are able to demonstrate interest salience, protections in the US are, so far, highly unlikely.

The pattern in the US of only protecting remote ocean spaces represents a particular form of norm localization that is quite distinct from how the large MPA norm diffused in other cases. This model of large-scale marine conservation is only available to a handful of other states with remote territories, most notably Chile (Easter Island), France, and the UK. In states without the luxury of overseas territories, stakeholder battles over ocean spaces tend to be more pronounced. The coalition between environmental groups and the state that emerged relatively smoothly in the US was not easily replicated in states whose marine protections were closer to population centers. Remoteness is key to this US conservation success story. Most nations do not boast remote, overseas territories within which they can play out their conservation ambitions. Campaigns for large MPAs closer to the hub of commercial activity are not as easy. If the Pacific Remote Islands tell the story of how environmental groups can triumph over industry power and influence, the campaign to protect Australia's Coral Sea tells the opposite.

5

A "Paper Park" in the Australian Coral Sea

Australia shares the Coral Sea with New Caledonia, Papua New Guinea, the Solomon Islands, and Vanuatu. The campaign to protect it was an effort to protect the 990,000 km^2 that falls within Australia's vast EEZ that is not already protected around the Great Barrier Reef through the GBRMP. Australia boasts the world's third largest EEZ, behind only the US and France. The Coral Sea Marine Park is adjacent to the 345,000-km^2 GBRMP, extending MPA coverage from the outer border of the reef all the way to the 200 nm limit of Australia's EEZ. It also connects to New Caledonia's 1,369,000-km^2 Natural Park of the Coral Sea. Taken together these three areas form a contiguous area of over 2.7 million km^2, by far the largest contiguous MPA network on the planet at the time of this writing. The 1975 GBRMP also makes Australia the only country to have had a large MPA before 2006. This preexisting experience with large-scale marine conservation would serve both to help facilitate the diffusion of the MPA norm into Australia and surprisingly to also generate backlash from specific stakeholder groups. Local economic interests drove that backlash. The story of a large MPA in the Australian Coral Sea is one of an ultimately futile attempt to reconcile conservation and extractive commercial activity.

The campaign to designate Australia's portion of the Coral Sea as an MPA reveals just how contentious large marine reserves can be. Early efforts to protect the Coral Sea began in 2005, leading to the Labor government of Julia Gillard (2010–2013) creating the Coral Sea Commonwealth Marine Reserve (CMR) in 2012. The initial reserve was short-lived, however, as subsequent governments undertook a concerted effort to water down regulations. That effort was successful, with a management plan now in effect that allows business-as-usual activity on the water. Those governments had gutted conservation measures for the reserve so thoroughly that the MPA was downgraded and renamed the Coral Sea Marine Park in 2017. The erosion of the reserve was the result of a contentious stakeholder battle between environmental groups and the commercial and recreational fishing industries. That struggle was highly politicized early in the process, with federal political

Conserving the Oceans. Justin Alger, Oxford University Press (2021). © Oxford University Press.
DOI: 10.1093/oso/9780197540534.003.0005

parties capitalizing on the divide to shore up support from these stakeholder factions. To further complicate the issue, Australia was undergoing a tumultuous political period with five different prime ministers between 2013 and 2018. The political economy of the Australian Coral Sea made the campaign for protections a veritable slog for environmental and industry groups alike.

Notably, the salience of industry interests in the Coral Sea had little to do with intensity of activity—industry presence in the region is actually quite small. The Coral Sea is the most remote portion of Australia's EEZ, with just a handful of commercial fishers, game fishers, and dive operators frequenting it. But many of those businesses are critically dependent on continued operation in the Coral Sea to remain profitable. That dependence gave them considerable bargaining leverage, with subsequent Australian governments catering to industry interests throughout the consultation process.

Environmental groups initially tried to apply the same model of large MPA advocacy in the Coral Sea that had proven successful in other cases (see chapter 4). With Pew and the Australian Marine Conservation Society (AMCS) taking the lead, they introduced the idea of a large, contiguous, no-take area into an ongoing, bipartisan government process to improve protections for the Coral Sea. That advocacy had the unintended consequence of further polarizing the debate over how to best protect the Coral Sea. Campaigners underestimated the influence that industry would have in an area with modest, at most, commercial activity. It may be tempting to attribute the erosion of regulations over time to party politics and a series of anti-conservationist, Liberal-led coalition governments following Gillard's initial designation. That narrative, I argue, fails to capture the fact that appeasing industry was central to both Labor and Liberal governments' positions throughout the 10-year consultation process. Regulations certainly eroded over time, but even the earliest management plan would have only marginally reduced commercial activity in the area. The political economy of extractive industry interests in the Coral Sea led to a pattern of norm diffusion characterized by close state-industry collaboration, undermining the conservation potential of Australia's large MPAs.

Conservation of Australia's Iconic Marine Hotspots

Australia has a unique history with large-scale marine conservation that no other nation can claim. The 1975 GBRMP was the first MPA in the world to exceed 200,000 km^2 and would be the world's largest for over 30 years. In 1998, the Australian government also started working toward a Nationally Representative System of Marine Protected Areas (NRSMPA) to protect essential biodiversity regions throughout the rest of Australia's biodiverse EEZ. In 2012, the Australian government formally announced 60 CMRs, which included the 272,000-km^2 South-West Corner CMR as well as the Coral Sea CMR. Both the GBRMP and the early efforts toward these CMRs predate the emergence of large MPAs as a global norm in the mid-2000s. Australia is, therefore, the only country to have previous experience with a large MPA before the mid-2000s. But despite this experience, these two initiatives only partially embody the characteristics of the large MPA norm. They do reflect a commitment to protecting large ocean spaces, but they did not emphasize the importance of large no-take zones, nor did they emphasize the importance of safeguarding pelagic waters.

Despite being the world's largest MPA for nearly 30 years, the Great Barrier Reef is in actuality a hub of commercial activity. The primary activity on the reef has by far always been ecotourism, and it remains the most significant economic contributor to the region. In 2013 (the most recent government reporting), tourism expenditures amounted to A$6.4 billion, or 91% of total direct spending on the Great Barrier Reef (Deloitte Access Economics 2013). It also contributed over 64,000 full-time jobs, which is more than 93% of the overall employment contribution of the reef. Until nearly 30 years after its designation, no-take protections for the Great Barrier Reef never exceeded just 4.6% of the park. The Australian and Queensland governments managed the Great Barrier Reef according to preexisting standards of behavior around what constituted appropriate marine conservation. Not even UNESCO's 1982 classification of the Great Barrier Reef as a World Heritage Area led the government to more fully protect it. So despite being a natural wonder of the world, a UNESCO World Heritage Area, and a commercial zone heavily reliant on ecotourism, the Great Barrier Reef did not include large no-take areas (De'ath et al. 2012).

Eventually, in 2004, the government rezoned the Great Barrier Reef to increase no-take zoning from the previous 4.6% to 33%. The reef had been in decline for decades due to the combined impacts of ocean warming, acidification, and coastal pollution. This rezoning was an effort by the Australian government to increase its resilience by reducing the impact of commercial and recreational fishing through an increase in no-take areas—what it called "green zones." The rezoning involved an extensive public consultation process that was intended, in part, to inform the government on how to limit the impact of new conservation measures on commercial and recreational fishers. The apparent disconnect between the primary sources of the Great Barrier Reef's decline (climate change and coastal pollution) and the intent of the rezoning (reducing fishing impact) became a major source of contention in Queensland marine politics in the ensuing decade. Some in the fishing industry—particularly high-level representatives from various fishing industry associations—felt aggrieved that the government unfairly targeted them when the main source of the problem lied elsewhere.[1] They admonished the rezoning as unscientific for locking out fishers who were not the primary source of the problem.[2]

There are three distinct sectors of the fishing industry in Queensland: commercial, charter, and recreational. Industry association representatives from all three groups strongly opposed the rezoning, but in reality, the issue divided fishers. According to one study about the social effects of the rezoning, three years after implementation 59% of recreational fishers supported it, compared to just 18% of charter fishers and 7% of commercial fishers (McCook et al. 2010). These figures represented a 10% increase in support from recreational and charter fishers in the three years after the rezoning, but a 10% decline in support from the commercial sector (McCook et al. 2010). The numbers indicated that the rezoning was unpopular within the charter and commercial sectors, and at best divisive within the recreational sector. Some recreational fishers were angered by the rezoning since it took away many of their favorite fishing spots.[3] This experience with rezoning led to the emergence of a vocal minority of recreational fishers that would go on to vigorously lobby against any and all closures in the region, including in the Coral Sea.[4]

Although fishers were not the most significant threat facing the Great Barrier Reef, MPAs are most effective in building ecosystem resilience when they are large and no-take (Edgar et al. 2014). A study of the Great Barrier Reef rezoning demonstrated that the increased protections had already started paying dividends by 2010 (McCook et al. 2010). Previously exploited fish stocks had partly rebounded in the new no-take areas, with some species of fish doubling in size and number. Further, there was no evidence that the protections just displaced fishing efforts, shifting exploitation to other areas, but instead represented a genuine improvement in fish stocks in the area. This study demonstrated the merits of no-take zones to marine ecosystem health, even in well-managed fisheries. The Great Barrier Reef rezoning to

33% no-take reflected the growing scientific consensus around the benefits of large, no-take marine reserves.

The NRSMPA that the government initiated in 1998 was a push for a nationwide network of mixed-use MPAs. One of the guiding principles of the process was to create, where possible, larger marine reserves. By the end of the process there were 60 reserves spread out across Australia's EEZ of varying size. These reserves themselves were carved up into various zones with varying levels of restriction on commercial access. Many marine scientists consider these types of representative and comprehensive networks to be a gold standard for marine conservation since they directly target the most vulnerable ecosystems for protection when governments design and manage them effectively (Roberts et al. 2001; Almany et al. 2009; Gaines et al. 2010). The Australian government undertook exhaustive scientific and socioeconomic study of these areas in preparation for the implementation of management plans for the reserves. Whether the NRAMPA would lead to a robust MPA network or a series of paper parks depended entirely on how the government planned to manage the areas.

Of these 60 MPAs, two meet the threshold for a large MPA: the Coral Sea Marine Park (990,000 km^2) and the South-West Corner Marine Park (272,000 km^2). The original idea was to manage these zones much in the same way that the Great Barrier Reef Marine Park Authority (GBRMPA) had managed the Great Barrier Reef for decades. Specifically, the intention was always to carve these large MPAs up into zones with a wide range of protection levels. This zoning practice was really just a continuation of what was then the standard practice of mixed-use MPA management. It did not represent the Australian government's adoption of the large MPA norm with its emphasis on large, contiguous, no-take areas.

Even the ENGOs that initially campaigned for better protections for the Coral Sea and South-West Corner were in favor of mixed-use zoning. Forming in the mid-1990s, the Protect Our Coral Sea and Save Our Marine Life campaigns advocated for better marine protections for the Coral Sea and South-West of Australia respectively. The campaigns involved a coalition of domestic and transnational environmental groups all in favor of better marine protections in Australia. Their goal for these two large MPAs was something in line with the Great Barrier Reef rezoning, with selective no-take areas in certain biodiversity hotspots, but otherwise with continued human use.

The NRSMPA initiative was also, notably, a bipartisan initiative. Marine conservation initiatives in Australia are frequently bipartisan for two reasons. First, more than 80% of the Australian population lives within 50 km of the coast, and marine ecosystems are a central feature of Australian life and industry. Second, the mixed-use approach to marine conservation appeals broadly across the political spectrum. How the government decides to manage a new MPA can range from strict prohibitions on use to integrating industry use quite explicitly. The Labor and Liberal parties find a lot of room to maneuver on the nature and extent of protections—which is where much of the debate ultimately happens—rather than on if they should protect an area.

The Coral Sea quickly became a high-profile component of the broader NRSMPA initiative: it is large, the most remote portion of Australia's EEZ, adjacent to the Great Barrier Reef, and home to a vast array of marine life, most notably large species of whale, ray, and shark.[5] It became the focal point for the battle between conservationists and fishers that ensued as the Coral Sea campaign progressed.[6] As one industry representative put it, they fought as hard as they did over the Coral Sea despite limited commercial interest because the "Coral Sea is the jewel in the crown [of the NRSMPA], so it is important for the long run."[7] The fishing industry chose the Coral Sea as the region to make its principled stand against closures in what they argued were sustainable fisheries.[8] The NRSMPA process was ongoing for nearly two decades, but the lobbying in Canberra revolved mostly around the Coral Sea throughout most of that time.

The initial environmental group proposals were what would now be considered industry friendly, so the early lobbying was reserved compared to what came later. The Cairns and Far North Environment Centre (CAFNEC) and the Northern Queensland Conservation Council (NQCC) submitted a proposal to the government in 2005 modeled after the 2004 Great Barrier Reef rezoning. The plan was to identify ecologically critical areas of the Coral Sea for full protection, while keeping the rest open to continued commercial fishing. CAFNEC and NQCC saw oil and gas and mining exploration as the main threats to the Coral Sea rather than commercial fishing.[9] Following a meeting with NQCC, the World Wide Fund for Nature (WWF) was convinced of the merits of this approach and adopted a similar proposal of its own.[10] While industry was not in favor of these proposals, it saw them as a continuation of the long-standing practice of mixed-use zoning, with a focus on stricter protection for reefs in lieu of protecting pelagic waters.[11] It was not until Pew's advocacy for a large, no-take Coral Sea MPA beginning in 2007 that tensions between conservationists and industry reached a boiling point.

From No-Take to Mixed-Use

The campaign for a large MPA in the Coral Sea was not just contentious between conservationists and industry, but even divided environmental groups at first. Pew's initial involvement in the Coral Sea came at the behest of WWF, which was by then pursuing a mixed-use MPA in the Coral Sea in the image of the 2004 Great Barrier Reef rezoning.[12] WWF approached Pew for funding support for the initiative, which Pew turned down.[13] The approach had nonetheless piqued Pew's interest, and, in August 2007, Global Ocean Legacy founder Jay Nelson partook in a WWF-arranged trip to the Coral Sea.[14] But ultimately, Pew was not enthusiastic about WWF's mixed-use approach to the Coral Sea and opted instead to launch a campaign for a fully no-take MPA.[15]

Pew was intrigued by the Coral Sea because it had an easy-to-sell name, numerous reefs, was adjacent to the GBRMP and a large MPA in New Caledonia, and was the most remote area of Australia's EEZ.[16] So the Coral Sea campaign began with two of the world's largest environmental groups running competing campaigns with different philosophical outlooks on how the Australian government should protect the Coral Sea. Although there was an internal debate at Pew about whether it was sensible to compete with WWF, eventually Pew's superior financial resources won out, with WWF soon withdrawing its initiative and supporting the Pew-led efforts.[17]

Pew worked alongside the Australian Marine Conservation Society to form a local coalition of environmental groups under the Protect Our Coral Sea banner. This alliance served two purposes. First, it acted as a focal point for advocacy efforts to improve protections in the Coral Sea, efficiently streamlining them into one devoted campaign. Second, it also attempted to mask Pew's influence throughout the process by embedding it as just one organization among the 15 members of the coalition.[18] Realistically, Pew was providing the bulk of the financial resources for the campaign, including funding full-time marine campaigner positions at other environmental groups.[19] Pew had the financial resources to escalate the comparatively low-key lobbying of local groups like CAFNEC and NQCC to a high-profile national campaign.[20] This campaign included a broad coalition of environmental groups, a documentary about the Coral Sea with regular screenings, extensive promotional material on TV, in cinemas, in shopping malls, and on airlines, and even a mascot in the form of Barry the Wrasse, used to instill a sense of bewilderment at the beauty of the Coral Sea.[21] This heavy influence led to a significant backlash against Pew, including from politicians opposed to the Coral Sea reserve.

During one parliamentary debate, MPs referred to Pew as "cancerous," "putrid," and "gangrenous" and lamented that they kept "hearing about the Pew foundation and them being everywhere" (House of Representatives 2013). This childish rhetoric aside, the problem was that Pew was a well-funded, influential US organization that many members of parliament and constituents saw as attacking Australian fishing culture through its advocacy for large-scale "lock-outs." Pew had good reason not to want to be seen as driving the Coral Sea efforts. Unfortunately for Pew, its efforts to stay out of the spotlight self-admittedly failed, hence these attacks in parliament.[22] CAFNEC—after years of providing a local advocacy voice in the campaign—even began to distance itself from Pew as a campaign strategy and stopped receiving funds from the organization in mid-2013.[23]

Fishers were already feeling aggrieved after the Great Barrier Reef rezoning, but two missteps exacerbated the public backlash to the Coral Sea campaign. First, Pew vastly underestimated the degree of public and industry opposition to a fully no-take Coral Sea: this ambitious goal had the unintended consequence of polarizing the issue of Coral Sea protections, with a large number of commercial and recreational fishers suddenly vehemently opposed to the reserve.[24] But the key issue with the Coral Sea—unlike Pew's other large MPA projects to date—was that it is adjacent to higher levels of ongoing commercial and recreational fishing. WWF, CAFNEC, and potentially others were more attuned to the prospective backlash, hence their reluctance to join, but Pew initially remained committed to the tried-and-true strategy of promoting large, no-take MPAs that had worked so well for it elsewhere.[25] Pew officials were inspired by the successes of Papahānaumokuākea and Chagos and wanted to replicate these models in Australia.[26] Eventually, Pew was forced to relent, abandoning the fully no-take proposal and instead consulting more closely with local and industry stakeholders.[27] But by then, much of the damage was already done, with clear dividing lines between pro-conservation and pro-industry more deeply entrenched.[28]

The second misstep was out of campaigners' hands entirely and instead was the result of a particularly enthusiastic environment minister* from 2007 to 2010, Peter Garrett. Garrett was the former president of the Australian Conservation Foundation (ACF), and Australian conservationists see him as a "rock star" in the conservation community (he also happens to be a literal former rock star as the vocalist for the band *Midnight Oil*).[29] Unbeknown to campaigners, Garrett spontaneously declared the Coral Sea a conservation zone in May 2009.[30] Under the 1999 Environmental Protection and Biodiversity Act (EPBA), an environment minister has the authority to declare a conservation zone as a temporary measure to protect the biodiversity in an area while it undergoes assessment for inclusion in a commonwealth reserve (Commonwealth of Australia 1999). This decision was controversial, because a conservation zone has no requirement for public consultations and is a prelude to a formal commonwealth reserve. The conservation zone proclamation only served to galvanize fishing industry opposition to a Coral Sea reserve further. Roughly 1,000 recreational fishers protested Garrett's decision in Cairns, appalled by what they saw as a cynical move to disenfranchise them.[31]

The Australian government began soliciting feedback from stakeholders following the surprise announcement. It received 566,377 submissions in the consultation process for the entire CMR network, a staggering 487,435 (86%) of which were for the Coral Sea (Marine Division 2012). Of the Coral Sea submissions, 99.76% were from formal advocacy campaigns, with the Protect Our Coral Sea campaign generating 87% of those. Of the Protect Our Coral Sea submissions, 76% were from overseas, demonstrating the global reach of the transnational environmental groups participating in the alliance, most notably Greenpeace, Pew, and WWF. These submissions indicated strong support for better marine protections in the Coral Sea, even excluding campaign submissions, as shown in Table 5.1. The commercial and recreational fishing lobbies, however, felt that the government consulted them too late in the process. By 2012, they were already feeling neglected and threatened.[32] There was significant concern about the social and economic impact of the reserve, expressed in nearly 30% of all non-campaign submissions.

* From 2007 to 2020, there were eight different formal (often verbose) titles for the federal environment minister. For consistency (and brevity), I refer simply to the "environment minister" throughout this chapter.

Table 5.1 Coral Sea CMR Submissions, 2012

Feedback	Proportion (Including Campaign)	Proportion (Excluding Campaign)
No support for marine reserve	< 0.1%	6.4%
Support for reserve as proposed	< 0.1%	7.8%
Support for stronger protections than proposed	99.9%	77.2%
Concern with protection of marine environment	< 0.1%	2.7%
Concern with social and economic impact	N/A[a]	29.6%
Concern with management	2.7%	14.2%

[a] Erroneously recorded as 96% in the official report. Correct figure unavailable.

In 2012, Garrett's successor Tony Burke formally proclaimed the Coral Sea CMR. The announcement was made alongside the rest of the NRSMPA network, making it a part of the world's most extensive MPA network. The three years between Garrett's proclamation of the Coral Sea Conservation Zone and Burke's announcement of the Coral Sea CMR consisted of ongoing campaigning and lobbying from stakeholder groups. During this time, the government was in the process of designing the entire NRSMPA network, while stakeholder groups simultaneously lobbied the government for favorable zoning. Although there was considerable stakeholder input into the process before 2012, the formal proclamation officially triggered legal requirements for public consultation on the Coral Sea, elevating what was already becoming a contested and lengthy stakeholder bargaining process.

Despite industry claims to the contrary, the Gillard government had engaged in extensive stakeholder consultations in designing the management plan for the reserve. The Australian Bureau of Agricultural and Resource Economics and Sciences (ABARES)—the poorly named research arm of the Department of Agriculture and Water Resources—produced a 155-page social and economic impact assessment report on the Coral Sea CMR. The report assessed the displacement of economic activity, its impact on the commercial fishing sector, and its effects on local ports and communities (ABARES 2012) and included six detailed case studies of how the reserve would impact specific businesses, industries, and cities. Producing this report involved extensive consultation with industry through workshops, meetings, and surveys of fishers (Marine Division 2012). Tony Burke met personally with many stakeholder groups, often quipping about how organizing meetings with the fishing industry equated to "herding cats" (much to the industry's chagrin) because of the diversity of groups and interests within it.[33]

The Coral Sea CMR process was one of the most rigorous research and public consultation processes of any large MPA at the time. One campaigner estimated that the research and consultation expenditures for the CMR network from the early 2000s were about A$9 million, much of which the government spent on new scientific research in the Coral Sea.[34] The result was a 10-year management plan that the Gillard government intended to put into effect in 2014, creating a mixed-use MPA in the Coral Sea with a no-take area of 502,654 km². The management plan would have displaced an estimated A$377,000 (51.7%) of the Coral Sea Fishery and A$3.8 million (9.7%) of the Eastern Tuna and Billfish Fishery (ETBF) (ABARES 2012). It also included a A$100 million funding commitment to buy out the select few businesses that would be unable to continue their operations under the management arrangements. At least some commercial fishing businesses were reportedly pleased with the buyout, seeing it as an opportunity to get out of an industry with increasingly small profit margins.[35]

The 2012 management plan incorporated extensive consultations with industry and mostly allowed for business-as-usual activity to continue on the water. It would have forced some businesses to target new fishing grounds, while the government would pay off others to shut down, but it ultimately reflected a concerted effort to compromise with the commercial fishing industry to minimize the economic impact of the reserve—a far cry from Pew's initial fully no-take proposal. Despite the compromise, industry continued to challenge the management plan. By 2012, the fishing industry was already galvanized in opposition to the reserve, so even this industry-friendly plan was not enough to appease opponents. The commercial fishing industry in particular had substantial bargaining power in the Coral Sea because it was able to clearly demonstrate that it relied on the region, even though commercial activity in the area was relatively modest.

In 2013, the election of Tony Abbott's Liberal coalition created a window of opportunity for industry to turn its opposition into policy action once again. Abbott ran a scathing campaign that criticized all aspects of the Labor government's environmental initiatives, including the Coral Sea reserve. Abbott's stance was that the Gillard government failed to engage in an adequate stakeholder consultation process, despite the extensive consultations. The NRSMPA system had a lot of bipartisan support, and most Australians favored new sanctuary zones, so repealing the Coral Sea CMR outright was a politically unattractive option (despite having the legislative authority to).[36] Even with a shift in the balance of power in the House of Representatives, Abbott faced a problem. The Gillard management plan had already been approved by the previous environment minister. Under Australian law, the plan would become official legislation with ministerial approval and after sitting in parliament for 15 days. Parliamentary approval was not necessary. As it had been sitting with parliament for the required 15 days before the election was called, the plan would soon be in full effect.

In what one conservationist called a "brilliant strategic move," Abbott found a legal loophole to get around this legislative problem. He reproclaimed the Coral Sea CMR, effectively resetting the clock on the management plan and creating a new legal precedent.[37] As a result, the Gillard management plan never actually came into effect. Instead, Abbott started anew the consultations for the Coral Sea CMR (and the rest of the network). This round of discussions was much like the last, with the government engaged directly with industry stakeholders to determine zoning for the Coral Sea.[38] The consultations would lead to a 2016 review of the management plan for the Coral Sea, ultimately completed under the government of Abbott's successor, Malcolm Turnbull. The overarching goal this time, however, skewed even further in industry's favor, with the government insisting that the plan not lead to business closures. Abbott swiftly retracted the A$100 million that was on the table for buyouts. The driving question that the government asked industry representatives in this new review was "how do we keep you in business?"[39]

The Political Economy of the Coral Sea

The Coral Sea CMR stakeholder consultations were as industry friendly as they were because industry had substantial bargaining leverage. That leverage was not simply because industry had a large presence in the region, which was not the case. Instead, it was the consequence of businesses in the region lacking mobility. They could not relocate in response to loss of resource access, so the Australian government always faced the unenviable choice of catering to them or sacrificing them in the name of conservation. The political economy of the Coral Sea led to a form of large MPA norm diffusion in Australia in which conservation policy and extraction went hand in hand. The result was good for business but accomplished little for

Table 5.2 Industry Interests in the Coral Sea Marine Park

Industry	Intensity of Activity	Factor Specificity	Asset Specificity	Exogenous Stressors	Overall
Commercial Fishing	Low	Moderate	Moderate	High	Moderate
Charter Fishing	Low	Moderate	Low	Low	Low
Recreational Fishing	Low	Low	Low	Low	Low
Ecotourism	Low	Moderate	Moderate	Moderate	Moderate

conservation. To fully appreciate why this happened in Australia—in contrast to the numerous large, no-take MPAs elsewhere—we need to look to the economic interest of key stakeholders. The bargaining leverage generated by those interests shaped the localization of the large MPA norm in Australia.

There are four primary industries in the Australian Coral Sea: commercial fishing, charter fishing, recreational fishing, and ecotourism. Each of the three fishing industry groups strongly opposed any closures within the Coral Sea and advocated against them. Commercial and charter fishers were concerned about the direct impact these closures might have on their businesses, while the recreational fishing lobby was more concerned about the precedent the closure would set rather than any direct effect. The ecotourism industry comprised just a few dive operators that ventured as far out from shore as the Coral Sea. It mostly avoided injecting itself in the debate between environmental groups and the fishing industry over protections for the broader region, instead concerning itself with gaining stronger protections for the handful of reefs within the Coral Sea on which it relied. Table 5.2 shows the values on the four key interest salience indicators for each industry active in the Australian Coral Sea. This section explains the rationale behind those values, as well as how industry was able to shape the policy process because of them, beginning with the extractive sectors.

Extraction

Commercial Fishing

A handful of Commonwealth and Queensland fisheries operate in the Coral Sea, but the two most prominently affected by the Coral Sea Marine Park are the Commonwealth ETBF and the Commonwealth Coral Sea Fishery (ABARES 2012). The other fisheries that overlap with the Coral Sea did so to such a small extent that ABARES did not include them in its 2012 impact assessment. The Coral Sea is too remote to significantly impact fisheries managed by the state of Queensland, so the bargaining around the reserve was between fishers and the federal government.[40]

The ETBF encapsulates the Australian Coral Sea, covering the entire east coast of Australia from Cape York at the country's northern tip down to the South Australia-Victoria border in the south. It includes albacore, bigeye, and yellowfin tuna, as well as broadbill swordfish and striped marlin. Fishers bring their catch to port all along the coast, with ETBF operators that use the Coral Sea based primarily out of Cairns and Mooloolaba. The Australian Fisheries Management Authority (AFMA) manages the fishery and by most accounts had managed it effectively. Representatives from Greenpeace and Pew, for example, acknowledge that Australia's fisheries management is adequate relative to other nations.[41] AFMA conducts frequent risk assessments and updates its catch limits annually.

Only a small amount of ETBF fishing actually occurs in the Coral Sea. The ETBF fishery is an expansive area of which the Coral Sea is only a small portion, so most operators are able to shift fishing effort fairly easily. The one exception to this is Great Barrier Reef Tuna, a vertically-integrated, family-run business based in Cairns. The entirety of the company's fishing effort throughout its more than 25-year history was in the Coral Sea and it was critically dependent on continued access. The company holds about 9% of the quota for the ETBF (ABARES 2012). The family that owns and operates the business—the Lamasons—was one of the focal points of government reporting and consultations for the then Coral Sea CMR. The Lamasons were caught in the middle of the differing Labor and Liberal views on the desirability of buyouts. Under the Labor management plan, the Lamasons were set to be offered a generous pay off to shutter their doors. One of the motives behind the 2016 review was to prevent such buyouts.

Throughout the process, the Lamasons fought to stay in operation and were bewildered by the initial government efforts to shut down a sustainably managed fishery.[42] After nine years of extensive consultations, the Lamasons desired certainty above all so they could run their business or move on (with buyout funds in hand).[43] The Lamasons were (and remain) heavily invested in the Coral Sea and could not shift efforts elsewhere.[44] Their home port and the retail portion of their business are in Cairns, with the next closest port

1,800 km away. The ETBF is not a highly productive tuna fishery, so profit margins are already small. The Lamasons lobbied against any closures because of their already vulnerable position.[45] They were concerned about increased fishing trip costs and being overcapitalized for a reduced fishing area.[46] For ETBF operators based out of other ports along the east coast, the Coral Sea closures were at most an inconvenience and perhaps a concerning precedent. But for the Lamasons, the future of their business depended on how the government decided to manage the Coral Sea.

The 2012 ABARES impact assessment was the most thorough reporting on how the Coral Sea CMR would affect the commercial fishing sector. The soon-to-be-scrapped 2012 Gillard management plan was going to designate 51% of the area as no-take, most of which was on the outer fringe of Australia's EEZ. The value of the entire ETBF fishery was A$31.1 million in 2014–2015, with the 2012 management plan estimated to displace about A$3.8 million, or about 12% of the fishery (AFMA 2016). The estimated total value of Australia's tuna fisheries in 2014–2015 was A$58.2 million, so the 2012 plan's displacement amounted to roughly 6.5% of Australia's overall annual tuna catch. Data are not available for the displacement value of a fully no-take Coral Sea, but the values would be similar since the no-take area set aside in the 2012 plan was mostly residual, with little tuna fishing occurring there anyway.[47]

The Coral Sea was not a major source of tuna for Australia at the national scale or within the ETBF itself. Most operators would be able to relocate their efforts elsewhere, which the displacement values above do not take into account. It was not the intensity of activity that gave tuna fishers bargaining leverage, but rather the factor and asset specificity of a few operators. It was that factor and asset specificity that drove much of the industry backlash throughout the process. Great Barrier Reef Tuna's catch value was only an estimated A$2.8 million annually (ABARES 2012; AFMA 2016). But unlike some competitors, the Lamasons were limited by geography because of their integration into the local economy in Cairns and slim profit margins. Seeking out new fishing grounds was not an option. The business needed Coral Sea access to survive and its assets in Cairns were non-transferable anyway. While most ETBF operators did not rely on the Coral Sea, this one operator critically depended on it.

The second fishery in the area—the Coral Sea Fishery—targeted reef fish for aquariums, as well as sea cucumber, lobster, and trochus, and a small line, trap, and trawl sector. The fishery exists only within the boundaries of the

Coral Sea CMR, with all of the fishing activity occurring around a handful of reef systems. A fully no-take Coral Sea would have put these operators out of business. The sector was heavily impacted by the 2004 rezoning of the Great Barrier Reef, losing access to 85% of offshore and 25% of onshore reefs.[48] Many operators took a one-off A$50,000 payment from the government to relinquish their licenses, while others went through a structural adjustment process.[49] Cairns Marine is the biggest collector of aquarium fish on the Great Barrier Reef and aggressively negotiated for a A$3.8 million settlement from the government.[50] This arrangement facilitated their shift toward using the Coral Sea instead, where it has been operating since.

The Coral Sea Fishery's annual gross value of production in 2011 was only A$730,000, so this fishery is not a significant source of national or regional revenue. A fully no-take Coral Sea would have been the end of the fishery. But even the industry-friendly 2012 management plan was set to displace about 52% of its take. This displacement would have shifted the intensity of fishing activity rather than ended it, but many operators were already forced to relocate to the Coral Sea after the 2004 Great Barrier Reef rezoning, so their relocation options were becoming increasingly limited.[51] The factor specificity of Coral Sea Fishery operators depended on the extent of the no-take zoning around reefs in the Coral Sea. Closing only some reefs to fishing would allow operators to relocate their fishing effort, but it also meant businesses were competing with each other on fewer reefs. One industry representative estimated that the 2012 plan would only allow three to five of the eight businesses operating in the area to stay in business.[52] A 2016 review that followed Abbott's re-proclamation of the Coral Sea CMR recommended freer access to reefs for operators in this fishery, as long as they continued to rotate their fishing effort to avoid depletions (Buxton and Cochrane 2016). And as with Great Barrier Reef Tuna, these businesses also had non-transferable assets, such as Cairns Marine's husbandry and shipping facility in Cairns.

Subsequent Australian governments made it clear that the Coral Sea Fishery was not the target of management provisions for the marine park. Under Gillard, that meant guaranteeing access to some reefs while closing off others, but with the intent of facilitating continued operations. The 2016 review went further, dismissing managing a fishery that was "low impact as long as [it] maintained [its] established pattern of rotational fishing on reefs . . . to avoid localised depletion" (Buxton and Cochrane 2016). The Abbott and Turnbull governments were not going to repeat the 2004 Great Barrier Reef rezoning that saw a large number of businesses bought out and displaced. Although there was some haggling between fishers and dive operators over which reefs the government should close to fishing, new regulations did not threaten companies in this fishery in the same way they did the Lamasons, despite its similar reliance on the Coral Sea.

The Australian commercial fishing industry is also under a lot of pressure from exogenous stressors. The same global tuna price decline experienced by the US industry affected Australian fishers as well. But beyond this, Australia's waters lack the nutrients needed to support more abundant fish stocks, so they host relatively unproductive pelagic fisheries (Hobday et al. 2006). The Australian government also carefully manages its fisheries to limit industry catch, albeit according to a maximum sustainable yield approach. As a result, Australia imports as much as 70% of its seafood to meet domestic demand for lower value products, primarily from Asian countries with more productive waters and less regulation (Ruello 2011). Australia exports half of its fisheries production (A$1.2 billion) to markets in Japan and elsewhere, predominantly of premium products such as rock lobster and bluefin tuna (Department of Agriculture 2015). Australia similarly relies on positioning itself as selling premium products in the aquarium species trade due to its inability to compete on price with competitors in countries with minimal sustainability regulation. Despite boasting the world's third largest EEZ, Australian industry struggles to compete in a global market characterized by overfishing and poor regulation.

Charter and Recreational Fishing

Only a handful of charter operators use the Coral Sea. One marine campaigner estimated that only a couple of charter operators would be affected by even a fully no-take Coral Sea and, even then, it would just affect 20–25% of their business.[53] Because of this minimal reliance, the initial consultations for the Gillard management plan neglected the charter fishing sector entirely.[54] The 2016 review looked to fill this gap.

The charter sector had two primary concerns: ensuring continued access to reefs in the Coral Sea and preventing a scaling up of commercial fishing efforts.[55] Chartered boats to the Coral Sea are high-end charters that target the wealthy, typically booking trips anywhere from three to four years in advance.[56] These charters rely on various reefs throughout the Coral Sea as staging areas on trips to more distant locations (Buxton and Cochrane 2016). Continued access to those reefs was a priority, but some charter operators also expressed concern about commercial fishing. One charter industry representative argued that longlining was not compatible with a marine reserve and that allowing it would "leave the door open for a super trawler."[57] A provisional application for a super trawler in the Coral Sea already existed at the time, so that concern was not just a hypothetical.[58] The charter sector's interests were therefore not perfectly aligned with the commercial fishing sector. That said, its concern was not with existing commercial fishing efforts, but instead with the long-term prospect of a dramatic upscaling of effort.

The charter sector's activity in the Coral Sea was limited, but for recreational fishers it was even more so. With the exception of a handful of professional game fishers, recreational fishers have virtually no direct stake in the Coral Sea because of its distance from shore: it is too far away to support any kind of viable industry. The recreational fishing lobby was nonetheless one of the most vocal opponents of the Coral Sea CMR. That opposition was baffling to many. Former environment minister Tony Burke (2010–2013) questioned lobbyists behind closed doors about why they cared given the minimal interest.[59] Many marine campaigners refer to the lobby's opposition as "irrational."[60] Others refer to the lobbyists in Canberra driving the opposition as "hardliners" and "not representative."[61]

The direct experience for recreational fishers throughout Australia is that they can and do fish in marine parks, yet campaigns such as the one opposing the Coral Sea create the perception that these parks are an attack on fishing rights (Meder 2016). Recreational fishers tend to overwhelmingly support MPAs after polarizing community debates about them subside with time, including 73% support for the 2004 Great Barrier Reef rezoning just three years later (Sutton and Li 2008; Meder 2016). There seems to be a disconnect between the hardliner lobbyists in Canberra and the lived experience of Australian recreational fishers; a divide of which the Australian government is acutely aware.

Even recreational fishing lobbyists themselves acknowledged that the Coral Sea CMR would not directly affect recreational fishing.[62] Those lobbyists also acknowledged the divide between the lobbyists' position on the reserve and the position of many recreational fishers, many of which were in fact supportive of the reserve.[63] One environmental advocate estimated that 30% of the membership of the Save Our Marine Life campaign were recreational fishers—between 40,000 and 50,000 people.[64] The recreational fishing lobby was vocal, but its influence was limited because it lacked bargaining leverage.[65] A large MPA in the Coral Sea was not going to impact the people these lobbyists represented, so they had a somewhat tenuous claim to representing the views of recreational fishers.

These lobbyists were not irrational or shortsighted, however. They opposed the Coral Sea CMR on principle rather than its anticipated (non-)impact on the sector. They opposed the reserve out of concern over the precedent it would set for what they consider to be unscientific "lock-outs."[66] Their argument was that recreational fishing was sustainable, so banning it amounted to arbitrary regulation with no conservation benefit—a common argument among industry detractors that neglects the scientific basis for no-take reserves. The issue is ultimately not about the science, but about the politics of whether a given area should be managed according to a fisheries management approach or a conservation approach, as discussed in chapter 2. As one campaigner put it, "MPAs are not fisheries management tools; they are conservation management tools."[67] Part of the challenge that the Australian government faces in managing recreational fishing is that accurate data are difficult to collect and official reporting underestimates catch levels.[68] The irony of lobbyists' opposition is that the spillover from closures in the Coral Sea could benefit recreational fishers in the Great Barrier Reef, contributing to healthier fish populations adjacent to recreational fishing hotspots.

There are two reasons, both alluded to earlier, that recreational fishing lobbyists opposed Coral Sea protections despite the potential benefits to their industry. First, some recreational fishers felt aggrieved by the 2004 Great Barrier Reef rezoning and saw closures in the Coral Sea as the next phase in a cumulative process that would lead to them losing their fishing rights in the region entirely.[69] Lobbyists used Pew's initial proposal for a no-take Coral Sea to galvanize support from a minority of Queensland recreational fishers.[70] The rezoning coupled with the no-take plan was enough to raise the ire of this vocal minority in the region.[71] By contrast, the proposed no-take areas off the coast of Western Australia received no recreational fishing backlash.[72] Second, the Coral Sea reserve was a high-profile initiative and considered the "crown jewel" of Australia's marine reserve network. Lobbyists saw it as symbolically important to their long-term goal of protecting recreational fishing rights.[73]

Neither the charter nor recreational fishing industries were heavily invested in the Coral Sea. Aside from a select few fishing sites that act as staging posts on more far-reaching, high-end charter vessels and a small amount of professional game fishing, these industries have a minimal stake. The intensity of activity is low, there is no shortage of alternative sites (particularly given the

Coral Sea's mixed zoning), their assets are suitable for alternative sites, and the industries do not face any challenges beyond business as usual. Because a select few charter vessels do rely on Coral Sea sites as stops on longer trips, the charter industry has some reliance on the area. But on all other measures of interest salience, the two sectors had little demonstrable stake.

Ecotourism

The Coral Sea was, however, important to a small subset of Australia's large dive tourism industry. Only five dive operators in Queensland have boats that traveled as far out as the Coral Sea CMR, while the rest of Queensland's substantial dive tourism industry operated in the more accessible GBRMP (Stoeckl et al. 2010). The Coral Sea requires a minimum three-day trip due to its distance from shore, with four- to seven-day trips being more common. Bougainville Reef and Osprey Reef are the two primary dive sites, located roughly 100 km from the Coral Sea CMR's border with the GBRMP. As a predominantly pelagic ecosystem, the Coral Sea CMR boasts larger marine species than the GBRMP and attracts divers willing to spend more time and money to see those larger species.

Diving further out in the Coral Sea is a small industry that caters to dive enthusiasts, in contrast to the more accessible diving within the GBRMP. According to one study, live-aboard dive tourism in the Cairns and Port Douglass region generates A$15–18 million of revenue per year, including indirect expenditures such as hotels and restaurants (Stoeckl et al. 2010). The dive tourism industry is vital to the Queensland economy, which gave the industry some bargaining power during the Coral Sea CMR consultations. Dive operators' foremost concerns were with protections for their main dive sites, and they mostly avoided getting involved with the broader debate about fishing rezoning throughout the Coral Sea.[74] For them, the bargaining revolved primarily around whether game fishers had access to a handful of reefs.[75] Dive operators were concerned about the impacts of fishing on these reefs because of the abundance of resident species, notably of reef sharks.[76] Reefs are far apart in the Coral Sea CMR, so these species do not exhibit the same migratory behavior that they do within the GBRMP (Barnett et al. 2012). The distance between reefs means that sustained fishing pressure in any one reef has the potential to dispro-portionately affect it.

These reefs are also highly vulnerable to climate impacts. Flinders Reef was decimated and rendered unusable by a bleaching event in 2002, forcing businesses to relocate from Townsville to Cairns.[77] Bougainville and Osprey experienced severe bleaching during the global mass coral bleaching event of 2016. Dive operators were deeply concerned about the vulnerability of the reefs they depended on, so they concentrated their efforts on ensuring the best local protections possible for these reefs.[78] Their stance was a pro-conservation stance in line with environmental groups, but, aside from a few public statements of support, they were not willing to go toe-to-toe with commercial fishers over the surrounding pelagic waters.

While the intensity of ecotourism activity in the Coral Sea was small, a handful of operators did rely on a healthy Coral Sea. The distinct ecosystems and species in Coral Sea reefs offered dive experiences distinct from those provided by most Queensland operators. The five businesses that do travel as far as Coral Sea reefs depend on offering a unique, high-end diving experience to distinguish themselves from the competition. To do that, they have invested in assets devoted to longer and more remote dive trips, such as larger live-aboard vessels. These businesses are not able to cost-effectively relocate dive sites or transfer assets to other activities because their business models depend on the Coral Sea's unique dive sites.

But all of this is moot if climate change continues to decimate the Great Barrier Reef. Climate change impacts, particularly coral bleaching, pose an existential threat to the ecotourism industry in the short-term—a danger that further motivated dive operators to advocate for greater marine protections for the Coral Sea.[79] Mass bleaching events in 2016, 2017, and 2020 devastated corals in the Great Barrier Reef. During the 2020 bleaching event, reefs in the cooler southern waters of the reef experienced their first severe bleaching events in recorded history. In February 2020, sea surface temperatures reached a record high since tracking began in 1900. Tragically, ecotourism in the Great Barrier Reef will increasingly become "last chance" tourism, as dive enthusiasts look to experience the reef while they still can.

Keeping the Coral Sea Open for Business

The importance of Coral Sea access to the commercial fishing and ecotourism sectors led subsequent Australian governments to adopt a stakeholder consultation process designed to minimize business impact. The seemingly never-ending consultations had managed to irritate stakeholders from virtually every major group. Representatives from the commercial fishing and ecotourism sectors alike were frustrated with constantly renegotiating zoning maps.[80] Many disparagingly refer to the consultations as being all about determining "lines on a map," implying a disconnect between the government process and local businesses' need for a more certain process.[81] One commercial fishing business owner claimed that they "became numb" to the consultation process and the uncertainty of not knowing if they would be bought out or expected to continue operations.[82] By the end of the 2016 review, not one representative of any of the major stakeholder groups claimed that the consultations were not extensive.

The government released the report for the review in September 2016, capping nine years of consultations. It recommended keeping the majority of the Gillard management plan intact across the CMR network, but with some notable changes in the Coral Sea. The review recommended reducing the no-take area of the Coral Sea by nearly 100,000 km^2—a concession that would allow Great Barrier Reef Tuna to stay in business (Buxton and Cochrane 2016). It also adjusted the zoning around reefs in the Coral Sea to allow greater access for fishers, reducing the impact of the reserve on the Coral Sea Fishery. Marine campaigners were naturally disappointed that the outcome of the review was to scale back protections. Fiona Maxwell, the Australian Marine Conservation Society's lead campaigner for the Coral Sea, was quoted in *ABC News* as saying that the Coral Sea was now "well and truly sliced and diced" (Smail 2016).

The 2016 review was on balance a loss for the ecotourism sector. While the review did recommend partly protecting reefs in the Coral Sea, including the area's major dive sites at Bougainville and Osprey reefs, it weakened protections overall. It advocated permitting collection of aquarium species at Bougainville and splitting Osprey in half, with one half protected and the other allowing fishing activity. The government consulted dive operators about reef zoning throughout both consultations but was only interested in safeguarding specific dive sites.[83] The ecotourism sector favored strong protections throughout the Coral Sea, but as one industry representative put it, "it's a political trade-off for how invested [we] want to get."[84] Although the sector is vital to the regional economy, its limited activity in the Coral Sea prevented it from influencing the process more broadly. The government was intent on allowing extractive and non-extractive activity to continue on reefs throughout the Coral Sea, to the chagrin of the ecotourism sector.

The recreational fishing lobby in Canberra, despite its hostility to no-take zones, ultimately accomplished very little. Its principled opposition to what it considered unscientific lock-outs did not make a compelling case given the sector's minimal activity in the Coral Sea. The changes that the government made during the review were to keep commercial fishers in business, not to appease the recreational fishing lobby. Recreational fishing will nonetheless continue around the remote Bougainville, Osprey, and Shark reefs, which particularly adventurous game fishers do frequent in small numbers.[85] But the review maintained over 200,000 km^2 of no-take zoning, meaning that even the heavily industry-friendly review rejected the stance that no-take zones were unprincipled.

In the end, the 2016 review was highly favorable to the commercial fishing industry. Despite the outcome, commercial fishing industry representatives insist that the mere fact that the government created the Coral Sea CMR signifies the pervasive influence of transnational environmental groups in Australian resource management. They refer to this influence as a "disgrace" and question why "environmental groups do not focus on areas that are not sustainably managed."[86] Two fishing industry representatives expressed disbelief that the Australian government wanted to limit tuna catch further in Australia only to have these migratory species caught in Papua New Guinea instead.[87] As in the US, the industry saw any and all large, no-take zoning as undermining sustainable fisheries management.

The Turnbull government was still not finished with diluting protections, however. The Bioregional Advisory Panel responsible for the 2016 review only had the authority to make recommendations to the government. In 2017, in a rejection of its own review, the Turnbull government decided to go forward with a plan that had even less stringent zoning. It reduced the no-take area (IUCN II) of the Australian Coral Sea to just 24%, in the process abandoning the CMR designation altogether and renaming the MPA the Coral Sea Marine Park. This further erosion of no-take zoning will, according to reports, prevent the displacement of an additional $4 million per year in the EBTF, roughly 0.03% of national annual fishing revenue (Reese 2017). Conservationists and marine scientists were confounded by the move, wondering how it was possible that the pendulum would swing so far in the direction of business interests. No-take zoning in the Coral Sea had deteriorated from an initial hope for a fully no-take Coral Sea, to 51% under Gillard, to 41% recommended in the 2016 review, to just 24% when a management plan finally came into effect in 2018 (see Table 5.3 and Figure 5.1).

Table 5.3 Coral Sea Zoning, 2012–2017

Zone[a]	IUCN Category	2012 Management Plan		2016 Review Recommendation		2017 Management Plan	
		Area (km²)	%	Area (km²)	%	Area (km²)	%
Sanctuary Zone (SZ)	IUCN Ia	0	0	5,212	0.53	0	0
Marine National Park Zone (MNPZ)	IUCN II	502,654	50.78	405,258	40.94	238,738	24.12
Habitat Protection Zones (HPZ)	IUCN IV	268,085	27.08	518,833	52.42	684,704	69.17
Multiple Use Zones (MUZ)	IUCN IV	194,232	19.62	0	0	0	0
Other	IUCN IV	24,870	2.51	60,540	6.12	66,482	6.72

[a] Sanctuary Zones (SZ) prohibit all human access; Marine National Park Zones (MNPZ) ban all extractive industry activity; Habitat Protection Zones (HPZ) and Multiple Use Zones (MUZ) permit mixed-use, with pelagic longline, purse seine, and mid-water trawl commercial fishing permitted in non-reef areas.

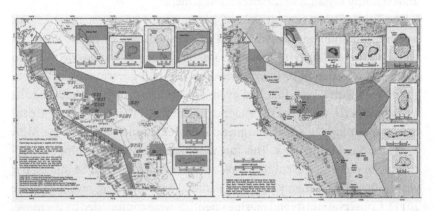

Figure 5.1 Coral Sea Zoning

Solid line represents the boundaries of the Coral Sea Marine Park (unchanged from 2016 to 2017). Dark grey denotes no-take zoning.

Sources: Buxton and Cochrane (2016), Parks Australia (2018).

Dynamic Management

Future Australian governments have the authority to extend protections in the Coral Sea, so the watered-down 2018 management plan is by no means final. Throughout the consultation process, the Australian government had the authority to design a management plan as it saw fit. EPBA provides the legal basis for CMRs and marine parks in Australia: under the EPBA, a management plan does not need parliamentary approval, as noted earlier. As with the US Antiquities Act, this legislation affords a high degree of authority to one decision-maker, in this case the environment minister. The minister has the power to proclaim a marine reserve in commonwealth waters, as well as to approve a management plan for the reserve. This high level of authority allows the governing party to pursue new marine reserves with near impunity. The EPBA requires a justification for a new reserve, public consultations, and tabling the management plan in parliament, but none of these requirements are veto points.

Where this Australian legislation differs significantly from that in the US is that it has weaker requirements for the permanence of new reserves. In fact, the EPBA even sets a maximum management plan duration of 10 years, meaning that the ministry frequently re-evaluates regulations by law. The requirement to reassess can lead to more responsive and effective protection of biodiversity, but it can also lead to the weakening of regulations over time. Moreover, the minister has the authority under the EPBA to revoke an existing management plan and issue a new one at any time. The management plan for a commonwealth reserve in Australia is therefore highly fluid and potentially subject to the whims of the sitting government. Revoking a reserve in full or in part is, on the other hand, more difficult, requiring a resolution to pass in both houses of parliament. The flexibility that the minister has in deciding how to manage reserves means that spending the political capital to revoke one is unlikely to be an attractive option. Instead, it seems more likely a minister would choose to alter the management plan to achieve her or his objectives, as was the case with the Abbott government's review of the Gillard government's Coral Sea management plan before it came into effect.

The flexibility afforded to the sitting environment minister under the EPBA means that the Coral Sea management plan could be under constant scrutiny. The 2017 management plan formally approved by environment minister Josh Frydenberg (2016–2019) was the first new set of regulations in the Coral Sea since the campaign began over a decade earlier. The stake-holder fatigue that characterized the Coral Sea process was palpable, so as of this writing it seems likely that it will be some time before this or a sub-sequent government decides to re-evaluate the area. The 2019 election of Scott Morrison's Liberal-led coalition means the 2017 plan will undoubt-edly stand for the foreseeable future. But the only barriers to altering it are political. The government can at any time choose to reinitiate a process that could strengthen or weaken Coral Sea protections. The sitting Australian government therefore has a high degree of flexibility to alter Coral Sea regulations, including in response to economic or environmental change in the region.

The Co-optation of Conservation

The salience of fishing industry interests led to close collaboration be-tween the Australian government and industry representatives throughout the Coral Sea process. It is this collaboration that best explains the mainly business-as-usual activity that will continue in the Coral Sea. This co-alition transcended partisan lines, with subsequent Labor and Liberal governments highly responsive to the fishing industry. Commercial fishing activity in the Coral Sea is not high. This process demonstrates that even when industry activity is modest, the power and influence that industry ac-tors wield can still be substantial. The dependence of a select few businesses on the Coral Sea to stay in operation proved to have a dramatic influence on government decisions. The Coral Sea Marine Park is a cautionary tale about how a state can adopt the large MPA norm, yet implement it in a way that is highly responsive to commercial interests. Conservation was very much secondary.

The Coral Sea in Australia was one of the Pew Global Ocean Legacy's four inaugural projects, making it one of the earlier large MPA campaigns. Pew's initial fully no-take proposal introduced the norm of large, contiguous, pe-lagic, and ideally no-take MPAs into an ongoing Australian process to create a national network of MPAs. This proposal further polarized environmental and industry groups in Australia and led to what is possibly the most drawn out large MPA campaign to date. It may be tempting to point to campaign missteps and overly ambitious environmental groups as the reason Coral Sea protections were so polarizing in Australia, which ultimately undermined conservation goals. I would argue that missteps and ambition were epi-phenomenal to the political economy of the region. They may have further polarized the issue and led to a more combative discourse throughout the process, but from the beginning it was clear that subsequent governments—Labor and Liberal—were driven foremost by a desire to limit the commercial impact of the MPA.

The Coral Sea Marine Park is nonetheless among the least remote large MPAs on the planet as of 2020, with ongoing commercial activity within and surrounding it. It has, in many ways, served as a learning experience for ocean campaigners looking to promote large MPAs globally. Despite the contested and lengthy process—summarized in Table 5.4—the result of the campaign was still a 990,000 km² MPA, with the final management plan designating 237,600 km² as no-take. The no-take zoning was residual, doing little to reduce commercial activity. But unlike the US, Australia does not boast overseas territories far removed from major commercial hubs. The distinct conservation outcomes in the Pacific Remote Islands and the Australian Coral Sea had less to do with each country's (or government's) respective conservation values. Both processes were driven by the array of commercial stakeholder interests in each region and industry's ability to leverage those interests into policy influence.

The politics of protecting Australia's Coral Sea demonstrate the perils of neoliberal environmentalism well. Pew's proposal for a fully no-take Coral Sea represented the introduction of the large MPA norm in Australia, but the political economy of the region all but guaranteed that the government would erode the tenets of the norm. The stakeholder bargaining process that dragged on for over 10 years was an attempt by the government to reconcile a new conservation norm with commercial interests. Pew, the Australian Marine Conservation Society, and others succeeded in persuading multiple Australian governments that designating large, no-take MPAs was the appropriate course of action just as they were beginning to grow in number around the world.

In the end, the localization of the large MPA norm in Australia reflects the Australian government continuing its practice of complex zoning within MPAs. The result still included large, contiguous no-take zones in the Coral Sea and South-West Corner unprecedented in Australian conservation history. But that zoning was quite clearly residual. It begs the question of what the point of such an exhaustive consultation process was. Extractive industry stakeholders with only moderate interests in the region still had enough

Table 5.4 Coral Sea Timeline

1975	Australian government establishes the GBRMP, the world's first MPA exceeding 200,000 km^2
1998	Australian government begins work with bipartisan support on NRSMPAs
2004	Australian government rezones the GBRMP, increasing no-take zoning from 4.6% to 33%
2005	WWF proposes zoning of Coral Sea similar to 2004 GBRMP rezoning (following CAFNEC and NQCC proposal)
2007	Pew launches campaign for large, no-take MPA in Coral Sea
	WWF joins Pew- and AMCS-led coalition for no-take Coral Sea
2009	Environment minister Peter Garrett declares the Coral Sea a conservation zone
2010	Julia Gillard replaces Kevin Rudd as leader of the Labor Party
2012	Gillard government formally declares 25 new or expanded marine reserves as part of the NRSMPA initiative, including the Coral Sea CMR
2013	Gillard government proposes initial 10-year management plan for Coral Sea, with 51% no-take zoning and A$100 million earmarked to buy out commercial fishers
	Tony Abbot's Liberal-led coalition wins election
	Abbott government re-proclaims the Coral Sea CMR
2014	Consultations for a revised management plan for the Coral Sea CMR begin
2015	Malcolm Turnbull replaces Abbott as leader of the Liberal Party
2016	Malcolm Turnbull's Liberal-led coalition wins re-election
	Consultations completed on revised management plan, with a recommendation to reduce the no-take zoning of the Coral Sea CMR by nearly 100,000 km^2 to 41%
2017	Coral Sea CMR renamed Coral Sea Marine Park
2018	Coral Sea Marine Park management plan comes into effect reducing the no-take zoning by an additional 165,000 km^2 to just 24%
	Scott Morrison replaces Malcolm Turnbull as leader of the Liberal Party
2019	Scott Morrison's Liberal-led coalition wins re-election

bargaining power to yield a management plan that effectively changed very little. In both Australia and the US extractive industries staunchly opposed new protections but had different results because of their respective interest salience. In Palau, the country's critical ecotourism sector played a very different industry role as a major advocate for a strict, comprehensive marine reserve.

6

A Dive Tourism Haven in Palau

The Palau National Marine Sanctuary (PNMS) was championed by Palauan President Tommy Remengesau Jr. and unanimously approved by the *Olbiil Era Kelulua*, the Palau National Congress, on October 22, 2015. The Palau National Marine Sanctuary Act was an ambitious piece of legislation. It established a 500,238-km^2 no-take zone covering 80% of Palau's EEZ, set aside the remaining 20% for the development of a small-scale domestic commercial fishing industry, banned most foreign fishing and fish exports, and substantially increased the penalties for illegal fishing in Palau. It phased these regulations in over time, with the initial goal of them coming into full effect on January 1, 2020. The legislation was designed to conserve marine biodiversity and protect Palau's ecotourism industry, but was also an effort to restructure commercial fishing in Palau from a primarily foreign-dominated enterprise to one in which the proceeds remained in Palau. Implementation will be an ongoing challenge, with many remaining unanswered questions about the feasibility of the commercial fishing restructure and about Palau's capacity to enforce the regulations on the water.

The overarching economic goal of the sanctuary legislation was to strengthen the Palauan economy by bolstering its critical tourism sector while ensuring that Palau was the primary benefactor of commercial fishing in its waters. Palau is a world-class dive destination, and tourism accounted for a staggering 54% of the Pacific Island nation's GDP in 2015 (Asian Development Bank 2016a). By comparison, only 2.2% (USD 5.5 million) of Palau's GDP in 2014 came from the fishing industry (Bureau of Budget and Planning 2014). Despite abundant high-grade tuna in its waters, Palau only received minor revenue from fleets based primarily out of Japan and Taiwan through modest license fees and a 35 cent/kg tax. Palau's two primary domestic fishing companies at the time—the Kuniyoshi Fishing Company (KFC) and Palau International Traders Inc. (PITI)—used predominantly foreign boats and workers, and even they immediately exported their high-grade tuna on chartered flights to sashimi markets in Japan and Taiwan, where it receives a premium price.[1]

Conserving the Oceans. Justin Alger, Oxford University Press (2021). © Oxford University Press.
DOI: 10.1093/oso/9780197540534.003.0006

Palau's high dependence on tourism and the poor performance of its commercial fishing sector (from a Palauan perspective) were the impetus for the sanctuary. The politics of Palau's large MPA stand in contrast to those of other large, no-take reserves, many of which were designated by governments because of their remoteness and the advocacy of powerful ENGOs. In Palau, the rationale emphasized both the conservation and commercial benefits of a reserve. The prevailing hope among reserve advocates in the Palauan government was nothing short of bolstering Palau's ecotourism sector while simultaneously restructuring its commercial fishing sector to better benefit Palauans. This hope led to a different kind of political process than for other no-take reserves—one with a powerful economic justification in favor of strict conservation. The central argument of this chapter is that industry can be the central driver of a large marine reserve, given a favorable configuration of extractive and non-extractive industry interests.

The PNMS in many ways represents the progression of the large MPA norm. The idea to close Palau's EEZ emerged out of the ecotourism industry rather than transnational environmental groups.[2] President Remengesau, who needed little convincing of the merits of a reserve, actually reached out to Pew for support after deciding to pursue a large MPA.[3] It was the first clear instance of a state leader embracing the large MPA norm without the need for a devoted advocacy campaign, suggesting that the norm was becoming further entrenched in global politics by 2015. But the underlying political economy of the sanctuary underscored Remengesau's support, highlighting a pattern of norm diffusion in which economic policy and conservation policy can truly go hand in hand. Unlike the greenwashing platitudes of many political leaders attempting to balance economy and environment, this was a case in which the two priorities seemed perfectly aligned rather than at odds and in need of balancing. This chapter will analyze the politics of this apparent alignment, in the process telling the story of how a small island nation of roughly 18,000 people enacted what was perhaps the most ambitious large MPA legislation at the time.

Conservation Culture in Palau

The PNMS was by no means Palau's first ambitious marine conservation initiative, nor even its first attempt at large-scale marine conservation. Marine conservation is embedded in traditional Palauan cultural practice,

primarily through the concept of "*bul*": a temporary fishing closure tradi-
tionally enacted by local chiefs in response to noticeable declines in reef fish
stocks. When fish in a specific reef became sparse, a local chief would impose a *bul* to give fish stocks time to recuperate. Fishers would then move
their efforts to another reef until the local chief formally ended the *bul*. These
buls would rotate regularly to ensure that fishers did not overfish any one
area. A chief could also enact a *bul* to reserve a particular fishing grounds
for special expeditions, usually surrounding an important cultural event
(Johannes 1978).

This practice was the primary method of marine conservation in Palau
before colonization (which began in 1885), with the country shifting toward
increasingly centralized methods of conservation in the time since (Gruby
and Basurto 2013). Initially, these took the form of colonial arrangements
imposed by Spain, Germany, Japan, and the US at various stages of Palau's
colonial history, leading to a de facto open access policy (Ueki and Clayton
1999; Gruby and Basurto 2013). Despite its declining use and significance in
Palauan marine conservation as more modern institutions replaced it, *bul*
still resonated strongly in Palau as an essential part of the local culture.[4] In
1994, Palau achieved independence from US administration after 47 years
as a UN Trust Territory. Palau remains in free association with the US, which
provides security, and the US dollar is Palau's official currency. Since independence, Palau has consistently enacted new legislation intended to protect its marine resources. Two high-profile pieces of conservation legislation
stand out: the 2003 Protected Areas Network (PAN) Act and the 2009 Shark
Haven Act.

The PAN Act created the institutional platform for a national system of
protected areas. Prospective member sites go through a nomination process
and if the government accepts them, they receive benefits in the form of access to technical assistance, participation in a national monitoring system,
and eligibility for federal funds (Palau National Congress 2003). Perhaps the
most significant consequence of the act was to bring marine conservation
under federal jurisdiction (Gruby and Basurto 2013). The act provided federal oversight and authority over marine conservation that was previously
the role of states or local governments. This reflected a shift toward a more
centralized Western-style institutional structure, but the motivations for it
mainly came from the traditional cultural understanding of the importance
of marine conservation embodied in *bul* (van Kerkhoff and Pilbeam 2015).
In other words, the PAN Act was a shift toward a more centralized form of

marine conservation that was still grounded in traditional Palauan practice. As one interviewee put it, "PAN is *bul*."[5] It is comparatively easy for state and local governments in Palau to create MPAs, or for the federal government to enact initiatives such as the PAN Act, because closures to manage marine areas are common throughout Palauan history.[6] The PAN Act has already yielded conservation benefits, with a scientific study of Palau's MPA sites showing that no-take areas in the network now contain twice the biomass of nearby unprotected areas, with larger MPAs seeing even stronger results (Friedlander et al. 2017).

The second major initiative, the 2009 Shark Haven Act, created the world's first ever shark sanctuary. It prohibited shark fishing, banned having sharks or shark parts on board vessels at any time, and imposed penalties for violations. But the sanctuary was not the first effort to protect sharks in Palau. In 2001, President Remengesau (then in his first term) passed laws to prohibit shark finning, but his political opponents ensured that they were watered down, unenforceable, and resulted in miniscule fines.[7] On May 6, 2003, Remengesau and his minister of justice, angry with the ineffectiveness of the laws, ordered officials to burn a sizeable illegal catch of shark fins found aboard a Taiwanese boat.[8] The government followed this high-profile burning by strengthening the laws later in 2003, increasing fines and banning foreign vessels from transporting sharks or rays.[9] Despite these efforts, Palau could not enforce the regulations given its roughly 630,000 km^2 EEZ and limited capacity.[10] These laws sent a strong message, but they were mostly symbolic given Palau's lack of credible enforcement and likely did little to slow down the rate of finning in Palau's waters.

In 2009, Johnson Toribiong assumed the Palauan presidency for a single term in what was a significant threat to Palau's anti-finning legislation. Toribiong was reportedly supportive of Bill 8-44, a proposal to repeal shark protection laws and to allow the sale of shark bycatch, and one of the first bills tabled after he took office.[11] A local environmental group called Shark Sanctuary—founded in 2001 by Dermot Keane, who also manages one of Palau's leading dive shops—aggressively lobbied against the bill.[12] Matt Rand from Pew, then the head of Pew's shark conservation program, and Ambassador Stuart Beck, Palau's representative to the UN, actively lobbied Toribiong on the bill, convincing him that he had more to gain from protecting sharks.[13] Pew's political and international influence helped convince Toribiong that the reputational benefits of creating the world's first shark sanctuary outweighed minor revenues from shark finning.[14] This advocacy reportedly convinced Johnson that declaring the sanctuary was the statesmanlike thing to do and that doing so would benefit him politically.[15] He announced the sanctuary at the UN on September 25, 2009, making international headlines as the founder of the world's first shark sanctuary at a time when conservationists were despairing at the lack of global progress to protect rapidly declining shark species.[16]

The advocacy campaign for the shark sanctuary also led to the first attempt to put a dollar value on Palau's pelagic marine resources as a contributor to the nation's ecotourism sector. A 2010 study by the Australian Institute of Marine Science (AIMS) estimated the lifetime value of a reef shark in Palau to the ecotourism industry at $1.9 million (Vianna et al. 2010). A fishery targeting these same sharks would only realize 0.00006% of this lifetime value—just over $100—if fishers extract them instead. The study emphasized the importance of live sharks to Palau, noting that sharks alone account for about 8% of Palau's GDP and 14% of its business tax revenue, while the tax revenue collected from shark diving is roughly 24 times higher than that collected from the fishing industry. The economic case for protecting sharks instead of harvesting them was an exceedingly strong one. The $1.9 million figure was so compelling during the shark sanctuary advocacy that the government and activists also used it liberally during the promotional push for the PNMS.[17] International recognition and the economics of shark protection were critical to Toribiong's reversal from considering a resumption of shark finning to declaring a shark sanctuary instead.[18]

For all of the fanfare surrounding the shark sanctuary, some observers note that it did not do much to slow down shark finning.[19] Data on both legal and illegal fishing in Palau's EEZ is limited, so it is difficult to measure the effectiveness of policies such as the shark sanctuary. Research institutes such as the Palau International Coral Reef Center (PICRC) and Coral Reef Research Foundation (CRRF) monitor and assess Palau's coral reefs, but there is no domestic research body currently devoted to pelagic waters. The Shark Haven Act was also an executive order rather than legislation, so a subsequent president could overturn it. The conservation-friendly Remengesau was not likely to reverse it when he resumed office in 2013, but the shark sanctuary lacked legislative permanence. This Shark Haven Act nonetheless provided much of the early foundation for the national sanctuary: it was a high-profile initiative with both transnational and domestic environmental group involvement, it focused on protecting species in Palau's pelagic ecosystems, and it explicitly connected Palau's pelagic resources to its integral ecotourism industry.

In sum, three main developments in Palau's marine conservation history set the stage for the PNMS. The first was the continued cultural relevance of *bul*, which despite being less prominent than in precolonial Palauan history, remains an essential concept in Palauan culture. The second is the shift toward marine conservation as a more centralized, national priority, most notably through the 2003 PAN Act. And third, the 2009 Shark Haven Act emphasized the non-extractive value of Palau's pelagic marine resources. Given these developments and combined with heavy reliance on the ecotourism industry, it is not surprising that there was high-level government support for the idea of a large, no-take marine reserve in Palau's EEZ.

Ecotourism-Driven Campaigning

With its rich conservation history and an influential ecotourism industry in favor of better protections, Palau was primed for a large MPA. Palau's two premier dive shops—Sam's Tours and Fish 'n Fins—have owners or senior management who also run small environmental groups. Sam's Tours, located on Malakal, used to be located next to a port that docked 40–50 longline fishing boats all smelling of uric acid from their shark fin catch. The contrast between a dive shop that relied on live sharks and the shark finning next door inspired the creation of Shark Sanctuary, a small environmental group founded and operated by the aforementioned manager of Sam's Tours, Dermot Keane. Shark Sanctuary was active in the push to strengthen Palau's poor shark finning regulations in the early 2000s and was one of the most vocal proponents of the 2009 Shark Sanctuary legislation. One state over in Koror, Fish 'n Fins owner Tova Harel founded the Micronesia Shark Foundation, another environmental group devoted to protecting sharks. The foundation uses dive guides to collect data about shark abundance (particularly less common pelagic species of shark) and publishes the results. These two businesses were strong advocates of robust conservation in Palau.[20]

To these businesses, the potential benefits of a large MPA were clear: it could lead to better diving by protecting marine species and, as one dive shop manager put it, is a "major marketing tool" that they can use to attract customers to Palau in a competitive international dive market.[21] The dive tourism industry emphasized that divers tend to be concerned about the health of the oceans and want to support conservation, including when choosing between prospective dive destinations (Uyarra, Watkinson, and

Cote 2009). A large MPA covering most of Palau's EEZ would give Palau a competitive advantage over other premier dive destinations in the region, such as Indonesia or the Philippines, which are home to some of the most at-risk coral reefs in the world (Jeffe-Bignoli et al. 2014). Sharks are the main attraction for Palau's dive tourism industry, so shark conservation is of particular importance to these shops (hence their emphasis on sharks in their advocacy efforts). A large MPA was not just about conservation to the ecotourism industry in Palau, but was also an initiative that would enhance their businesses.

It is little surprise, then, that the idea to designate a large MPA emerged out of the ecotourism sector. In a text message exchange with a government consultant in 2013, Keane proposed an outright ban on commercial fishing in Palau's EEZ as the next step for Palau's conservation policy.[22] That proposal immediately made its way to the top.[23] In March 2013, Remengesau was set to host Prince Albert of Monaco—a renowned philanthropist—so he wanted to be prepared with a clear proposal for the prince.[24] He held a meeting with a small group of advisers to brainstorm ideas.[25] The government consultant and Keane had their text exchange during the meeting when Keane proposed the fishing ban, so the consultant took the opportunity to relay the idea to Remengesau.[26] He was enthusiastic and later presented it to Prince Albert at a meeting on the prince's yacht.[27] The prince was similarly enthusiastic, offering his moral and financial support.[28] Shortly after, Remengesau announced his intention to pursue a large MPA—the PNMS (see Figure 6.1)—covering the vast majority of Palau's EEZ. The reserve would cover 80% of Palau's EEZ, with the remaining 20% initially reserved for a domestic commercial fishing zone.

The next step was to secure support for the sanctuary from environmental groups and the Palauan people. Remengesau wrote letters to several transnational environmental groups requesting their support, including Pew, National Geographic, and The Nature Conservancy (TNC), among others. All were on board to varying degrees and contributed to various aspects of the sanctuary. Pew once again, however, played a leading role in campaigning for the sanctuary before its passing into law, providing critical resources and organizing campaigning efforts. What was different this time for Pew was that this was the first time that a government approached them with the idea for a large MPA, rather than the other way around. Pew had not budgeted for the surprise project, so the project team had to request additional funding from its backers, which it received. It proved to be Pew's

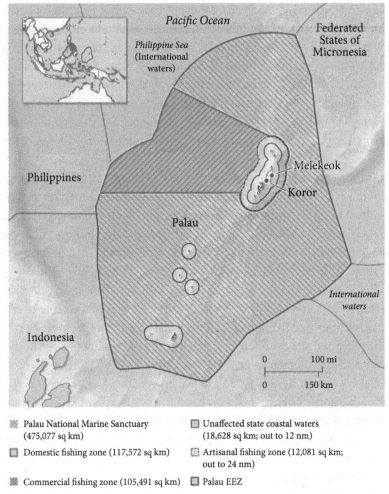

Figure 6.1 Palau National Marine Sanctuary Map

most cost-effective project at the time on a per-km²-protected basis, costing only \$2 per km² relative to the average of \$5 per km².[29] For its part, National Geographic conducted an expedition, producing a documentary to showcase the rich biodiversity of Palau's waters. TNC has a long history in Palau, was influential in the sanctuary process, and has one member sitting on the sanctuary's executive committee.[30] During the process, it undertook an assessment of Palau's tuna fishery, where data are sorely lacking, to improve fisheries management.[31] These organizations all played a role in garnering support for the reserve, though local environmental groups such as the Ebiil Society were more important for shepherding the reserve through congress, as discussed later in this chapter.

Palau's long cultural tradition of conservation meant that the campaign for the PNMS did not need to convince constituents of the benefits of conservation—they were widely taken as a given.[32] The scientific studies that environmental groups compiled for other large MPA campaigns were not prominent in the campaign. Instead, the campaign reaffirmed local knowledge that closures work by adapting the familiar concept of *bul*.[33] The idea was to translate this traditional practice into modern practice. Remengesau positioned himself as the "chief" of the waters under his jurisdiction as president, merging centralized conservation with *bul* further.[34] Early in the campaign, Pew provided marketing materials ranging from t-shirts to bumper stickers for the sanctuary that prominently displayed the word *bul*.[35] These marketing materials were still highly visible throughout Palau several years after the start of the campaign. The sanctuary's congruence with preexisting local norms meant that the campaigners had less work to do convincing constituents of the merits of large no-take MPAs than has been the case with other large MPAs. But even with this strong cultural congruence, a more powerful explanation of why a robust marine reserve was so popular in Palau was the particularly strong economic case for it.

The Business Case for Conservation

The ecotourism industry was in many ways the driving force behind the sanctuary. Not only did the idea emerge out of it, but it ardently supported Remengesau's push to pass legislation in congress. But even more so than that support, the economic rationale that Palau's critical dependence on ecotourism provided was a powerful argument in support of the reserve that detractors struggled to counter. The ecotourism and commercial fishing industries were the two primary industry stakeholders in the PNMS, with some vested interest from a small but growing recreational fishing industry. Because the sanctuary legislation was to regulate the entirety of Palau's EEZ, the industry stakeholders comprised the entirety of the national industry rather than a subset of industry, as was the case for large MPAs in both Australia and the US. The massive disparity between the salience of

Table 6.1 Industry Interests in the PNMS

Industry	Intensity of Activity	Factor Specificity	Asset Specificity	Exogenous Stressors	Overall
Ecotourism	High	High	High	High	High
Commercial Fishing	Low	Moderate	Moderate	Moderate	Moderate

ecotourism and fishing industry interests empowered the Palauan govern-ment to enact robust conservation measures that, as of this writing, seek to radically transform the country's commercial fishing sector.

The commercial fishing sector was so vulnerable—despite the privi-lege that governments typically afford extractive industry (see chapter 2)—because domestic investment and interests were minimal. Foreign fleets took the majority of profits from Palau's tuna resources out of the country, which limited their political influence during the process. These foreign fleets were relatively small and originated from nations much wealthier than Palau, so they were unable to convincingly claim that they were critically dependent on Palau's resources. Table 6.1 presents the breakdown of the salience of in-dustry interests for the ecotourism and commercial fishing industries in the PNMS.

Ecotourism

Ironically, the PNMS does not directly protect Palau's tourist hot spots. All of these hot spots are within 12 nautical miles of shore—where the national sanctuary begins—and therefore under state jurisdiction under Palauan law, so the economic argument in favor of the reserve was more compli-cated than citing overall contribution to GDP. The benefit of the sanctuary to Palau's ecotourism sector was from protecting the transitory species that frequented both pelagic waters and reefs, but also branding. Palau is a world class dive destination, so much so that CEDAM International—an environ-mental group comprised of divers devoted to marine conservation—lists Palau's reefs as one of the seven wonders of the underwater world. Existing regulations already protected dive sites, so the sanctuary was not going to di-rectly protect the geographical spaces that attract tourists to Palau in droves year upon year. Some observers have been critical of the campaigning for the sanctuary because the images used are frequently of reefs and reef species (especially turtles and reef fish) that the sanctuary does not directly protect, rather than the pelagic species it does (such as tuna and sharks).[36] The PNMS nonetheless serves a broader purpose for Palau's ecotourism industry, which is why the industry has been categorically supportive of the initiative. It attracts high-value tourists to Palau, which was becoming an increasingly important priority.

Palau has historically had a steady number of tourist visitors from Japan, South Korea, and Taiwan, with a smaller but stable number from Europe and the US. But the number of visitors began to skyrocket in the 2010s, straining Palau's infrastructure and ecosystems alike.[37] Palau's population was only about 18,000 people in 2015, but in that same year alone the country had nearly 170,000 visitors (PITI-VITI 2020), more than double the 81,000 visitors in 2010. Much of that increase was due to a sudden and rapid influx of tourists from mainland China, up from 9,100 in 2013 to 91,000 in 2015—a dramatic tenfold increase in just two years. Figure 6.2 depicts this rapid tourism growth broken down by nationality. According to one prominent Palauan scientist, tourism levels in 2016 had surpassed what Palau's marine resources could provide at sustainable levels.[38] Palau is in the middle of trying to find the right balance between growing its critical tourism sector without overstressing its marine environment.

Palau's tourism challenges are not only the number of tourists but the type of tourism. The influx of mainland Chinese tourists coincided with an

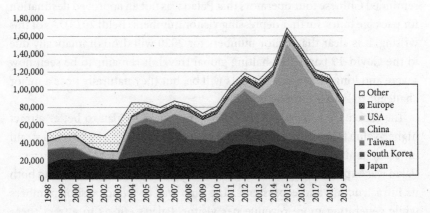

Figure 6.2 Visitors to Palau by Nationality
Source: PITI-VITI (2020).

increase in low-value tourism: tourists that primarily enter Palau on chartered flights with package tours prepaid at the point of origin. This model reduces the revenue that the Palauan government and local businesses receive from visitors. In 2015, the total income earned from each visitor to Palau dropped by 12.7% from the previous year, and the income collected per visitor-night fell by 7.8% (PITI-VITI 2020). Visitors were spending much less on average. Spending per tourist was a modest $891 in 2015 and was trending in the wrong direction (Asian Development Bank 2016b). According to an Asian Development Bank private sector assessment of Palau, the costs imposed on "Palau's tourism resources in the form of overcrowding and degradation may not be offset by the benefits to the country as a whole" (Asian Development Bank 2016b).

The sudden increase in package tours was putting undue strain on Palau's infrastructure, while also yielding a lower marginal gain per new visitor.[39] It put additional pressure on Palau's reef resources because mainland Chinese tourism tends to be more seafood focused, with visits to Palau motivated in part by the desire to sample exotic marine life such as giant clams.[40] President Remengesau expressed concern that it was unhealthy to rely too much on tourists from one location, fearing it could create a dependency (Remengesau 2016). But visitor numbers contracted each year between 2015 and 2019, for a number of reasons. In part, the decline was due to Delta Airlines' cancellation of commercial flights to Palau from Tokyo, while at the same time the Palauan government began limiting charters from Hong Kong (Asian Development Bank 2019). In what was reportedly an attempt to punish Palau for maintaining relations with Taiwan, the Chinese government also reminded Chinese tour operators that Palau was not an approved destination for package tours, further depressing visitor numbers (Beldi 2018). As of this writing, it is clear that visitor numbers for 2020 will drop dramatically due to the Covid-19 pandemic halting global travel. It remains to be seen how severe and long-lasting the impacts will be, but they naturally pose a major challenge to Palau's tourism industry.

The sanctuary was nonetheless a way to rebrand Palau to better attract higher-value tourists that would spend more while putting less overall strain on ecosystems. In 2015—at the height of the campaign for the sanctuary— Palau was experiencing record high visitor levels that were threatening both its infrastructure and ecosystems. The plan was to reduce visitor numbers while generating more revenue per visitor. Palau's efforts to attract these high-value tourists coalesced around the slogan, "Pristine Paradise Palau."

The Palau Visitors Authority (PVA) markets Palau as an untouched island paradise, with a strong conservation record. The hope is that this branding will help it to differentiate Palau from other tropical island locations and premium dive destinations.[41] The government saw the sanctuary as an extension of the Pristine Paradise Palau branding, hoping that such an ambitious conservation initiative would attract ecotourists.[42]

Palau nonetheless faces many challenges in encouraging high-value tourism. Part of the problem is that deciding what counts as high-value is not straightforward.[43] Palauan officials acknowledged the need for high-value tourism, but there was no clear sense for precisely what counts as high-value nor how to go about attracting it (Asian Development Bank 2016a). Another challenge is that Palau has no nationally integrated tourism plan. The 16 states each issue tourism permits, with Koror, the largest state, benefitting more than even the national government.[44] As of this writing, work on a national tourism strategy was underway in Palau, with the sanctuary a key component. According to the Asian Development Bank the challenges to developing such a strategy are many: there is little data available on Palau's carrying capacity; there is a significant shortage of the skills required to operate high-end tourist operations; Palau's existing policies and regulations are insufficient; and the rules that are in place are poorly enforced (Asian Development Bank 2016b). The ecotourism industry is fully supportive of leveraging the sanctuary to attract an influx of high-spending tourists,[45] though some operators remain deeply skeptical.[46]

Tourism operators see two key ways in which the PNMS can enhance their businesses. The first is that it does help tour operators sell their businesses in a globally competitive market.[47] Tour operators were already including the sanctuary in their promotional material as early as 2016 to attract customers to Palau. Such a high-profile conservation initiative only helps to attract conservation-minded divers (Whatmough, Van Putten, and Chin 2011).[48] The second is that it should lead to better diving, mainly through the protection of sharks.[49] Unlike the local inhabitants of Palau's coral reefs, sharks also frequent Palau's pelagic waters, so the sanctuary does directly protect them. The illegal, unregulated, and unreported fishing of sharks will undoubtedly continue in Palau's waters, but the sanctuary legislation cements Palau's existing policy against the harvesting of sharks or shark parts. These sharks are for many divers the main attraction of diving in Palau, and the sanctuary is further recognition that shark species are more valuable alive than dead.

No matter the challenges of enhancing Palau's ecotourism sector, it was and remains essential to Palau. No other country relies on tourism activity as much as Palau does for its economic welfare (roughly half of its GDP). The critique that the sanctuary does not encompass Palau's tourist attractions was therefore somewhat overstated given the fluidity of marine species. The $1.9 million lifetime value of a shark in Palau is quite high. Though dive operators do not frequent the sanctuary waters, these sharks certainly do. The geographic disparity between the sanctuary zoning and tourist operations does not diminish the importance of pelagic protections for the ecotourism sector. The value of the resources contained within the PNMS to Palau's ecotourism industry are what matter for measuring the intensity of industry activity. Despite protections that are physically displaced from dive sites, industry's reliance on pelagic species that frequent both pelagic waters and reefs is quite high.

As with the vast majority of tourism operations, both the factor and asset specificity of Palau's ecotourism industry are high. Dive sites are fixed, typically determined by the location of coral reefs and ocean currents, which create hot spots for marine life. Dive operators rely heavily on these dive sites and cannot relocate. Tourism operators cannot efficiently redeploy the dive shops, boats, and dive equipment that they use. Palau's dive boats are small, typically around 30 feet, and intended for day trips. There are a handful of larger, live-aboard vessels that operate in and around Palau with a more extensive range, but these ships are the exception. Palau's dive tourism industry predominantly uses assets suited to visiting Palau's close-range dive sites. In addition to dive operators, hotels, of course, have a high degree of factor and asset specificity since they rely on geographically fixed ecological attractions and buildings.

Finally, Palau's tourism industry faces considerable exogenous stressors. Maintaining sustainable tourism will be doubly difficult given the impact of climate change. Another of Palau's major tourist attractions—the iconic Jellyfish Lake—saw a massive die-off of jellyfish in 2016 due to a combination of climate change and the even warmer and drier conditions brought on by an El Niño year. The government closed the lake for two years to allow jellyfish to recover. It reopened in January 2019 after a successful recovery effort, but the event highlighted the vulnerability of marine ecosystems to diffuse environmental stressors caused by climate change. An unsustainable number of tourists will only increase ecosystem strain as sites receive more visitors, to say nothing of the higher reef and pelagic fishing levels (primarily the latter) required to feed so many visitors. Palau's challenge is to find a way to profit more from its tourism industry without relying on growth in numbers that will strain its marine resources and infrastructure even further.

Commercial Fishing

Before the sanctuary was designated, Palau's commercial fishing industry was comprised mainly of foreign-based fleets operating primarily out of Japan and Taiwan and two local companies (KFC and PITI) that are also mostly foreign-operated. The initial legislation for the sanctuary banned both foreign fleets and exports, with the goal of excluding foreign-based fleets from fishing in Palau's EEZ. The Palauan government would eventually walk back that commitment in response to fears of declining fishing revenue and supply, as well as pressure from the Japanese government to allow some continued fishing (Dacks et al. 2020). Nonetheless, in an uncommon twist, these relatively large-scale commercial operators found themselves with limited political influence throughout the process because of their minimal contribution to the Palauan economy. Aside from the modest tax revenue and licensing fees noted earlier, these foreign fleets contributed little to the Palauan economy while extracting Palau's valuable marine resources. Naturally, these foreign-based fleets were staunch opponents of a piece of legislation that would force them to relocate to more contested or more remote fishing grounds. The majority of the resistance to the sanctuary came from these commercial fishing interests.[50]

A few Palauan politicians used the initial foreign fleet ban as a political tool in the debate over the PNMS legislation in congress. Palau has a handful of oligarchs in congress with close ties to individual fishing businesses and, according to some interviewees, these oligarchs looking for kickbacks were the main political opposition to the sanctuary.[51] This kind of resource grabbing is a common challenge for environmental policymakers in resource-rich countries, and Palau was no exception (Le Billon 2013). These oligarchs had leverage during the negotiations in the form of $5–6 million in government revenue from fishing licensing fees (PITI-VITI 2020). Though the amount was not high, it accounted for roughly 5% of Palau's annual federal budget. The government needed to find a way to replace this lost revenue, and these oligarchs knew it. Losing this revenue was perhaps the main barrier to passing the legislation, discussed in more detail later. For their part, the foreign fleets relied almost entirely on just these few senators to represent their interests. They lacked influence themselves because their benefactors and constituents were located predominantly in Japan and Taiwan. They represented a small industry, with limited benefit to Palau, and the government initially seemed willing to sacrifice them despite some diplomatic pressure.

Commercial fishing activity in Palau is rather modest given the country's large EEZ. Part of the reason for this is that Palau's waters are not highly productive for tuna.[52] The fleet of roughly 30 Japanese boats based out of Okinawa, for example, reported an extracted value of only $15 million in 2014, although they undoubtedly underreport catch.[53] This underreporting proved to be a problem for the Japanese government, which initially struggled to justify its opposition to the sanctuary given such a small reported catch value.[54] During the sanctuary campaign, in 2015, commercial fishing was the eleventh biggest contributor to Palau's GDP, accounting for just 1.5%. As Figure 6.3 shows, the importance of fishing to Palau's economy had been consistently modest for the previous 20 years. Figure 6.4 shows a similarly minor contribution to employment, with the sector contributing just 79 full- and part-time jobs in 2015, or 0.7% of Palau's labor force. Fleets that went to port in Japan and Taiwan were also long-range fleets, so it was possible for them to seek fishing grounds elsewhere, further reducing any leverage they might have had.

The politics of the local Kuniyoshi Fishing Company and Palau International Traders Inc. commercial fishing businesses are more complicated, not least because of the uncertainty at the time about how the government intended to regulate the proposed domestic fishing zone. These

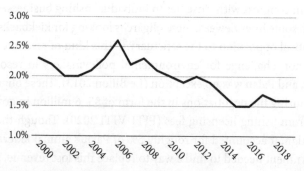

Figure 6.3 Commercial Fishing Contribution to GDP
Source: PITI-VITI (2020).

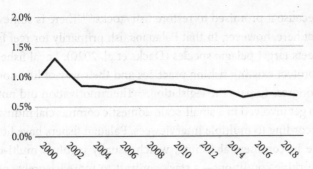

Figure 6.4 Commercial Fishing Contribution to Employment
Source: PITI-VITI (2020).

companies are only partly Palauan-owned—as are many tour operators and hotels—and are operated almost entirely by foreign workers. Crews tend to consist of workers from China, Indonesia, and the Philippines, and typically only have one legally required Palauan observer on board.[55] To call them local is in many ways a misnomer. PITI, for example, has close ties to a partner corporation in Hong Kong, and one of its local owners has taken an increasingly diminished management role over the years.[56] One conservationist described the local ownership component of these companies as "amounting to a rounding error."[57] Further, both export their high-grade tuna directly to sashimi markets in Japan and Taiwan via chartered flights—an activity that the initial sanctuary legislation banned.[58] Despite being Palau's only local commercial fishing businesses, KFC and PITI both faced uncertainty about how the legislation would impact their operations.

To survive in Palau, KFC and PITI depended on a continued fishing presence in Palau's EEZ. Palau is too remote from major fish markets to act as a hub for long-haul fishing expeditions, and KFC and PITI's facilities were not transferable, so both businesses lacked mobility. The majority of KFC and PITI's boats were foreign-owned, however, so they could potentially be redeployed in other markets. While KFC and PITI's contribution to the economy was modest, that they were Palau-based businesses meant it would have been considerably more difficult for the government to enact legislation that would undermine them.

One of the aspirations of the PNMS legislation was to empower local fishers to develop a small-scale, locally owned and operated, commercial industry. Palauan fishers frequently voice their displeasure at how much further out they have to travel to fish and how much smaller the fish they catch are due to decades of commercial exploitation.[59] These fishers supported the reserve because it promised to restore fish stocks.[60] There is somewhat of a disconnect here, however, in that Palauans fish primarily for reef fish while foreign fleets target pelagic species (Dacks et al. 2020). Local fishers, motivated to protect existing fishing practices and their way of life, nonetheless lobbied congress to pass the legislation.[61] Their motivation did not include a desire to get involved in a small-scale domestic commercial industry, however.[62] According to multiple interviewees, Palauan fishers have little desire to partake in commercial fishing, which usually involves multi-day trips in hard working conditions—a stark contrast to more leisurely coastal day trips.[63] Palau has historically relied on foreign workers to meet some of its labor demands (Pierantozzi 2000). Palauan fishers like that the reserve had the potential to improve costal fishing, but seemed to have little appetite for pelagic commercial fishing. This aversion to pelagic fishing foreshadowed concerns over the supply of pelagic fish to the Palauan market years later, especially to feed tourists (Dacks et al. 2020).

Finally, the exogenous stressors faced by the commercial fishing industry in Palau were those facing tuna fisheries writ large. The ongoing global decline in tuna stocks and increasing competition for licenses made it difficult for fishers to relocate, including fleets out of Japan and Taiwan. The sanctuary did not immediately terminate their licenses, but instead called for a gradual phase out, giving these fleets until 2020 to strategize about how to relocate their efforts or, in the case of the Okinawa fleet, convince the Palauan government to let them stay. Declining global tuna stocks, fishing restrictions throughout the Pacific, and a growing number of fishing closures made for a competitive, low-margin tuna industry that would impact foreign and domestic operators alike. The relatively small amount of fishing activity in Palau and its remoteness have contributed to a less competitive environment than in other fishing grounds in the Pacific, however. To pass the legislation, though, the Palauan government would need to overcome the challenge of appeasing not only the commercial fishing sector, but its influential supporters in congress.

The Pushback

The sanctuary became contentious among a handful of senators due to the $5–6 million in lost fishing revenue that would result from the foreign fishing ban. This income came from two sources. The first was direct licensing of vessels mainly out of Japan and Taiwan. With these boats banned, the government would lose this portion of revenue. The other source was through the Nauru Agreement Concerning Cooperation in the Management of Fisheries of Common Interest. The Nauru Agreement is between eight Pacific island states and imposes vessel limits, effort limits (fishing days), and restrictions on certain types of gear. The Parties to the Nauru Agreement (PNA) have agreed upon effort limits based on a combination of historical catch (60%) and biomass (40%) within each country's EEZ. The PNA has also agreed to a cap-and-trade system by which a state can sell its allocated fishing days to other countries for them to resell and distribute as they see fit. Palau's sale of its allotted fishing days makes up a portion of this $5–6 million in government revenue. The fear was that, when the sanctuary came into full effect, Palau's allocation would decline over time as its catch numbers dropped. The sanctuary's proponents needed to find a way to assuage these concerns to pass the legislation.

One initial plan was for a donor-funded endowment to replace the revenue. But according to one senator, a consultation with Pew revealed that the government would need a $200 million endowment with a 5% growth rate—an outcome Pew considered highly unlikely.[64] The government instead found alternatives to replace the lost revenue. The legislation included a doubling of Palau's "green fee" from $50 to $100 per visitor, and congress also attached a rider bill that imposed a $50 visa fee on most nationalities (Palau had no visa requirements before that).[65] The doubling of the green fee alone would amount to an extra $7.5 million based on 2015 visitor numbers.[66] But only $12.50 of the $50 increase to the green fee was earmarked for replacing lost fishing revenue, with the rest going to the pension program ($25) and enforcement ($12.50).[67] Critics of the sanctuary argued that nearly $4 million of the lost revenue was still unaccounted for.[68] The visa was one way to partially recover this lost revenue. Many sanctuary advocates did not widely support it due to the impact it could have on discouraging tourists from going to Palau (especially when compounded with the increased green fee).[69] The visa rider bill was nonetheless a victory for those senators concerned about lost revenue.

Proponents of the PNMS labeled this concern about the lost fishing revenue "fake scare tactics" or "just politics."[70] They considered the fears disingenuous for a few reasons. The first was that Palau would not lose all of its allocated fishing days under the Nauru Agreement. It would retain the 40% allocation based on biomass (which could increase if the sanctuary succeeded in replenishing tuna stocks), and some level of fishing would continue in the domestic fishing zone. Second, the plans to develop a small-scale national commercial fishing industry would theoretically replace some of the lost revenue, though there is still a lot of uncertainty over how. Third, since the announcement of the sanctuary the government has received financial commitments from various environmental groups to provide support for it. That support, although earmarked for conservation initiatives, would nonetheless raise overall government revenue, albeit redistributed revenue. Finally, and perhaps most importantly, the figure only amounts to 5% of government revenue. Given that the government would not lose all of the revenue, and that there were new sources of income to replace it, proponents felt that critics had overstated their concern.

Despite some of these reassurances, many congressional opponents were steadfast in opposing the legislation. Some opposed it because they felt it prioritized marine life over the Palauan people, neglecting issues like Palau's infrastructure problem.[71] During the 2016 election campaign, Remengesau's opponents sarcastically called for a "human sanctuary" in Palau—a critique of the administration's conservation focus.[72] Some senators also have ties to the commercial fishing sector and were perhaps reluctant to support any changes that would threaten their status or wealth. In either case, proponents' reassurances about the lost fishing revenue were not enough on their own to convince congressional opponents to change their vote.

In response to the deadlock in congress, Remengesau decided to change tack to focus on the importance of the sanctuary for the Palauan people. Ann Singeo, the founder of the Ebiil Society, a local environmental group, convinced Remengesau that this shift was necessary to increase the pressure on detractors to support the bill. Ebiil works closely with local fishers and already had a sustainable fishing campaign underway. Singeo began an aggressive promotional campaign involving frequent radio appearances, community events, and fishers' forums, all focused on the foreign exploitation of Palau's marine resources in their messaging. Campaigners argued that commercial fishing in Palau made foreign countries richer while bringing no economic benefit to Palauans, instead profiting just a select few elites with the most notable among them being the select few Palauan senators responsible for blocking the legislation.[73]

The new messaging effectively motivated local fishers to advocate for the sanctuary. A crucial turning point was at the September 2015 funeral of Francis Blelai, a prominent local fisherman and vocal proponent of the sanctuary.[74] Members of congress attended the funeral, where fishers had posted banners supporting the sanctuary in honor of Francis and called out the senators delaying the passage of the bill.[75] One fisherman even put the lead signatory on the bill, Senator Hokkens Baules, on the spot asking for a renewed commitment to getting it passed after nearly two years of stagnation.[76] Fishers then began attending sessions of congress in groups to increase the pressure on detracting senators further.

In October 2015, KFC's partial owner and Palauan senator Quincy Kuniyoshi gave a speech in congress supporting the PNMS in a room filled with local fishers. His motivation was reportedly that KFC's tuna catch was less than one-fifth of what it was in the 1970s due to declining stocks.[77] He saw legislation banning KFC's competition as good for business, even though it was also poised to prevent KFC from exporting tuna.[78] The commercial fishing industry was therefore not categorically opposed to the legislation. KFC, for its part, seemed willing to hedge its bets on the hope that it would benefit from Palau's plans for a small-scale domestic commercial fishery to service the local market. PITI did not taken this position, with its co-owners vocally opposed to the sanctuary and feeling excluded from the process.[79]

KFC's position was a gamble due to the uncertainty around the future of commercial fishing in Palau. The Palauan government lacked the data on its coastal and pelagic fisheries to develop a sophisticated fisheries management plan.[80] The government sees the sanctuary as an opportunity to improve its data collection, in large part through the help of various environmental groups.[81] TNC's work to enhance Palau's fisheries management information since 2014 is an example of this, but it had not yet produced results at the time of the sanctuary bargaining.[82] The paucity of information made it unclear how Palau intended to manage its domestic fishing zone, but the prevailing hope was that the government or companies would deploy fish aggregating devices (FADs) closer to shore, which combined with replenished stocks would allow smaller-scale fishers to profit from pelagic fish, especially tuna.[83] The idea was that encouraging small-scale fishers to target pelagic fish closer to shore would relieve the pressure on Palau's overfished coastal fisheries, which had seen increased strain due to the rapid tourist influx discussed earlier.[84] There was also no precise estimate of how long it would take fish stocks to rebound, nor how diffuse stressors like climate change might affect migration patterns or the health of Palau's coastal fisheries.[85]

Palau's initial management plan for the domestic fishing zone was largely aspirational. The legislation required a concrete plan to be in place by 2020, so the government expected some degree of malleability. Kuniyoshi was taking a chance by endorsing the sanctuary, given the number of unknowns at the time, but he seemed to have faith the process would evolve in a way that would not undermine his interests.[86] According to one of the lead campaigners, Kuniyoshi's senate speech was a turning point for the legislation.[87] The combined pressure from a representative of the domestic commercial fishing industry and the presence of local fishers in the room shamed the senators with ties to foreign commercial fishing interests into silence.[88] With the plans to recover the lost fishing revenue in place, a concession in the form of the visa rider bill, and this public shaming of individual senators, the opposition to the bill had crumbled, and it passed unanimously.

This unanimous passage was not unusual in Palauan politics. Palau modeled its political system after the US system, with distinct executive, legislative, and judicial branches, with a division of power between its 16 states and the federal government. One of the key differences, however, is that Palau operates under a norm of consensus decision-making—a continuation of longstanding cultural practice (van Kerkhoff and Pilbeam 2015). As arduous as that may sound, it was manageable in Palau because of its small size, with its 13-member senate. Once it became clear that momentum on the legislation was moving it toward passage, detractors fell in line to vote in favor of the reserve. Whereas in the US requiring congressional approval would likely be a death knell for large MPAs, in Palau it was a surmountable obstacle.

Why the legislation floundered in the senate for nearly two years before its passage depends on who you ask. Either it was the political opportunism of a handful of senators seeking personal gain by withholding their support, or it was genuine concern about how to recover the $5–6 million per annum in lost fishing licensing revenue. Both reasons undoubtedly have some truth to them. The sanctuary was nonetheless a relatively clear-cut case in which conservation and the economy were in sync. Overcoming the opposition to the reserve boiled down to recovering a small amount of revenue and subverting the parochial interests of a select few elites.

The Capacity Challenge

For all of its promises, much of the sanctuary legislation was aspirational. The legislation was a commitment to protect biodiversity and revolutionize Palau's commercial fishing industry, but to what extent the government would be able to implement it was unclear. Government representatives acknowledge that the legislation was aspirational and that the government made the commitment knowing that there was a lot of uncertainty over implementation.[89] The government and environmental groups began conducting a host of studies about the logistics of implementing the reserve, including studies to determine a tourism strategy for the sanctuary, assessing Palau's tuna stocks and the viability of a domestic market, and the critical issue of whether Palau can enforce the legislation on the water.[90] These are the core promises of the legislation, but it was not clear how the government would deliver on them.

The uncertainty meant that aspects of the legislation were always likely to be malleable. For example, many commentators argued that a ban on fish exports was far too restrictive, and within a year of the legislation passing there was already discussion underway about a proposal to export surplus catch.[91] Similarly, the visa rider bill that was so important to the bill's initial passage also came under threat. In 2016, the senate tabled a supplemental budget bill intended to remove the requirement.[92] In 2019, Remengesau requested that congress amend the legislation to allow some Okinawa-based long liner boats access to the domestic fishing zone, citing Palau's close relationship with Japan and the generations of fishers from Okinawa who have fished in Palau's waters (Pojas 2019). Congress acquiesced. Part of the rationale at the time was, undoubtedly, that there was little sense of what kind of demand there would be for high-grade tuna domestically. Government officials argue that the exemption will not undermine the conservation potential of the reserve (Pojas 2019). Nonetheless, it seems clear that the management plan for the sanctuary will be iterative as Palau wrestles with how to restructure the commercial fishing sector to better benefit Palau.

Given the uncertainty about the feasibility of certain parts of the legislation, it is reasonable to expect more amendments as plans evolve. While the central tenets of conservation, bolstering ecotourism, and domesticizing commercial fishing are likely to remain in some form, the details of implementation could end up being highly variable, particularly around commercial fishing. The Phoenix Islands Protected Area (PIPA) in Kiribati was subject to criticism because of the nearly 10-year process of phasing in regulations. Given Palau's similar capacity challenges, the implementation process will take considerably longer than the initial 2020 completion goal. Some aspects of the bill have already changed, and it seems likely that more concessions will come.

Palau also faces capacity challenges with monitoring and enforcement in the sanctuary—a problem that critics of large MPAs often note (De Santo, Jones, and Miller 2011; De Santo 2013). Monitoring and enforcement are indeed significant challenges for Palau given its limited resources. As of 2020, the Division of Marine Law Enforcement has just two patrol boats, relies on donations to provide fuel to make trips out to sea, and struggles to staff boats regularly.[93] As government officials acknowledge, the division currently does little to deter illegal fishing.[94] The government did produce a monitoring and enforcement plan for the sanctuary in November 2015, but it lacked detailed cost information (Terrill et al. 2015). One commentator referred to it as a "laundry list of wants rather than a practical monitoring plan."[95]

The government is dependent on third-party contributions to monitor and enforce the sanctuary. The hope was that the sanctuary would help to attract donor support, and it has. Pew committed to providing satellite monitoring through its Eyes on the Sea project. The Nippon Foundation also pledged a patrol boat, a new wharf, and a 10-year commitment to provide fuel and a crew of 15 people. The Nippon contribution doubled the number of patrol boats in Palau from one to two, and it more than doubled Palau's patrolling-days capacity by covering some of the associated fuel and staffing deployment costs. The Palauan government is in the unenviable position of needing a comprehensive monitoring and enforcement plan, but is reliant on attracting piecemeal contributions to do so.

It seems unlikely that third-party support would ever be on the scale required to yield a viable solution. Capacity challenges are not a strictly Palauan problem but are common across many large MPAs throughout the Pacific, especially those in the global South. But Palau faces these challenges irrespective of whether or not the sanctuary exists. Illegal fishing is already commonplace in Palau's EEZ, so if the sanctuary attracts donor support to allow Palau to better combat it that is a net gain. The legislation also dramatically increased illegal fishing fines, promoting a new seizure mentality to deter illegal fishers. The government has burned illegal fishing boats to send the message to other unlawful fishers that the cost of getting caught will be high, in part to make up for the low likelihood of getting caught. The burnings even led to a high-profile piece in the *New York Times* highlighting the problem of illegal fishing in Palau and efforts to address it (Urbina 2016). The sanctuary does not, of course, solve Palau's illegal fishing problem, but it does aid in the effort.

Revitalizing the Economy

The PNMS was the first clear instance of a state pursuing an MPA of its own volition, absent an advocacy campaign to persuade it. It showed the growth of the large MPA norm globally from requiring norm entrepreneurs to advance it to having a life of its own. Remengesau so readily accepted the idea of a large MPA in 2013 in part because large MPAs were becoming increasingly common in global conservation. The growth of the large MPA norm, Palauan conservation culture, and Remengesau's leadership were all important to the government's designation of the sanctuary, but, as this chapter has argued, the economic rationale for the reserve provides a more powerful explanation of what drove it. This was not just a conservation initiative, but a plan to revitalize the national economy.

The arguments to support the reserve were many, but central to them was its potential to facilitate a national economy that would better serve Palauans. In that sense, cooperation between the Palauan government and the ecotourism industry led to a different kind of large MPA politics. By 2015, most large MPAs came about as a result of ENGO-driven advocacy campaigns to convince a target government of the merits of large-scale conservation. Advocates needed to argue that a reserve would not unduly undermine economic interests. In Palau, the rationale for the reserve was different. The argument was instead that one of its core benefits was to bolster the economy. Because advocates were able to convincingly position the reserve as, on aggregate, good for business in Palau, it was much easier to build a broad coalition in favor of it that included the government, tourism industry, local fishers, and general public alike.

The diffusion of the large MPA norm in Palau was relatively smooth because of this coalition, but this type of norm diffusion is unlikely to be common for a few reasons. First, Palau exhibits a unique combination of traits that, in tandem, greatly increased the potential for a robust large MPA; namely, it is a small country with a large EEZ, it is uniquely dependent on ecotourism, and its pelagic fisheries are not all that productive. Alone, each of these factors would not be enough, but in combination they amount to an ideal political economy for the designation of a robust large MPA. Second, and related to that, tourism contributes an exceptionally large portion of Palau's GDP, both in absolute terms and relative to the commercial fishing sector. The ratio between the two is nearly a staggering 25:1. This kind of disparity is unusual, so such clear-cut ecotourism-driven large MPAs are likely to be rare.

The diffusion of the large MPA norm in Palau still falls within a neoliberal paradigm of environmentalism. The reserve is an important and ambitious achievement for Palau as the country looks to honor its conservation heritage while simultaneously building a Palauan economy that better benefits Palau. To acknowledge the economic drivers of the reserve is in no way intended to diminish the hard work of those devoted to seeing it through. But Palau was, in a sense, the perfect storm for a large MPA that so seamlessly looked to merge conservation with economic development.

7

Conclusion

A Solution to Ocean Decline?

For better or worse, large MPAs are now pervasive in global marine conservation. On the one hand, they allow governments to protect marine biodiversity at an entirely unprecedented rate, closing off millions of square kilometers of ocean space to commercial activity since 2006. But on the other, they are still often remote from commercial activity, potentially directing attention away from the immediate sources of ocean decline. The final question that this book will address is whether these large MPAs are a desirable solution to ongoing ocean decline. The answer to this question is not a simple "yes" or "no." Large MPAs undoubtedly lead to healthier ecosystems and abundant biomass when they are well managed. The question of whether MPAs are desirable is not, however, strictly scientific, but deeply political. It matters why governments make certain conservation policy choices: not just for an assessment of any given MPA but also for whether or not this paradigm shift in marine conservation has the power and potential to significantly alter the fate of the oceans.

The PRIMNM, Coral Sea Marine Park, and PNMS reveal three different types of large MPA policymaking, but they nonetheless all represent states embracing the large MPA norm. In each case, the idea of large, contiguous, pelagic, and no-take MPAs permeated advocacy efforts and government processes for marine conservation. The uptake of this large MPA norm is dramatically changing what state decision makers see as a feasible scale for ocean protection. The political economy of a targeted marine area is nonetheless a vital predictor of the robustness of its eventual protections. Governments are highly responsive to industry, even in instances where industry seems to have a minor stake in a region. But industry influence can be a boon for conservation, and government responsiveness does have its limits. A stakeholder-based global environmental norm diffusion framework deconstructs industry interests to provide insight into when and under what conditions industry gets its way, and when it does not.

Conserving the Oceans. Justin Alger, Oxford University Press (2021). © Oxford University Press.
DOI: 10.1093/oso/9780197540534.003.0007

So, do the politics of large MPAs suggest that they are a desirable solution to ocean decline? I make two seemingly at odds arguments in this chapter. The first is that the move toward large-scale protections in the mid-2000s is an important paradigm shift in marine conservation. It is a manifestation of the growing awareness that we have woefully underestimated our impact on the oceans for too long. That awareness is not limited to environmental advocates but has transformed what states see as being within the realm of possibility for ocean protection. It is no coincidence that the emergence of large MPAs in the mid-2000s was shortly thereafter followed by negotiations for the first ever multilateral environmental agreement to allow states to establish MPAs on the high seas (more on this later).

The second argument is less generous. The case studies in this book suggest that, while notions of scale may have changed, states are still in the old habit of designing conservation policy around business interests and not the other way around. The fate of an MPA depends on the political economy of a given space. Some states will establish robust, no-take MPAs that allow ecosystems to thrive while others will establish paper parks. But all countries will be making those decisions based on whether or not the price is right. This means that, at the global level, the world's large MPAs so far only put a minor dent in combatting over-extraction, to say nothing of the threat posed by climate change. The rise of large MPAs is, in its current form, still inherently consistent with a neoliberal environmental project grounded in incrementalism that has proven to be woefully inadequate at combating the most pressing environmental issues. This is not to deny the important ecological contribution of any given MPA but to recognize that if our goal is nothing short of stopping and preventing global ocean decline, we need more, with MPAs only one component.

The rest of this chapter is devoted to exploring these two arguments in depth. To begin, it is worth revisiting the four theoretical expectations introduced in chapter 3 for a comparative analysis of how well they explained the politics of my three large MPA case studies.

The Politics of Large MPAs

The theoretical expectations that I introduced in chapter 3 explain a great deal about MPA political processes: how the state aligns and forms its interests for a given MPA; how influential industry actors are likely to be;

and how likely we are to see an ambitious, well designed MPA versus a paper park. Those expectations were:

Expectation 1   The state is more likely to form an informal coalition with an industry partner if that industry can demonstrate salient interests in a prospective large MPA site.

Expectation 2   Holding interest salience equal, governments are more likely to privilege extractive industry interests over non-extractive industry interests.

Expectation 3   Political and legal institutions that allow a government to circumvent veto points make it more likely a coalition will achieve its policy goals.

Expectation 4   a) An extractive industry coalition is more likely to yield weak or ineffective environmental policies.

b) A non-extractive industry, environmental group, or local community coalition is more likely to yield more robust environmental policies.

A comparative analysis of these expectations across large MPA cases in Australia, Palau, and the US reveals much about what is driving the large MPA norm, but also what is holding it back from making a bigger contribution to better protecting the oceans.

The three case studies selected for this research each represent a different coalition type. President Obama's expansion of PRIMNM from 225,000 km^2 to 1,270,000 km^2 demonstrated limited industry influence and close collaboration with environmental groups (an environmental group coalition). In contrast, the 990,000 km^2 Coral Sea Marine Park was a veritable battleground for over 10 years between fishers and environmental groups, with the government ultimately aligning its interests with the former (an extractive industry coalition). Finally, Palau's critical dependence on its ecotourism industry and President Remengesau Jr.'s commitment to a 500,238 km^2 marine reserve facilitated close collaboration between the ecotourism industry and the state (a non-extractive coalition). These three coalition types each demonstrate a distinct brand of conservation politics. This section will tease out some of the key insights of these cases.

Expectation 1: Industry Influence

Being able to demonstrate that an area is commercially important is the key to industry's ability to influence government conservation policy. In Australia, Palau, and the US, industry groups worked tirelessly to influence already announced MPAs. In each case, a period of consultations followed the initial announcement of the new MPA, providing industry and other stakeholders the opportunity to influence boundaries, zoning, access restrictions, and other regulations.

The efforts of the US Western Pacific fleet to retain access to fishing grounds in the Pacific Remote Islands is a cautionary tale for industry looking to influence policy without a strong resource claim. The fleet was besieged by a number of exogenous stressors including losing its fishing licenses around Kiribati, a federal minimum wage hike, and volatile tuna prices, among others, but industry influence was fairly minimal. Because the area targeted for protections accounted for such a small portion of fishing revenue—only 0.09% of the national total (Sala et al. 2014)—the industry lacked leverage. The 37-boat Western Pacific fleet simply was not overly dependent on the proposed area (which provided less than 5% of its annual catch). Industry was nonetheless adamant, organizing local town halls, aggressively lobbying politicians, and submitting a report to the White House making the case for continued fishing access. Those efforts fell short, with the Obama administration unconvinced. The expansion of the marine monument went ahead in 2014.

Despite a vocal and at times vehement opposition, the commercial fishing industry was unable to demonstrate significant adverse effect on its operations. Government decision makers were unresponsive to the industry's concern that it could be more reliant on specific zones as species migrated, either as a part of their natural migration patterns or in response to warmer oceans. Wespac tried to make this argument about the Pacific Remote Islands, providing historical catch data to suggest higher take in the region in individual years. The Obama administration was unpersuaded. The concession that the Obama administration did make—to not expand the monument in two of the five zones—was in part because their surrounding seamounts had higher catch rates. That is, the administration showed a willingness to respond to immediate extractive industry interests but was less responsive to attempts to hedge against uncertain migratory patterns years and even decades into the future.

Industry opposition to no-take zoning on principle also fell flat in both Australia and the US. Many industry stakeholders—and a few experts—argue that a strict no-take plan is counterproductive to working toward sustainable fisheries. Governments were unresponsive to this as well. The Australian recreational fishing lobby had no real stake anywhere in the Coral Sea, instead using it as a high-profile case for voicing their opposition to no-take zones on principle. Government decision makers routinely met with recreational fishing lobbyists, but there is little evidence to suggest that these lobbyists influenced the zoning of the MPA. The reduction in no-take zoning that came out of the review of the management plan was explicitly intended to keep commercial fishers in business. Similarly, neither the Bush nor Obama administrations took Wespac's principled opposition to no-take zoning as unscientific seriously.

But when industry can demonstrate salient interests, the narrative shifts to one of the highly influential industries that significantly shape conservation policy. In Australia, the commercial fishing industry—bolstered by support from the recreational fishing lobby—did successfully undermine the Coral Sea conservation initiative. After years of consultations and rezoning, the Coral Sea Marine Park does virtually nothing to alter business-as-usual operations on the water. Like the Pacific Remote Islands, fishers account for a relatively small regional and national portion of the fishing revenue. But unlike the US case, they are critically dependent on fishing areas within the Coral Sea to remain in operation. Many of their operations—especially of Cairns owned and operated Great Barrier Reef Tuna and Cairns Marine, an aquarium fish supplier—are vertically integrated into the local economy in Cairns. Relocation is not an option. By demonstrating high factor and asset specificity, commercial fishers put the federal government in the position of catering to their interests or risking considerable political backlash. Subsequent federal governments wavered between buying them out and zoning that would allow continued operations, with the latter winning out in the end.

Palau is an unambiguous case of a government doing its part to protect an essential industry. Palau's massive reliance on its ecotourism industry was the driving force behind the reserve, with arguments in favor often suggesting the reserve's potential to bolster this critical sector of the economy. The 2010 study that estimated the value of a reef shark in Palau to ecotourism as $1.9 million, compared to the roughly $100 value of a harvested shark, was often cited by reserve advocates. Figures such as this were instrumental as President Remengesau Jr., environmental groups, and local community stakeholders worked to build a coalition to support the reserve. The eco-tourism industry was critical to the Palauan economy and, as is typical of ecotourism operations, relied on non-transferable factors of production (i.e., coral reefs) and assets (i.e., short-range dive boats).

The common theme across all three case studies was that a vocal industry lobby was not enough to sway policymakers. Industry fortunes were tied di-rectly to its ability to demonstrate that it was dependent on an area in a con-crete way. Once businesses in a sector invest in a geographic region, sunk costs begin to accumulate, which tend to make businesses more rigid in their decision-making and reduce their resource mobility (Barham and Coomes 2005). Arguments about migratory species or future fishing potential were, on their own, unconvincing. To convince, industry needed to demonstrate some combination of high-intensity activity, high-factor specificity, and high-asset specificity. One of the central conclusions of this book is that if we want to better understand the limits of industry power and influence, we need to pay more attention to these variables.

Expectation 2: Extractive Privilege

Not all industries are equal in their capacity for influence. Extractive indus-tries have an outsized effect on government conservation policy, even when non-extractive industries are similarly reliant on an area. Put simply, they tend to receive preferential treatment.

The power and influence of extractive industries in developed and de-veloping countries alike are well documented (Salant 1976; Vernon 1980; Freudenburg 1992; Ferguson 2005; Bebbington et al. 2008; Haufler 2010; Gamu, Le Billon, and Spiegel 2015). These industries can generate large profits over short periods of time, often contributing substantial revenue to government coffers through tax revenue and licensing. Governments are reluctant to impose limitations on industries that provide income, em-ployment, and usually have powerful lobby groups. The continued over-capitalization and subsidization of the commercial fishing industry despite widespread overfishing is indicative of this trend (DeSombre and Barkin 2011; Barkin and DeSombre 2013). Governments do not just restrain them-selves from regulating extractive industry, they pay to keep it in business (oil subsidies are a common example). Overwhelming evidence of the environ-mental consequences of over-extraction tends to fall on deaf ears.

Protected area regulations also tend to target extractive activities rather than non-extractive. Prohibiting or limiting extraction is often incompatible with economic priorities, so governments tend to seek compromise. States can more easily design a large MPA that allows for ecotourism activity than one that reconciles commercial fishing with conservation goals. Protected areas by definition limit or prohibit commercial activity, and extractive activity has a much higher environmental impact than non-extractive activity. Most large MPAs in fact specifically target commercial fishing (and oil and gas development), and advocacy campaigns rally support by evoking images of pristine, no-take marine ecosystems. But governments are still responsive to even minor extractive interests. For example, it was not clear that the US Western Pacific fleet would lose a single dollar in revenue because of the Pacific Remote Islands monument, but President Obama partially conceded to extractive industry demands and scaled back the expansion anyway.

The politics of protecting the Australian Coral Sea demonstrates this extractive privilege especially well. Dive tourism outfits were as critically dependent on the Coral Sea as their commercial fishing counterparts, yet the final management plan was a clear win for commercial fishers. It is no secret that the Great Barrier Reef is in decline, including reefs located in the Coral Sea Marine Park. Though the most severe threats to the Great Barrier Reef are climate change and terrestrial run-off, not commercial fishing, large no-take areas are one way to build ecosystem resilience. Rather than taking a precautionary approach, the Australian government decided it could have it all and facilitated the continued operations of extractive and non-extractive commercial activity alike in its design of the Coral Sea management plan. The government's zoning became so convoluted that aquarium fish collectors and divers were in some cases granted access to different parts of the same reefs.

The Coral Sea illustrates extractive privilege in two ways. First, the commercial fishing and ecotourism sectors had similar reliance on the Coral Sea. Neither commercial fishers nor dive operators had the option of relocating their operations or assets. In these scenarios, governments tend to cater to extractive industries to maximize economic activity, tax revenue, and political support. Second, three subsequent prime ministers were committed to a business-as-usual approach to conservation in the Coral Sea. Although the Julia Gillard Labor government (2010–2013) proposed buying out commercial fishers, this option was only on the table as a part of a meticulously zoned Coral Sea that would minimize the commercial impact of conservation. The Coral Sea becoming a paper park was not simply the result of the anti-environment Tony Abbott (2013–2015) or Malcolm Turnbull (2015–2018) governments watering down legislation. They certainly watered it down, but from the beginning the Coral Sea consultations were about creating an MPA that would minimize commercial impact, however modest that impact would be (albeit not so modest to the businesses affected).

Even Palau was not entirely immune to extractive privilege. A few political elites in the country had ties to the Japanese and Taiwanese fleets that did most of the commercial fishing in Palau. Though commercial fishing licenses lined a few pockets in Palau, the industry's contribution to Palau's economy was small, at no more than 2.6% of GDP or 1.3% of employment (PITI-VITI 2020). The profits and jobs were mainly out of country. In addition, Japanese and Taiwanese fleets further hamstrung their political influence with their own underhanded business practices. For years, they had massively underreported their catch to the Palauan government, so when the time came for them to make the economic case for their continued access to Palauan waters, they could not demonstrate their dependence without revealing their misreporting. But despite minimal benefits to the Palauan economy and this misreporting, the Palauan government eventually amended its legislation to allow Okinawa-based boats to fish in Palau's (formerly) domestic fishing zone.

Holding all else equal, extractive industries tend to be more influential than their non-extractive counterparts. In all three case studies, we can see extractive industries winning concessions from policymakers beyond what we might expect by looking solely at their interest salience relative to their non-extractive counterparts. Conservation outcomes are not only a function of demonstrable industry interests, but also of a neoliberal global economic system that prioritizes resource extraction in the name of profit maximization (Princen 1997; Jacques and Lobo 2018).

Expectation 3: Veto Points

Whether a state aligns its interests with environmental groups, industry, or local communities, the next concern is whether it will be able to pursue those interests effectively. Most governments face checks and balances. The ability of an informal coalition to push through its desired policy outcome therefore depends on its legislative authority—the number of possible veto points in its way and its ability to circumvent them. Institutions are not as powerful an explanatory variable of conservation outcomes as the composition of industry interests, but they are an important intervening variable. Without the Antiquities Act, for example, the US large MPAs almost certainly would not exist, because of congressional opposition. This institution—a relic from 1906—was essential not just to US large MPAs but to the emergence of the large MPA norm, given the US role as an influential early promoter of the norm. The composition of industry interests does most of the explanatory work in the framework presented in this book, but institutions do matter.

These cases are all positive case studies, so they do not reveal much about legislative failures. They nonetheless reveal distinct forms of legislative authority. As noted earlier, President Obama expanded the Pacific Remote Islands monument under the auspices of the Antiquities Act. The act has only recently come under fire from Republicans, but historically both Democrat and Republican presidents have used it extensively, with its first use under Republican President Teddy Roosevelt. Although Palau's political institutions are modeled after the US, it lacks similar legislation. President Remengesau Jr. needed approval from Palau's 13-person senate, where several senators who benefited financially from foreign-based commercial fishing created an initial deadlock. But Palau's consensus-based political culture meant that when local fishers publicly shamed senators opposed to the reserve (at a funeral, no less), the hold-outs in the senate were compelled to fall in line. In Australia, the Coral Sea designation in 2012 came as part of a broader national initiative that, historically, had bipartisan support. The political battle over the reserve revolved around its management plan rather than its initial designation. That battle has been compounded by a series of minority and coalition governments dating back to 2010. In each case, conservation legislation shaped what was possible for governments. In Palau and the US, it enabled robust conservation measures despite varying levels of congressional opposition. In Australia, it did the opposite, allowing subsequent governments the flexibility to continually undermine previous efforts.

After the preferred legislation has been successfully passed by a coalition, the next concern becomes its permanence. The Trump administration took the unprecedented step of issuing an executive order in April 2017 to review the 27 uses of the Antiquities Act since 1996, with the Pacific Remote Islands among them. As of this writing, the administration has not taken steps to reduce protections in the Pacific, though they are certainly at risk despite an ongoing challenge to the legality of the executive order. In both Australia and Palau, overturning the MPAs would be politically unpopular, so the more likely path to altering them would be to adjust their management plans. In Australia, management plans are typically for a finite 10-year span, so they tend to have a high degree of malleability, for better or worse. Because of Palau's capacity challenges, implementation and enforcement is likely to be an ongoing process. The reserve's management plan is likely to be more dynamic, evolving over time in response to non-compliance as well as varying levels of external financial and technical support from other states or environmental groups. Adaptive management is important so conservation policy can be responsive to environmental change, though overly flexible management plans risk permitting subsequent governments to water them down as well (Webster 2009).

Expectation 4: Robust Protections versus Paper Parks

In chapter 3, I noted that there is no one-size-fits-all approach to what counts as effective conservation of marine ecosystems (Claudet 2011). But identifying clearly ineffective conservation can be easier. It is clear that the Coral Sea adds little to protecting ecosystems and species in the region, whereas protections in the Pacific Remote Islands and Palau are more robust with their large, no-take (or virtually no-take) zones. Government coalitions with environmental groups and with the ecotourism industry shaped large MPA political processes in the US and Palau, respectively. Environmental groups evoked imagery of a pristine marine haven in the relatively commercially inactive Pacific Remote Islands, spurring action. In Palau, the ecotourism industry and the Palauan government cited the many economic (and ecological) benefits of a reserve, having little trouble convincing the broader public of its value. Whether a government forms a coalition with environmental groups, non-extractive industry, or local communities (this last not explored in depth in this book) shapes the content and political dynamics of a conservation campaign, but they all tend to produce more robust MPAs. When a government forms a coalition with extractive industry, on the other hand, it is a powerful predictor of a weak or ineffective MPA. If the political economy of an area favors close government–extractive industry cooperation, a paper park is the most likely outcome.

In assessing MPA effectiveness, capacity is also a factor. The US has the resources and legal institutions to credibly enforce regulations, even in such a remote space, but Palau faces a considerable challenge. Its enforcement plan is ambitious, but as of this writing lacked detailed cost information and was largely aspirational (Terrill et al. 2015). Capacity challenges are a reality for smaller or underdeveloped countries, but they are not the whole story. Whether or not Palau is able to put an end to illegal fishing in its EEZ is not a reasonable benchmark for success. Motivation and level of ambition matter. As noted in chapter 3, the comprehensiveness of a large MPA management plan and the steps a state takes to implement it can reveal much about its commitment to stronger ocean protections. Palau's ability to police its EEZ is understandably limited with just two active patrol boats. But Palau is partnering with other states and foundations to enhance its capacity, and the marine sanctuary will help to attract those very partners. Palau's large MPA will not end illegal fishing in Palau (and no one claims it will), but it will help to make meaningful progress toward that goal.

A Paradigm Shift in Marine Conservation

The norm of large MPAs is a significant step forward in marine conservation. It has only been strengthening since its emergence in the mid-2000s, and it has changed the scale of what states see as possible for marine protection. The paradigm shift in marine conservation that I refer to here is that shift of scale. Whereas smaller, sometimes networked, MPAs have long been standard practice (and they still are), states now have a new tool in their policy toolkit for protecting marine ecosystems. The dedicated advocacy efforts of environmental groups have been central in putting large MPAs on states' agendas and there is growing evidence that states have embraced them as well.

Thinking Big: The Role of Environmental Advocacy

The push for large MPAs is driven by a desire to scale up ocean protections, with ENGOs acting as norm entrepreneurs. Though how the large MPA norm diffused was rooted in domestic political economies, with mixed results, the initial emergence of the norm was undoubtedly driven by conservation goals. The norm's emergence and spread were broadly consistent with the predominant pattern of international norm diffusion: with norm entrepreneurs advocating for a new standard of behavior, building support gradually over time until a critical mass of states buy in to the new norm (Meyer 1979; Finnemore 1993; Finnemore and Sikkink 1998; Price 1998; Sunstein 1999; Kelley 2008). Environmental groups—most notably Pew, National Geographic, and Conservation International—conceived the idea of large MPAs then worked tirelessly to persuade states of its value (Finnemore and Sikkink 1998). This is not to detract from the important contributions of the politicians, civil servants, local environmental groups, local communities, or indigenous groups that played a role in any given large MPA case. In many, they were essential. But as a global norm, as an idea that has gone on to reshape global marine conservation, it primarily owes its spread to the determined efforts of a select few groups.

The politics of the Coral Sea and Pacific Remote Islands MPAs reveal the importance of these transnational environmental groups well. The same is true of Papahānaumokuākea and PIPA, both of which I briefly explored in chapter 2. In all four of these large MPA campaigns, environmental groups conceived of the idea of a large MPA, presented it to high-level officials, and actively campaigned for its establishment through lobbying, public outreach, and research. In both the Pacific Remote Islands and Coral Sea, stakeholders from government, industry, and civil society itself saw environmental groups as the primary drivers of large MPA advocacy efforts.

Environmental groups successfully framed the large MPA norm to appeal to state leaders, positioning large MPAs as an appropriate response to ocean decline, but also one that was politically expedient (Snow et al. 1986; Finnemore and Sikkink 1998; Payne 2001). Throughout the Papahānaumokuākea campaign, environmental groups documented and presented the richness of biodiversity located in the region, but also conducted a thorough economic analysis of the likely impact on US commercial fisheries. The biodiversity report and documentary *Voyage to Kure* appealed to decision makers on an emotional level, instilling a sense of stewardship over these waters. On the other hand, the economic analysis was intended to reassure the administration that this would not be a costly decision and that the political benefits of such a significant conservation announcement far outweighed the minimal impact it would have on the commercial fishing industry. A similar pattern emerged in both the Coral Sea and Pacific Remote Islands, with environmental groups adhering to a consistent playbook for large MPA advocacy. Though it did not always work as planned—the Coral Sea is an apt cautionary tale—the overall success of these campaigns seemed to justify this consistent approach.

That just a select few transnational environmental groups undertook the brunt of the advocacy work for large MPAs is, however, somewhat unusual. Most environmental norms emerge through the efforts of a fairly large, cohesive international coalition of environmental groups working through multilateral venues, such as conferences of states parties to the CBD or the UN Framework Convention on Climate Change (UNFCCC) (Gulbrandsen and Andresen 2004; Allan and Hadden 2017). The norm diffusion literature in international relations emphasizes the influence that large coalitions of NGOs can have on international negotiations, usually through multilateral venues such as treaty negotiations or international conferences (Betsill and Corell 2001; Gulbrandsen and Andresen 2004; Humphreys 2004; Betsill and Corell 2008). Typically, the better access that NGOs have to multilateral negotiations, the more influence they can have on outcomes (Böhmelt and Betzold 2013; Tallberg et al. 2015). The evolution of the large MPA norm does not, however, fit the mold of advocacy through multilateral venues.

One of the more important reasons that large MPA advocacy efforts have not focused on multilateral venues is the lack of a cohesive multilateral coalition of environmental groups. Transnational environmental groups frequently have competing visions for marine conservation that do not align with Pew and National Geographic's preference for large, contiguous, no-take marine reserves. In Australia, WWF opposed Pew's proposal for a no-take Coral Sea, instead preferring mixed-use zoning more in line with that of the GBRMP. TNC initially opposed the Palau sanctuary, instead preferring to focus on improving fisheries management.[1] Even Pew and National Geographic disagreed about whether to include state waters in the PNMS (where the majority of Palau's rich biodiversity is), with Pew opposed because of the political difficulty of doing so.[2] Greenpeace, for its part, prefers to focus on less remote marine areas where commercial activity is prevalent, as well as the high seas, though it does maintain an ambitious 30% global marine area protected goal.[3] Although Greenpeace, TNC, WWF, and others tend to endorse large MPA campaigns eventually, their role is minimal, often limited to contributing their extensive networks for campaign outreach. Despite their eventual support, these influential transnational environmental groups often have competing visions for what the best way to combat ocean decline is.

A second reason that Pew and National Geographic have not focused their efforts in multilateral venues is that there is no need for a new legislative or institutional framework to support large MPAs. As discussed in chapter 2, this framework already exists through the CBD, most notably through the

Aichi target of 10% marine area protected. The institutionalization of a new norm is usually necessary to increase its uptake beyond early adopters, but existing CBD commitments already provide the institutional basis for large MPAs. Large MPAs were simply a new way of meeting existing legal obligations, allowing environmental groups to direct their efforts toward domestic uptake of the norm instead.

Pew and National Geographic did precisely that. They adopted a bottom-up approach to expanding the large MPA norm, building support for the norm through targeted campaigns, one domestic jurisdiction at a time (Alger and Dauvergne 2017b). These campaigns were not an effort to convince individual states to agree to large MPAs in abstract terms, but rather for the creation of specific large MPAs. Environmental groups worked hard to identify politically feasible large MPA sites, recognizing that these sites would set an important precedent for large-scale marine conservation. These sites are politically viable in part because they are relatively remote from commercial activity (but not wholly remote, as the Australia and Palau cases demonstrate). Pew and National Geographic instead worked to form ad hoc national coalitions for individual large MPA campaigns, relying on local knowledge and expertise to bolster their knowledge base and political resources. Both the Pacific Remote Islands and Coral Sea campaigns adopted this approach, with Pew in both cases identifying each area as a prospective large MPA site and overseeing a domestic campaign with the support of local environmental groups.

This bottom-up strategy also explains another curious feature of the spread of the large MPA norm: it spread concurrently in the global North and South. Most environmental norms begin in the global North and eventually spread to the South. In some cases the reverse is true (Clapp and Swanston 2009; Stalley 2018), but rarely have we seen the simultaneous emergence of a new norm in both. The Kiribati and US governments announced PIPA and Papahānaumokuākea nearly simultaneously. Since then, states in both the North and South have followed suit. Chile, Kiribati, and Palau have been just as enthusiastic about large MPAs as Australia, the UK, and the US. The concurrent North and South adoption is in part due to geography, with many countries in the global South (especially Pacific island nations) boasting large EEZs. Conservation International and Oceana, among others, have focused their efforts on the global South, helping to facilitate the spread of the large MPA norm there.

By targeting specific large MPA sites, environmental groups have been able to use their limited resources efficiently. Targeted campaigns allow them to devote those resources to where they can make an immediate short-term impact. The announcements of Papahānaumokuākea and PIPA in 2006 nonetheless did not preordain a global uptake of large MPAs. By targeting politically feasible sites, environmental groups have gradually built momentum toward a global norm that inspires the protection of large swaths of previously unprotected ocean. These high-profile initiatives raise the profile of marine conservation generally, and they send the signal that more ambitious solutions to ocean decline are not only needed but are achievable now.

Taking the Lead: State Efforts

As of 2020, ENGO-led environmental advocacy campaigns still characterize many large MPA efforts, but increasingly less so as states take on a more prominent role. By the mid-2010s, states were advancing the large MPA norm in a number of ways, including through state-driven MPA initiatives, organizing multilateral conferences, and beginning to pursue multilateral protections on the high seas. These developments, I argue, emerged because of the success of the large MPA norm in radically altering the scale of marine conservation initiatives. The power of a norm is not limited to just discrete instances of its adoption—to the ecological benefits of specific large MPAs—but extends to how it reshapes standards of behavior in a given issue area writ large. This reshaping began at the national level, with several governments taking it upon themselves to expand ocean protections in the absence of pressure from environmental groups.

The 2015 PNMS provides a clear and early indication of this shift. The executive branch of the Palauan government was the primary driver of the sanctuary. Environmental groups played a pivotal role in helping to initiate and run a campaign in support of the sanctuary, but only once the Palauan government actively sought their assistance, having already committed to the idea of a large MPA. Although Palauan officials viewed the sanctuary as the right thing to do for the environment, there was also a pervading sense of what it would mean for Palau's standing as a global leader in marine conservation. Palauan President Tommy Remengesau Jr. has been invited to speak at countless international conferences and has been the recipient of several environmental awards, including the UN Environment Programme's Champion of the Earth award. As the president's political opponents will tell you, reputation and esteem for both Remengesau and Palau motivated the decision to pursue the sanctuary. The primary norm entrepreneur in Palau was not an environmental group, but the government itself.

Every new large MPA that a state establishes builds momentum toward embedding the large MPA norm in global marine conservation practice. As this norm strengthens, countries will take a more active role in furthering it. The UK announced the Ascension Island Marine Reserve (445,000 km^2), the St. Helena Marine Reserve (445,000 km^2), and the Tristan da Cunha Reserve (750,000 km^2) in 2016. Although domestic advocacy groups were prominent supporters of these reserves, the advocacy campaigns for them were not nearly as involved as the eight-year campaign for the UK's Pitcairn Islands Marine Reserve (Alger and Dauvergne 2017a). This heightened state role manifested through a growing sense of competition between the UK and the US to demonstrate global leadership in marine conservation in the final years of the Obama presidency. At the 2016 *Our Ocean* conference in Washington, UK Foreign Office Minister Alan Duncan playfully quipped:

> Well this was going to have been my big moment, because until last week the Pitcairn MPA would have been the largest in the world. But President Obama sort of rather blew that out of the water by announcing an even bigger MPA in Hawaii—trust the Yanks to indulge in a bit of one-upmanship over us poor Brits. (Duncan 2016)

This amusing quip was telling of a major shift in how states thought about marine conservation. It was no longer just the realm of technical experts or policy wonks, but the realm of political leaders and a source of friendly competition between states.

The *Our Ocean* conferences became the main multilateral venue for this friendly competition. The first conference was held in 2014, hosted by then US Secretary of State John Kerry, who had taken a particular interest in ocean protection. The conference emerged as a way for states to coordinate their large-scale conservation efforts. It is no coincidence that *Our Ocean* was initially led by the US, where the large MPA norm had its early roots and was internalized through three large MPA designations and two expansions in less than a decade. US leadership turned to unscientific anti-environment crusading during the Trump presidency, but other countries remain to assume the mantle, with conferences hosted in the EU in 2017, Indonesia in 2018, and Norway in 2019, with Palau hosting the next meeting in 2021. The *Our Ocean* conference is where states outline their marine conservation plans, with a slew of new commitments made each year.

Canada serves as a useful example of the power of the large MPA norm to shape state behavior. As recently as 2015, Canada had one of the world's worst marine conservation records with less than 1% of its waters protected. Under the Liberal government of Justin Trudeau, Canada made an ambitious push to meet the 10% Aichi target by 2020. In 2015, the government began aggressively designating protected areas throughout the country's vast ocean space. This included, in August 2019, the designation of the 320,000 km^2 Tuvaijuittuq MPA in the Canadian Arctic, which will ban all but a select few Inuit activities in the region for an initial five-year period. The name Tuvaijuittuq means "the place where ice never melts," and the area is expected to be the last in the world to retain sea ice year-round. Along with the announcement of Tuvaijuittuq came the declaration of another 107,000 km^2 area to be protected: the Tallurutiup Imanga National Marine Conservation Area. Together, these areas will push Canada's coverage up to 14%, surpassing the government's own target handily. There were no high-profile advocacy campaigns around Canada's ambitious push for protected areas. Canada does, however, have the world's seventh largest EEZ. By the time of Trudeau's election in 2015, Australia, France, the UK, and the US had already designated large MPAs of their own. Canada was the only western nation with a top-10 EEZ that did not have a large MPA. Most of Canada's MPAs are paper parks and the country has a long way to go to correct that, but this was a decisive shift in rhetoric and ambition for a country that had woefully neglected marine conservation throughout its history.

The large MPA norm has put marine conservation on the global agenda, and it is having a ripple effect. For example, it is already leading to an increase in what we can think of as medium-sized MPAs that do not cross the 200,000 km^2 threshold. In November 2017, Mexico announced the Revillagigedo National Park to protect what is colloquially known as the "Galapagos of North America." The 148,000 km^2 park was the largest MPA on the North American continental shelf at the time. It was announced as a fully no-take reserve, despite some prior commercial activity in the area and resistance from the fishing industry. In 2006, the Revillagigedo reserve would have been a ground-breaking conservation commitment. It would have been among the largest MPAs on the planet, but today there is a long list of MPAs that are larger, and in some cases orders of magnitude larger. It also would have demonstrated Mexico's global leadership in marine conservation. Now it signifies Mexico is conforming to what has become standard practice in global marine conservation. It does, however, represent an extension of that practice. The Revillagigedo reserve's location on the North American continental shelf shows how designating remote large MPAs can, over time, also make the protection of coastal ecosystems that are prone to more commercial activity more likely. The large MPA norm may have emerged through environmental groups and governments targeting remote, politically feasible areas, but as momentum builds these areas will get closer and closer to shore and the hubs of commercial activity. Revillagigedo is a momentous conservation achievement, but a feat made more likely by the emergence in the previous decade of the large MPA norm. The large MPA norm changed the baseline for what counts as ambitious in global marine conservation.

The ripple effects of the large MPA norm also extend to multilateral initiatives. In October 2016, the Commission on the Conservation of Antarctic Marine Living Resources (CCAMLR), after years of failed negotiations, established a 1.55 million km^2 MPA in Antarctica's Ross Sea, the world's first multilateral large MPA, and when announced, the largest MPA on the planet. The Ross Sea MPA is the culmination of years of protracted negotiations between countries with a stake in the area. China and Russia held out the longest, fearing that their geopolitical influence in the region would diminish if their commercial fishing fleets no longer had access to it. Proponents of the MPA worked to convince the Russian government in particular that monitoring and enforcement of activities and scientific research within this large MPA would ensure their continued presence. CCAMLR decisions are by consensus, so the creation of the Ross Sea large MPA is a significant multilateral accomplishment—one that paves the way for future multilateral collaboration on marine protection. The large MPA norm makes developments such as the Ross Sea MPA much more likely by legitimizing and giving prominence to large-scale marine conservation initiatives.

The United Nations also ramped up its efforts to establish measures for the protection of marine areas beyond national jurisdiction. Despite nine working group sessions between 2006 and 2015 that coincided with the emergence of large MPAs (Sumaila et al. 2007), it was not until December 2017, through resolution 72/249, that the UN General Assembly agreed to convene an intergovernmental conference to negotiate an instrument. Those negotiations are underway as of this writing, but have made considerable progress. The agreement will allow states to establish multilateral MPAs on the high seas, opening up an entirely new frontier for large MPAs. The details have yet to emerge, but it seems clear at this stage that the agreement will also facilitate sustainable use of marine resources and any new MPAs will be subject to fairly extensive stakeholder consultations (UNGA 2019). The June 2019 draft agreement includes a provision for states parties to make MPA decisions by consensus, which is a high threshold for protections (UNGA 2019: 18). The agreement will certainly allow states to move toward the 30% global ocean protected target that many environmental groups and scientists advocate, but curbing extractive activity does not seem to be on the table. Nonetheless, for the first time, the world is on the cusp of being able to protect areas on the high seas—the final frontier for conservation.

State-driven large MPAs, the *Our Ocean* conferences, the multilateral Ross Sea MPA, and invigorated UN efforts to protect the high seas have all benefited from the emergence and spread of the norm of large MPAs. The efforts that began in the mid-2000s to designate a select few sites as large MPAs spurred a paradigm shift in ocean conservation. That is no small victory, but it does not tell the full story.

The Unrelenting Neoliberalism of Environmentalism

It speaks volumes about the hegemonic power of neoliberalism as a model of environmentalism that even a norm about closing off millions of square kilometers of ocean can be consistent with it. On the surface, this should not be the case. The purpose of protected areas is, after all, to limit or prohibit commercial or other human uses of a given space. A paradigm shift in ocean conservation toward such large-scale protections should challenge the neoliberal model. Instead, states have so far masterfully merged the two.

Incrementalism

Despite the dramatic shift in scale of ocean conservation efforts since the mid-2000s, this progress is still in many ways incremental. Many large MPAs are residual, protecting areas that are too remote from commercial interests to directly target the main sources of ocean decline (Toonen et al. 2013). While the growth in MPA coverage is hardly incremental (it is, in fact, exponential), the reduction in commercial activity such areas have brought certainly is. Simply put, they are so far not reducing overall extractive activity and, in many cases, are hardly displacing it. This incremental approach allows governments and activists alike to celebrate progress, but it can breed a dangerous complicity (Allan 2019).

Incremental progress in many ways subverts environmentalism to the very neoliberal power structures that have fueled environmental decline (Cox 1983; van der Pijl 1989). When Pew launched its Global Ocean Legacy program, it decided early on to target politically feasible prospective large MPA sites.[4] That decision is completely understandable and, as a result of it, Pew was successful in its large MPA advocacy, playing a major role in shepherding a new environmental norm into global politics. Had Pew decided to target commercial hotspots instead, this would likely be a very different book. Pew, understanding the neoliberal paradigm of environmentalism that it was working within, made its choice about how to pursue large MPAs by accepting certain constraints rather than fighting against them. Those constraints are that economic growth and development are effectively off the table for environmentalism (Bernstein 2000, 2001, 2002). The hegemony of neoliberalism is not just that it privileges businesses, but that it provides environmentalists with a playbook for operating within it if they want to be successful. That playbook says that if environmentalists want to be taken seriously, they need to recognize certain limits.

The large MPA norm has, so far, conformed to neoliberal environmentalism. It makes an important contribution to ecological resilience and to raising the profile of ocean conservation, which I will return to later, but it has done so within limits. The politics of large MPA campaigns in Australia, Palau, and the US reveal those limits as being defined by domestic political economies. In all three cases, despite variance in conservation outcome, the political process of designating a large MPA was one grounded in economic cost-benefit analysis. Subsequent administrations in all three states repeatedly proved unwilling to make conservation decisions that would be overly costly to the private sector. While some minor costs were deemed acceptable, such as displacing some fishing effort, this approach to conservation is still one that fundamentally rejects the idea that reducing extractive commercial activity is necessary to prevent ecological decline and collapse.

On the one hand, the contribution of this book to international relations theory of norm diffusion is to reinforce that environmental norms are still very much constrained by neoliberalism, even a large MPA norm explicitly intended to limit or prevent extractive activity. On the other hand, it identifies some of the specific mechanisms through which businesses exert power and influence over environmental policy deliberations. That power and influence depends on intensity of activity, factor and asset specificity, and exogenous stressors. It also depends on the composition of interest salience between extractive and non-extractive industry. Recognizing these mechanisms as a source of industry leverage over governments creates new possibilities for environmental advocates (Levy and Newell 2005). It can perhaps even help environmentalists to develop strategies to better challenge industry.

Take the empirical claim that large MPAs are residual, for example. It is certainly accurate that large MPAs tend to be remote, but many nonetheless overlap with commercial activity, some much more so than others. Palau's marine sanctuary legislation is intended to facilitate certain types of commercial activity, both extractive and non-extractive. Palau's waters were also at risk of overfishing from foreign fleets and remain at risk of illegal, unreported, and unregulated fishing. In this case, the importance of ecotourism to the Palauan economy was one of the leading motivators for the MPA. Even if Palau's reliance on ecotourism makes it somewhat of an exception, this pattern is evident in other cases as well. The Coral Sea Marine Park encompasses the entirety of a small, but locally significant, fishery. It is also critically important to one commercial tuna business integrated into the local economy. Commercial fishing in the Pacific Remote Islands is more diffuse, and the US Western Pacific fleet is unlikely to be meaningfully impacted by closures there. Large MPAs are residual relative to areas of high (extractive) commercial activity, but the underlying political economy of large MPA sites varies, and that variance has significant implications for how governments make conservation policy decisions.

Residuality is not just a function of where a government sets an area's boundaries, but also its zoning. UK and US large MPAs are so far all located around their highly remote overseas territories rather than around their respective continental shelves. The Australian Coral Sea is of course much less distant by comparison. The zoning of the Coral Sea, however, reflects a similar tendency toward residuality. No-take zoning in the Coral Sea was reserved only for areas where there was virtually no extractive commercial activity. Both are manifestations of residuality. There are distinctions between these two types of residuality, but they have similar outcomes. Remotely located large MPAs are precautionary in that they can protect potential future commercial interests, but they do fail to mitigate the immediate sources of ocean decline. Large MPAs with residual zoning, on the other hand, directly address areas of more immediate concern, but run the risk of being paper parks that fail to protect species and ecosystems effectively. Some residually zoned MPAs, such as the Coral Sea Marine Park, do nonetheless safeguard against future extraction in their no-take zones (if we generously assume zoning continuity). Given their adjacency to commercial fishing zones, these residually zoned MPAs still have the potential to prevent future commercial activity, much in the way of their more remote counterparts.

On balance, these protections still matter. They do not tend to have an immediate impact on reducing the overall catch of various fishing industries, so far, although there may be some exceptions (e.g., Palau). They also do nothing to mitigate carbon emissions. But setting aside large, pristine marine areas protects against future commercial exploitation and builds ecosystem resilience to climate (and other) impacts. Large MPAs insulate us somewhat from the problem of shifting baselines (Pauly 1995). Shifting baselines refer to the tendency to evaluate fishery health based on continually eroding benchmarks for what counts as normal. Having these pristine areas not only protects the areas themselves, but serves as a reminder of what a pristine marine environment should look like. Sylvia Earle refers to these areas as "hope spots," and rightly so. Commercially exploited ocean space is the norm. These areas, despite their residuality, challenge that commercial exploitation is inevitable.

Equity

The large MPA norm has, on balance, fared better promoting equity within a neoliberal paradigm of environmentalism. By environmental equity, I am referring to the idea that disenfranchised or marginalized groups should not bear a disproportionate burden of harmful environmental effects or of solutions to them. In a large MPA context, this means that large MPAs should not adversely impact those with limited political or economic power and influence. The risk that they do so is potentially quite high. Large MPAs are centrally managed conservation measures dictating access rights across vast spaces. The potential for government abuse of conservation policy to achieve other political or social goals is ever present (Peluso 1993).

Other scholars of large MPAs have expressed exactly this concern, for good reason (Bennett, Govan, and Satterfield 2015; De Santo, Jones, and

Miller 2011). The large MPA norm got off to an especially rough start. I mentioned the Chagos MPA in chapter 3, but it warrants revisiting here. The UK designated the 640,000 km² Chagos MPA in 2011, making it among the first handful of large MPAs. It was also one of Pew's inaugural four Global Ocean Legacy projects. It was, in that sense, an early large MPA success and received considerable fanfare as the largest MPA in the world at the time. The problem with the Chagos reserve was that it also served the purpose of reinforcing the UK's claim to the Chagos Islands. The British government undemocratically detached the islands from Mauritius in 1965, then evicted about 1,500 islanders in 1971 when it leased the islands to the US for an air base (Bowcott 2019). In 2018, the UN General Assembly voted overwhelmingly to refer the case to the International Court of Justice (ICJ)—the UN's highest court. In 2019, the ICJ also ruled overwhelmingly in favor of Mauritius, condemning the UK's claim to sovereignty over the islands. For its part, the UK seems unmoved by the ruling as of this writing. Chagos is another example of the UK's waning global prestige in a post-Brexit world, but it also rang alarm bells for conservationists.

Chagos taught an important lesson to environmental groups about the importance of equity in their large MPA advocacy. They were blindsided by the political ramifications of the Chagos reserve. Moreover, they were disappointed that what was meant to be an ambitious conservation initiative had (rightfully) become a referendum on 21st century colonialism.[5] Neglecting local community groups in large MPA advocacy risks further marginalizing or disenfranchising them. After Chagos, transnational environmental groups changed their approach, though not solely on their own. The peoples, activists, scientists, and scholars that worked hard to enforce the imperative that large MPAs promote equity rather than undermine it deserve credit for this change.

A neoliberal environmental paradigm provides a framework for pursuing certain kinds of equity, specifically related to individual human rights and self-determination. The application of those ideals is often woeful, and environmental injustice is widespread in both the global North and South (e.g., Bullard 1990; Schlosberg 2007; Nixon 2011; Klinsky et al. 2017). Those ideals themselves can also be a source of injustice, notably in undermining indigenous forms of governance (Altamirano-Jiménez 2013). Neoliberalism provides a language and structure for pursuing certain kinds of injustice claims, as Chagossians did. Large MPAs are high-profile initiatives, so it is less likely that the injustices they perpetuate or create can be easily hidden.

Governments have had to be responsive to equity lest another celebration of ambitious conservation turn into a repudiation.

Two examples reveal this shift in how governments and environmental groups have integrated equity into large MPA initiatives. Chile's Easter Island Marine Park—discussed briefly in chapter 3—was initially a major concern because the Chilean government seemed poised to impose restrictions on the islanders without adequate consultation. Instead, the Chilean government conducted consultations, held a referendum on the island, and the islanders themselves voted in favor a large MPA. That large MPA does not reduce their access, it instead prohibits commercial fishing around the islands. In this case, a large MPA ultimately empowered an indigenous group to continue managing its land absent outside commercial pressures. The Trudeau government in Canada took a similar approach to the Tuvaijuittuq MPA. The August 2019 announcement of that MPA was in fact a joint announcement by the Canadian government and the Inuit, with some form of joint-governance likely as of this writing.

There are many other examples of large MPAs promoting equity. The government of Palau designed the PNMS legislation so as to find ways to ensure that Palauans were the main beneficiaries of its ecological resources. The UK—its nose bloodied from the Chagos experience—was more careful about involving Pitcairn islanders in its large MPA plans there. The islanders voted unanimously in favor of the reserve, which guarantees their continued access while denying commercial access (Alger and Dauvergne 2017a). There is variation in how well large MPA processes internalize equity issues, but the overall trend appears to be toward large MPAs as tools for empowering local communities and indigenous groups, at least for now. That trend will only continue if governments and environmental groups are held to account, but, so far, the evolution of the large MPA norm has been encouraging given its dubious start.

The large MPA norm is not, however, a so-called equity norm in that its main tenets do not revolve around correcting environmental injustice. Equity norms, such as the common heritage of mankind (CHM) and common but differentiated responsibility (CDR) principles, explicitly seek to address injustice, but even they have their limits (Okereke 2008). While states are generally willing to acknowledge the importance of equity in international agreements, the content and power of equity norms to alter state behavior is constrained by their fit with neoliberalism (Bernstein 2000; Okereke 2008). Put simply, even norms explicitly intended to correct environmental injustice can only do so in a way that does not undermine the main tenets of neoliberalism. So, caution is certainly warranted in labelling the large MPA norm as promising for environmental equity. Its environmental justice potential depends entirely on its application.

The large MPA norm may be able to promote certain types of equity around human rights and self-determination, but it cannot address structural and diffuse sources of injustice. Overfishing is perpetrated mainly by commercial operations originating in the global North, but the impacts of fisheries collapse and biomass drain will be felt most severely by people in the global South and future generations. The large MPA norm does not address overextraction, and the framework and case studies introduced in this book demonstrate the lengths to which governments will go to ensure that it does not. Displacing fishing effort so far seems to be the best a conservationist can hope for, but displacement does not address the core structural injustice of overextraction.

The moral content of certain ideas and norms still matters, however (Okereke 2008). The promise of the norm of large MPAs, I would argue, is that embedded within it is a clearer understanding of the impact of human activity on oceans that are no longer widely viewed as boundless. This understanding is important for efforts to subvert certain aspects of neoliberalism and the primacy it places on extractive economic activity. Business-driven norms—such as those for corporate social responsibility (CSR) or sustainability certifications—are quite clearly designed to validate and strengthen economic growth and market-based solutions to environmental problems (Dauvergne and Lister 2013). The large MPA norm, on the other hand, promotes prohibitions on extractive activity as appropriate (and necessary) to protect the oceans.

The problem lies in the "responsibility deficit" that characterizes global environmental governance (Okereke 2008). While states are willing to acknowledge the ecological and equity impacts of overextraction, efforts to address the problem domestically are quite thin on the ground. Rather than taking the costly steps needed to reduce extraction and the difficult steps needed to overcome an arduous global collective action problem, states are content to establish large MPAs that at best displace extractive activity rather than reduce it. Most environmental groups follow suit, content to pursue achievable gains with short-term payoffs rather than historically futile efforts to address the structural causes of ecological decline. The hegemonic power of neoliberalism is that even when states, environmentalists, and others recognize an environmental problem and are committed to solving it, they will inevitably pursue solutions that are compatible with it.

Conclusion: The Desirability of Large MPAs

I opened this chapter by stating that there is no simple "yes" or "no" answer to whether large MPAs are a good thing for global marine conservation. So far, I have made the "yes" case by showing how the large MPA norm spread to new countries, leading to millions of square kilometers of ocean protection. Scientific evidence suggests large, no-take areas build ecosystem resilience and lead to more abundant species biomass. The scientific consensus surrounding large-scale marine conservation will only grow in the coming years. The quantity of area protections and the conservation potential of large marine reserves are not, however, enough to make a convincing case in favor of large MPAs.

There are a number of criticisms and shortcomings of large MPAs that strengthen the "no" case. Issues such as residuality and business co-optation of large MPA processes undermine their value. The staunchest critics would go so far as to say that these residual or coopted large MPAs threaten global marine conservation. They create the illusion of progress, all the while marine resource extraction and greenhouse gases continue to devastate ocean ecosystems. Critics argued that the UK's large MPAs, for example, distracted from the poor state of protections on the UK continental shelf. The British government had committed to protecting these waters in a 2015 pledge, but progress was slow and it was overshadowing its reticence with high-profile large MPA announcements (Jones and De Santo 2016). President Obama proved willing to expand remote MPAs in the Pacific, but shied away from protection for Cashes Ledge in the Atlantic, closer to shore. Critics claim that these "easy wins" do not reflect a meaningful commitment to reducing strain on the world's oceans and instead allow leaders to paint themselves as conservation heroes undeservedly.

Detractors overstate some of these claims. Large MPAs are by no means a panacea for marine conservation, as both these critics and this book can confirm. But expecting them to be would be too high a benchmark. Marine conservation is not a zero-sum game. In fact, it cannot be a zero-sum game if the world is ever to make meaningful progress on ocean protection. As marine issues gain traction, environmental groups, governments, and the public will devote more time and money to them. Campaigns for remote, large MPAs do not make coastal or commercial hubs less likely for marine protections, but more. In May 2019, the British government expanded the "blue belt" of MPAs on its continental shelf, now covering an area twice the size of England (Barkham 2019). The government's designation of multiple large MPAs did not allow it to neglect conservation at home. Instead, it drew attention to it. This new norm changes ideas about what is achievable in marine conservation. Environmental groups' targeting of remote, pristine marine environments is only a first step. These areas may be politically expedient, but they also invest governments and publics in marine conservation. They contribute to a normative shift toward the idea that we should do more to protect ocean ecosystems. That normative shift matters.

Of course, ambitious protections only matter if they make a difference on the water. They need to change practices that degrade ecosystems in some way. Another common criticism of large MPAs is that they are unenforceable and therefore an inefficient way to improve biodiversity protection. Technological advancements have helped to mitigate this problem, allowing for remote monitoring of vast ocean spaces. Monitoring is only one part of the equation. Governments also need to commit to prosecuting noncompliance. That prosecution requires policing capacity on the water and punitive legal institutions. Wealthier states will have an easier time of this than developing countries with limited resources. From a capacity perspective, there is undoubtedly merit to the critique of large MPAs as difficult to enforce.

But this critique is also overstated. It underestimates the importance of voluntary compliance with large MPA regulations. Industry stakeholders are, by and large, law-abiding and likely to adhere to rules. They fight adamantly against new regulations in part because they intend to comply. Palau's foreign fishing restrictions will lead most Japanese and Taiwanese boats to find other fishing grounds rather than illegally fish in Palau's EEZ. The Okinawa fleet that will retain access will do so not illegally, but as a result of diplomatic pressure from Japan. Some might fish illegally, but the majority likely will not. Similarly, the majority of the US Western Pacific fleet will undoubtedly adhere to zoning restrictions. Its avenue for fishing in those protected waters is through changes to the law, which it has pursued through lobbying congress and President Trump. Widespread compliance does require some level of monitoring and enforcement commitment, but critics overstate the willingness of many industry actors to risk noncompliance in most cases, especially when penalties are harsh. Illegal fishing will surely continue both within and outside of MPAs, but improved monitoring and stricter penalties within large MPAs can help to combat this pervasive problem as well.

The emergence of the large MPA norm has certainly changed global marine conservation efforts for the better. Criticisms of large MPAs are valid, and in many cases, they point toward a need to design better reserves through more collaborative processes. They also bring attention to conservation blind spots, ensuring that individual countries cannot rest on the laurels of residual MPAs in their marine conservation strategy. But the large MPA norm has already altered states' relationship with marine conservation, giving it a heightened priority in the face of ocean decline. It is helping to bring an unprecedented level of attention to ocean issues and expanding the scope of what governments see as feasible conservation commitments. The direct benefit of millions of square kilometers of protected area coverage combined with these indirect benefits make large MPAs desirable, albeit with many shortcomings.

The central argument of this book is nonetheless that governments make conservation policy decisions based on the political economy of a given space. It is consistent with the established view that there is a global paradigm of environmentalism that requires that protections do not undermine economic growth and development (Bernstein 2001). This paradigm characterizes ocean governance as well, with its emphasis on maximum sustainable yield (Lobo and Jacques 2017; Jacques and Lobo 2018). This book reveals why and how the large MPA norm fits into this paradigm, but there is also an inherent tension here in that large MPAs by definition are intended to shut out (at least some) industry interests over large swaths of ocean. The framework and case studies that I present in this book reveal the lengths to which states will go to find compatibility between conservation and economic interests. As it stands, that compatibility is a precondition for conservation. States and many environmental groups have shied away from challenging the tenets of neoliberal environmentalism. The large MPA norm is a paradigm shift in marine conservation, but it is a paradigm shift that follows the rules of the global liberal order. That order is one that inherently privileges the interests of businesses first and foremost.

Business power and influence is ubiquitous in global environmental politics. The normative commitment of this research is to better understand why, how, and under what conditions businesses influence environmental outcomes so that activists and scholars can more effectively work toward solutions. The scaling up of marine conservation efforts through large MPAs in the mid-2000s to address ocean decline is encouraging, albeit not a panacea. Governments are still working within a paradigm of environmentalism that treats economic growth and development as sacred—not to be touched. Policies that adhere to this paradigm are not enough to reverse or even slow the ongoing global ecological crisis. This book highlights the ubiquity of industry interests and influence in environmental policymaking, but also its limitations as states protect millions of square kilometers of ocean space from current and future commercial exploitation. There is optimism to be found in the emergence of the large MPA norm, but we have a long way to go to truly challenge a neoliberal system that has caused considerable ecological decline.

APPENDIX

List of Interviewees

Civil Society

Campaign Manager, Australian Marine Conservation Society, phone, Brisbane, QLD, May 17, 2016.

Campaigner, Greenpeace Australia, Sydney, NSW, March 29, 2016.

Consultant, Pew Charitable Trusts, Koror, June 17, 2016.

Coordinator, Global Climate Change Alliance+, Koror, June 24, 2016.

Executive, Blue Frontier, Koror, June 15, 2016.

Executive, Conservation International, Arlington, VA, September 17, 2015.

Executive, Ebiil Society, Koror, July 7, 2016.

Executive, Environmental Defense Fund, phone, Raleigh, NC, September 23, 2015.

Executive, Marine Conservation Institute, phone, Glen Ellen, CA, September 24, 2015.

Executive, Palau Conservation Society, Koror, July 6, 2016.

Executive, The Environment Inc., Koror, June 23, 2016.

Former Campaigner, Cairns and Far North Environment Centre, Skype, Italy, May 31, 2016.

Former Executive, Cairns and Far North Environment Centre, Cairns, QLD, June 2, 2016.

Former Executive, Pew Charitable Trusts, phone, Juneau, AK, October 7, 2015.

Former Marine Campaigner, Australian Conservation Foundation, phone, Melbourne, VIC, May 27, 2016.

Former Program Director, Pew Charitable Trusts, phone, Brisbane, QLD, May 15, 2016.

Manager, Pew Charitable Trusts, phone, Washington, DC, August 11, 2015.

Manager, Rare, Koror, July 5, 2016.

Marine Campaigner, Australian Marine Conservation Society, phone, WA, June 3, 2016.

Program Director, Greenpeace USA, Washington, DC, September 17, 2015.

Program Director, Marine Conservation Institute, Washington, DC, September 24, 2015.

Program Director, National Geographic Society, Washington, DC, September 17, 2015.

Program Director, Pew Charitable Trusts, Canberra, ACT, May 6, 2016.

Program Director, Pew Charitable Trusts, phone, Perth, WA, April 4, 2016.

Program Director, Pew Charitable Trusts, Washington, DC, September 16, 2015.

Program Director, The Nature Conservancy, Koror, June 29, 2016.

Ecotourism Industry

Manager, dive tourism business, Cairns, QLD, May 30, 2016.
Manager, dive tourism business, Koror, June 30, 2016.
Owner, dive tourism business, Koror, June 23, 2016.
Owner, dive tourism business, phone, Port Douglass, QLD, June 1, 2016.
Owner, kayak tour business, Koror, July 6, 2016.

Fishing Industry (Commercial and Recreational)

Board Member, Palau Aquaculture Cooperative Association, Koror, July 5, 2016.
Executive, Australian National Sportfishing Association, Sydney, NSW, May 10, 2016.
Executive, Palau Aquaculture Cooperative Association, Koror, July 5, 2016.
Executive, Queensland Seafood Industry Association, Hendra, QLD, May 30, 2016.
Executive, Saving Seafood, phone, Washington, DC, October 15, 2015.
Executive, Sunfish Queensland, phone, Margate, QLD, June 3, 2016.
Executive, Western Pacific Regional Fishery Management Council, phone, Honolulu, HI, October 1, 2015.
Manager, commercial fishing business, Cairns, QLD, May 30, 2016.
Manager, Saving Seafood, phone, Washington, DC, October 15, 2015.
Manager, Western Pacific Regional Fishery Management Council, phone, Honolulu, HI, October 1, 2015.
Owner, charter fishing business, Koror, June 21, 2016.
Owner, commercial fishing business, Koror, June 28, 2016.
Owner, commercial fishing business, phone, Cairns, QLD, May 30, 2016.
Program Director, US commercial fishing business, phone, January 22, 2016.

Government

Advisor, Australian Navy, Koror, July 7, 2016.
Branch Manager, US Fish and Wildlife Service, Arlington, VA, September 22, 2015.
Campaigner, Zoological Society of London, phone, London, August 28, 2015.
Chief of Staff, Member of US Congress, Republican Party, phone, Washington, DC, September 22, 2015.
Coordinator, Ministry of Finance, Koror, June 21, 2016.
Former Program Director, Bureau of Marine Resources, Koror, July 1, 2016.
Former Researcher, Australian Department of Environment, phone, Hobart, TAS, May 6, 2016.
Manager, Ministry of Natural Resources, Environment & Tourism, Koror, June 29, 2016.
Member of Parliament, Conservative Party, House of Commons of the United Kingdom, email, London, July 20, 2015.
Member of Parliament, Labour Party, House of Commons of the United Kingdom, phone, London, July 27, 2015.

Policy Officer, Fisheries Queensland, phone, Brisbane, QLD, May 13, 2016.

Program Coordinator, US Fish and Wildlife Service, Arlington, VA, September 22, 2015.

Program Director, Ministry of Justice, Koror, July 7, 2016.

Program Director, National Oceanic and Atmospheric Administration, Silver Spring, MD, September 24, 2015.

Program Director, Office of the President, Koror, June 29, 2016.

Program Director, Parks Australia, phone, Hobart, TAS, May 16, 2016.

Program Director, US Department of State, phone, Washington, DC, September 15, 2015.

Senator, Green Party, Australian Parliament, Canberra, ACT, May 3, 2016.

Senator, Palau National Congress, Koror, July 6, 2016.

Senior Policy Analyst, UK Foreign and Commonwealth Office, phone, London, October 30, 2015.

Volunteer, Office of the President, Koror, June 21, 2016.

Volunteer, Office of the President, Koror, June 30, 2016.

Research Organizations

Consultant, Sea-Scope, phone, England, August 7, 2015.

Executive, Coral Reef Research Foundation, Koror, June 17, 2016.

Executive, Palau International Coral Reef Center, Koror, July 6, 2016.

Fisheries Scientist, University of British Columbia, Vancouver, BC, October 29, 2015.

Officer, Palau International Coral Reef Center, Koror, June 28, 2016.

Program Director, Sea Around Us, University of British Columbia, Vancouver, BC, August 17, 2015.

Researcher, EconMAP, Koror, July 6, 2016.

Researcher, geospatial research organization, Koror, June 24, 2016.

Senior Scientist, Sea Around Us, University of British Columbia, Vancouver, BC, August 17, 2015.

Notes

Chapter 2

1. Interview with Former Executive, Pew Charitable Trusts, phone, Juneau, AK, October 7, 2015.
2. Interview with Program Director, National Geographic Society, Washington, DC, September 17, 2015.
3. Interview with Program Director, National Geographic Society, September 17, 2015.
4. Interview with Program Director, National Geographic Society, September 17, 2015.
5. Interview with Consultant, Sea-Scope, phone, England, August 7, 2015; Interview with Director, Sea Around Us, University of British Columbia, Vancouver, BC, August 17, 2015; Interview with Senior Scientist, Sea Around Us, University of British Columbia, Vancouver, BC, August 17, 2015.
6. Interview with Senior Policy Analyst, UK Foreign and Commonwealth Office, phone, London, October 2015.
7. Interview with Senior Policy Analyst, UK Foreign and Commonwealth Office, October 30, 2015.
8. Interview with Program Director, National Geographic Society, September 17, 2015.
9. Interview with Former Executive, Pew Charitable Trusts, October 7, 2015.
10. Interview with Former Executive, Pew Charitable Trusts, October 7, 2015.
11. Interview with Former Executive, Pew Charitable Trusts, October 7, 2015.
12. Interview with Former Executive, Pew Charitable Trusts, October 7, 2015.
13. Interview with Former Executive, Pew Charitable Trusts, October 7, 2015.
14. Interview with Former Executive, Pew Charitable Trusts, October 7, 2015.
15. Interview with Former Executive, Pew Charitable Trusts, October 7, 2015.
16. Interview with Former Executive, Pew Charitable Trusts, October 7, 2015.
17. Interview with Former Executive, Pew Charitable Trusts, October 7, 2015.
18. Interview with Former Executive, Pew Charitable Trusts, October 7, 2015.
19. Interview with Executive, Environmental Defense Fund, phone, Raleigh, NC, September 23, 2015.
20. Interview with Program Director, Marine Conservation Institute, Washington, DC, September 24, 2015.
21. Interview with Program Director, Marine Conservation Institute, September 24, 2015.
22. Interview with Program Director, Marine Conservation Institute, September 24, 2015.
23. Interview with Executive, Conservation International, Arlington, VA, September 17, 2015.

24. Interview with Executive, Conservation International, September 17, 2015.
25. Interview with Executive, Conservation International, September 17, 2015.
26. Interview with Executive, Conservation International, September 17, 2015.
27. Interview with Executive, Conservation International, September 17, 2015.
28. Interview with Executive, Conservation International, September 17, 2015.
29. Interview with Executive, Conservation International, September 17, 2015.
30. Interview with Executive, Conservation International, September 17, 2015.
31. Interview with Executive, Conservation International, September 17, 2015.
32. Interview with Executive, Environmental Defense Fund, September 23, 2015.
33. Interview with Executive, Marine Conservation Institute, phone, Glen Ellen, CA, September 24, 2015.
34. Interview with Former Executive, Pew Charitable Trusts, October 7, 2015; Interview with Program Director, National Geographic Society, September 17, 2015.
35. Interview with Former Executive, Pew Charitable Trusts, October 7, 2015.
36. Interview with Manager, Pew Charitable Trusts, phone, Washington, DC, August 11, 2015.
37. Interview with Manager, Pew Charitable Trusts, August 11, 2015.
38. Interview with Manager, Pew Charitable Trusts, August 11, 2015.
39. Interview with Executive, Environmental Defense Fund, September 23, 2015.

Chapter 4

1. Interview with Program Director, Sea Around Us, University of British Columbia, Vancouver, BC, August 17, 2015.
2. Interview with Executive, Environmental Defense Fund, phone, Raleigh, NC, September 23, 2015.
3. Interview with Branch Manager, US Fish and Wildlife Service, Arlington, VA, September 22, 2015; Interview with Program Coordinator, US Fish and Wildlife Service, Arlington, VA, September 22, 2015.
4. Interview with Branch Manager, US Fish and Wildlife Service, September 22, 2015; Interview with Program Coordinator, US Fish and Wildlife Service, September 22, 2015.
5. Interview with Branch Manager, US Fish and Wildlife Service, September 22, 2015; Interview with Program Coordinator, US Fish and Wildlife Service, September 22, 2015.
6. Interview with Program Director, National Oceanic and Atmospheric Administration, Silver Spring, MD, September 24, 2015.
7. Interview with Program Director, National Oceanic and Atmospheric Administration, September 24, 2015.
8. Interview with Executive, Marine Conservation Institute, phone, Glen Ellen, CA, September 24, 2015.
9. Interview with Former Executive, Pew Charitable Trusts, phone, Juneau, AK, October 7, 2015.

10. Interview with Former Executive, Pew Charitable Trusts, October 7, 2015.

11. Interview with Executive, Marine Conservation Institute, September 24, 2015.

12. Interview with Former Executive, Pew Charitable Trusts, October 7, 2015.

13. Interview with Program Director, Marine Conservation Institute, Washington, DC, September 24, 2015; Interview with Program Director, National Geographic Society, Washington, DC, September 17, 2015.

14. Interview with Executive, Environmental Defense Fund, September 23, 2015.

15. Interview with Executive, Marine Conservation Institute, September 24, 2015.

16. Interview with Executive, Conservation International, Arlington, VA, September 17, 2015.

17. Interview with Executive, Marine Conservation Institute, September 24, 2015.

18. Interview with Former Executive, Pew Charitable Trusts, October 7, 2015.

19. Interview with Program Director, Marine Conservation Institute, September 24, 2015.

20. Interview with Program Director, Marine Conservation Institute, September 24, 2015.

21. Interview with Program Director, Marine Conservation Institute, September 24, 2015.

22. Interview with Program Director, Marine Conservation Institute, September 24, 2015.

23. Interview with Program Director, Marine Conservation Institute, September 24, 2015.

24. Interview with Program Director, Marine Conservation Institute, September 24, 2015.

25. Interview with Program Director, Marine Conservation Institute, September 24, 2015.

26. Interview with Program Director, Marine Conservation Institute, September 24, 2015.

27. Interview with Executive, Environmental Defense Fund, September 23, 2015.

28. Interview with Program Director, Marine Conservation Institute, September 24, 2015.

29. Interview with Program Director, Marine Conservation Institute, September 24, 2015

30. Interview with Program Director, Marine Conservation Institute, September 24, 2015

31. Interview with Executive, Environmental Defense Fund, September 23, 2015.

32. Interview with Former Executive, Pew Charitable Trusts, October 7, 2015.

33. Interview with Former Executive, Pew Charitable Trusts, October 7, 2015.

34. Interview with Chief of Staff, Member of US Congress, Republican Party, phone, Washington, DC, September 22, 2015.

35. Interview with Program Director, US commercial fishing business, phone, January 22, 2016.

36. Interview with Program Director, US commercial fishing business, January 22, 2016.

37. Interview with Program Director, US commercial fishing business, January 22, 2016.

38. Interview with Program Director, US commercial fishing business, January 22, 2016.

39. Interview with Program Director, US commercial fishing business, January 22, 2016.

40. Interview with Program Director, US commercial fishing business, January 22, 2016.

41. Interview with Program Director, US commercial fishing business, January 22, 2016.

42. Interview with Executive, Western Pacific Regional Fishery Management Council, phone, Honolulu, HI, October 1, 2015.

43. Interview with Chief of Staff, Member of US Congress, Republican Party, September 22, 2015.

44. Interview with Executive, Western Pacific Regional Fishery Management Council, October 1, 2015.

45. Interview with Manager, Western Pacific Regional Fishery Management Council, phone, Honolulu, HI, October 1, 2015.

46. Interview with Executive, Western Pacific Regional Fishery Management Council, October 1, 2015.

47. Interview with Executive, Western Pacific Regional Fishery Management Council, October 1, 2015.

48. Interview with Fisheries Scientist, University of British Columbia, Vancouver, BC, October 29, 2015.

49. Interview with Executive, Western Pacific Regional Fishery Management Council, October 1, 2015.

50. Interview with Program Director, Marine Conservation Institute, September 24, 2015.

51. Interview with Executive, Western Pacific Regional Fishery Management Council, October 1, 2015.

52. Interview with Executive, Western Pacific Regional Fishery Management Council, October 1, 2015.

53. Interview with Executive, Western Pacific Regional Fishery Management Council, October 1, 2015.

54. Interview with Manager, Western Pacific Regional Fishery Management Council, October 1, 2015.

55. Interview with Executive, Saving Seafood, phone, Washington, DC, October 15, 2015; Interview with Manager, Saving Seafood, phone, Washington, DC, October 15, 2015.

56. Interview with Program Director, Marine Conservation Institute, September 24, 2015.

57. Interview with Manager, Western Pacific Regional Fishery Management Council, October 1, 2015.

58. Interview with Executive, Western Pacific Regional Fishery Management Council, October 1, 2015.

59. Interview with Executive, Western Pacific Regional Fishery Management Council, October 1, 2015.

60. Interview with Manager, Western Pacific Regional Fishery Management Council, October 1, 2015.

61. Interview with Program Coordinator, US Fish and Wildlife Service, September 22, 2015.

62. Interview with Program Coordinator, US Fish and Wildlife Service, September 22, 2015.

63. Interview with Program Coordinator, US Fish and Wildlife Service, September 22, 2015.

64. Interview with Program Coordinator, US Fish and Wildlife Service, September 22, 2015; Interview with Branch Manager, US Fish and Wildlife Service, September 22, 2015; Interview with Program Director, Pew Charitable Trusts, Washington, DC, September 16, 2015.

65. Interview with Program Director, National Oceanic and Atmospheric Administration, Silver Spring, MD, September 24, 2015.

Chapter 5

1. Interview with Executive, Australian National Sportfishing Association, Sydney, NSW, May 10, 2016.

2. Interview with Executive, Australian National Sportfishing Association, May 10, 2016.

3. Interview with Former Program Director, Pew Charitable Trusts, phone, Brisbane, QLD, May 15, 2016.

4. Interview with Former Program Director, Pew Charitable Trusts, May 15, 2016.

5. Interview with Program Director, Pew Charitable Trusts, Canberra, ACT, May 6, 2016; Interview with Executive, Australian National Sportfishing Association, May 10, 2016.

6. Interview with Program Director, Pew Charitable Trusts, May 6, 2016.

7. Interview with Executive, Australian National Sportfishing Association, May 10, 2016.

8. Interview with Executive, Australian National Sportfishing Association, May 10, 2016.

9. Interview with Former Campaigner, Cairns and Far North Environment Centre, Skype, Italy, May 31, 2016.

10. Interview with Former Campaigner, Cairns and Far North Environment Centre, May 31, 2016.

11. Interview with Former Campaigner, Cairns and Far North Environment Centre, May 31, 2016.

12. Interview with Former Program Director, Pew Charitable Trusts, May 15, 2016.

13. Interview with Former Program Director, Pew Charitable Trusts, May 15, 2016.

14. Interview with Former Program Director, Pew Charitable Trusts, May 15, 2016.

15. Interview with Former Program Director, Pew Charitable Trusts, May 15, 2016.

16. Interview with Former Program Director, Pew Charitable Trusts, May 15, 2016.

17. Interview with Former Program Director, Pew Charitable Trusts, May 15, 2016.

18. Interview with Former Program Director, Pew Charitable Trusts, May 15, 2016.

19. Interview with Former Program Director, Pew Charitable Trusts, May 15, 2016.

20. Interview with Former Program Director, Pew Charitable Trusts, May 15, 2016.

21. Interview with Former Program Director, Pew Charitable Trusts, May 15, 2016.

22. Interview with Former Program Director, Pew Charitable Trusts, May 15, 2016.

23. Interview with Former Executive, Cairns and Far North Environment Centre, Cairns, QLD, June 2, 2016; Interview with Former Campaigner, Cairns and Far North Environment Centre, May 31, 2016.

24. Interview with Former Marine Campaigner, Australian Conservation Foundation, phone, Melbourne, VIC, May 27, 2016.

25. Interview with Former Marine Campaigner, Australian Conservation Foundation, May 27, 2016.

26. Interview with Program Director, Pew Charitable Trusts, Canberra, ACT, May 6, 2016.

27. Interview with Program Director, Pew Charitable Trusts, May 6, 2016.

28. Interview with Program Director, Pew Charitable Trusts, May 6, 2016.

29. Interview with Former Program Director, Pew Charitable Trusts, May 15, 2016.

30. Interview with Former Program Director, Pew Charitable Trusts, May 15, 2016.

31. Interview with Former Program Director, Pew Charitable Trusts, May 15, 2016.

32. Interview with Program Director, Pew Charitable Trusts, phone, Perth, WA, April 4, 2016.

33. Interview with Executive, Australian National Sportfishing Association, May 10, 2016.

34. Interview with Program Director, Pew Charitable Trusts, April 4, 2016.

35. Interview with Former Campaigner, Cairns and Far North Environment Centre, May 31, 2016.

36. Interview with Program Director, Pew Charitable Trusts, April 4, 2016.

37. Interview with Program Director, Pew Charitable Trusts, May 6, 2016.

38. Interview with Program Director, Pew Charitable Trusts, May 6, 2016.

39. Interview with Owner, commercial fishing business, phone, Cairns, QLD, May 30, 2016.

40. Interview with Policy Officer, Fisheries Queensland, phone, Brisbane, QLD, May 13, 2016.

41. Interview with Campaigner, Greenpeace Australia, Sydney, NSW, March 29, 2016; Interview with Program Director, Pew Charitable Trusts, May 6, 2016.

42. Interview with Owner, commercial fishing business, May 30, 2016.

43. Interview with Owner, commercial fishing business, May 30, 2016.

44. Interview with Owner, commercial fishing business, May 30, 2016.

45. Interview with Owner, commercial fishing business, May 30, 2016.

46. Interview with Owner, commercial fishing business, May 30, 2016.

47. Interview with Former Marine Campaigner, Australian Conservation Foundation, May 27, 2016; Interview with Marine Campaigner, Australian Marine Conservation Society, phone, Brisbane, QLD, June 3, 2016.

48. Interview with Manager, commercial fishing business, Cairns, QLD, May 30, 2016.

49. Interview with Manager, commercial fishing business, May 30, 2016.

50. Interview with Manager, commercial fishing business, May 30, 2016.

51. Interview with Manager, commercial fishing business, May 30, 2016.

52. Interview with Manager, commercial fishing business, May 30, 2016.

53. Interview with Former Campaigner, Cairns and Far North Environment Centre, May 31, 2016.

54. Interview with Executive, Sunfish Queensland, phone, Margate, QLD, June 3, 2016.

55. Interview with Executive, Sunfish Queensland, June 3, 2016.

56. Interview with Executive, Sunfish Queensland, June 3, 2016.

57. Interview with Executive, Sunfish Queensland, June 3, 2016.

58. Interview with Executive, Sunfish Queensland, June 3, 2016.

59. Interview with Executive, Australian National Sportfishing Association, May 10, 2016.

60. Interview with Former Marine Campaigner, Australian Conservation Foundation, phone, Melbourne, VIC, May 27, 2016.

61. Interview with Marine Campaigner, Australian Marine Conservation Society, June 3, 2016.

62. Interview with Executive, Australian National Sportfishing Association, May 10, 2016.

63. Interview with Executive, Australian National Sportfishing Association, May 10, 2016; Interview with Marine Campaigner, Australian Marine Conservation Society, June 3, 2016.

64. Interview with Marine Campaigner, Australian Marine Conservation Society, June 3, 2016.

65. Interview with Marine Campaigner, Australian Marine Conservation Society, June 3, 2016.

66. Interview with Executive, Australian National Sportfishing Association, May 10, 2016.

67. Interview with Marine Campaigner, Australian Marine Conservation Society, June 3, 2016.

68. Interview with Campaigner, Greenpeace Australia, Sydney, NSW, March 29, 2016.

69. Interview with Former Program Director, Pew Charitable Trusts, May 15, 2016.

70. Interview with Former Program Director, Pew Charitable Trusts, May 15, 2016.

71. Interview with Former Program Director, Pew Charitable Trusts, May 15, 2016.

72. Interview with Former Program Director, Pew Charitable Trusts, May 15, 2016.

73. Interview with Executive, Australian National Sportfishing Association, May 10, 2016.

74. Interview with Manager, dive tourism business, Cairns, QLD, May 30, 2016.

75. Interview with Manager, dive tourism business, May 30, 2016.

76. Interview with Manager, dive tourism business, May 30, 2016.

77. Interview with Manager, dive tourism business, May 30, 2016.

78. Interview with Manager, dive tourism business, May 30, 2016.

79. Interview with Manager, dive tourism business, May 30, 2016.

80. Interview with Owner, commercial fishing business, May 30, 2016; Interview with Manager, dive tourism business, May 30, 2016.

81. Interview with Owner, commercial fishing business, May 30, 2016.

82. Interview with Owner, commercial fishing business, May 30, 2016.

83. Interview with Manager, dive tourism business, May 30, 2016.

84. Interview with Manager, dive tourism business, May 30, 2016.

85. Interview with Marine Campaigner, Australian Marine Conservation Society, June 3, 2016.

86. Interview with Executive, Queensland Seafood Industry Association, Hendra, QLD, May 30, 2016; Interview with Owner, commercial fishing business, May 30, 2016.

87. Interview with Executive, Australian National Sportfishing Association, May 10, 2016; Interview with Owner, commercial fishing business, May 30, 2016.

Chapter 6

1. Interview with Owner, commercial fishing business, Koror, June 28, 2016.

2. Interview with Consultant, Pew Charitable Trusts, Koror, June 17, 2016.

3. Interview with Consultant, Pew Charitable Trusts, June 17, 2016.

4. Interview with Executive, Palau International Coral Reef Center, Koror, July 6, 2016; Interview with Consultant, Pew Charitable Trusts, June 17, 2016; Interview with Manager, dive tourism business, Koror, June 30, 2016; Interview with Program Director, Office of the President, Koror, June 29, 2016.

5. Interview with Coordinator, Global Climate Change Alliance+, Koror, June 24, 2016.

6. Interview with Coordinator, Global Climate Change Alliance+, June 24, 2016.

7. Interview with Manager, dive tourism business, June 30, 2016.

8. Interview with Manager, dive tourism business, June 30, 2016.

9. Interview with Manager, dive tourism business, June 30, 2016.

10. Interview with Manager, dive tourism business, June 30, 2016.

11. Interview with Manager, dive tourism business, June 30, 2016; Interview with Owner, dive tourism business, Koror, June 23, 2016.

12. Interview with Manager, dive tourism business, June 30, 2016.

13. Interview with Manager, dive tourism business, June 30, 2016.

14. Interview with Manager, dive tourism business, June 30, 2016.

15. Interview with Executive, Coral Reef Research Foundation, Koror, June 17, 2016.

16. Interview with Manager, dive tourism business, June 30, 2016.

17. Interview with Consultant, Pew Charitable Trusts, June 17, 2016.

18. Interview with Consultant, Pew Charitable Trusts, June 17, 2016.

19. Interview with Owner, kayak tour business, Koror, July 6, 2016.

20. Interview with Owner, dive tourism business, June 23, 2016; Interview with Manager, dive tourism business, June 30, 2016.

21. Interview with Manager, dive tourism business, June 30, 2016.

22. Interview with Consultant, Pew Charitable Trusts, June 17, 2016.

23. Interview with Consultant, Pew Charitable Trusts, June 17, 2016.

24. Interview with Consultant, Pew Charitable Trusts, June 17, 2016.

25. Interview with Consultant, Pew Charitable Trusts, June 17, 2016.

26. Interview with Consultant, Pew Charitable Trusts, June 17, 2016.

27. Interview with Consultant, Pew Charitable Trusts, June 17, 2016.

28. Interview with Consultant, Pew Charitable Trusts, June 17, 2016.

29. Interview with Consultant, Pew Charitable Trusts, June 17, 2016.
30. Interview with Program Director, The Nature Conservancy, Koror, June 29, 2016.
31. Interview with Program Director, The Nature Conservancy, June 29, 2016.
32. Interview with Consultant, Pew Charitable Trusts, June 17, 2016.
33. Interview with Consultant, Pew Charitable Trusts, June 17, 2016.
34. Interview with Program Director, Office of the President, June 29, 2016.
35. Interview with Program Director, Office of the President, June 29, 2016.
36. Interview with Executive, Coral Reef Research Foundation, June 17, 2016.
37. Interview with Executive, The Environment Inc., Koror, June 23, 2016.
38. Interview with Executive, Palau International Coral Reef Center, Koror, July 6, 2016.
39. Interview with Researcher, EconMAP, Koror, July 6, 2016.
40. Interview with Executive, The Environment Inc., June 23, 2016; Interview with Executive, Palau Aquaculture Cooperative Association, Koror, July 5, 2016; Interview with Owner, charter fishing business, Koror, June 21, 2016.
41. Interview with Manager, dive tourism business, June 30, 2016.
42. Interview with Manager, Ministry of Natural Resources, Environment & Tourism, Koror, June 29, 2016.
43. Interview with Executive, The Environment Inc., June 23, 2016.
44. Interview with Manager, dive tourism business, June 30, 2016.
45. Interview with Owner, dive tourism business, June 23, 2016; Interview with Manager, dive tourism business, June 30, 2016.
46. Interview with Owner, kayak tour business, July 6, 2016.
47. Interview with Manager, dive tourism business, June 30, 2016.
48. Interview with Owner, dive tourism business, June 23, 2016.
49. Interview with Owner, dive tourism business, June 23, 2016.
50. Interview with Program Director, Office of the President, June 29, 2016.
51. Interview with Consultant, Pew Charitable Trusts, June 17, 2016; Interview with Executive, Ebiil Society, Koror, July 7, 2016.
52. Interview with Executive, The Environment Inc., June 23, 2016.
53. Interview with Consultant, Pew Charitable Trusts, June 17, 2016.
54. Interview with Consultant, Pew Charitable Trusts, June 17, 2016.
55. Interview with Consultant, Pew Charitable Trusts, June 17, 2016.
56. Interview with Owner, commercial fishing business, June 28, 2016.
57. Interview with Consultant, Pew Charitable Trusts, June 17, 2016.
58. Interview with Consultant, Pew Charitable Trusts, June 17, 2016.
59. Interview with Owner, charter fishing business, June 21, 2016.
60. Interview with Owner, charter fishing business, June 21, 2016.
61. Interview with Executive, Ebiil Society, July 7, 2016.
62. Interview with Executive, Ebiil Society, July 7, 2016.
63. Multiple interview sources.
64. Interview with Senator, Palau National Congress, Koror, July 6, 2016.
65. Interview with Senator, Palau National Congress, July 6, 2016.
66. Interview with Senator, Palau National Congress, July 6, 2016.
67. Interview with Senator, Palau National Congress, July 6, 2016.

68. Interview with Senator, Palau National Congress, July 6, 2016.
69. Interview with Manager, dive tourism business, June 30, 2016.
70. This paragraph draws from multiple interview sources from Palauan civil society.
71. Interview with Senator, Palau National Congress, July 6, 2016.
72. Interview with Senator, Palau National Congress, July 6, 2016.
73. Interview with Executive, Ebiil Society, July 7, 2016.
74. Interview with Executive, Ebiil Society, July 7, 2016.
75. Interview with Executive, Ebiil Society, July 7, 2016.
76. Interview with Executive, Ebiil Society, July 7, 2016.
77. Interview with Executive, Ebiil Society, July 7, 2016.
78. Interview with Executive, Ebiil Society, July 7, 2016.
79. Interview with Owner, commercial fishing business, June 28, 2016.
80. Interview with Manager, Ministry of Natural Resources, Environment & Tourism, June 29, 2016.
81. Interview with Manager, Ministry of Natural Resources, Environment & Tourism, June 29, 2016.
82. Interview with Program Director, The Nature Conservancy, June 29, 2016.
83. Interview with Executive, The Environment Inc., June 23, 2016.
84. Interview with Executive, Palau International Coral Reef Center, July 6, 2016.
85. Interview with Executive, The Environment Inc., June 23, 2016.
86. Interview with Executive, Ebiil Society, July 7, 2016.
87. Interview with Executive, Ebiil Society, July 7, 2016.
88. Interview with Executive, Ebiil Society, July 7, 2016.
89. Interview with Program Director, Office of the President, June 29, 2016.
90. Interview with Program Director, Office of the President, June 29, 2016.
91. Interview with Former Program Director, Bureau of Marine Resources, Koror, July 1, 2016.
92. Interview with Program Director, Office of the President, June 29, 2016.
93. Interview with Program Director, Ministry of Justice, Koror, July 7, 2016.
94. Interview with Program Director, Ministry of Justice, July 7, 2016.
95. Interview with Executive, Coral Reef Research Foundation, June 17, 2016.

Chapter 7

1. Interview with Volunteer, Office of the President, Koror, June 21, 2016.
2. Interview with Consultant, Pew Charitable Trusts, Koror, June 17, 2016.
3. Interview with Program Director, Greenpeace USA, Washington, DC, September 17, 2015.
4. Interview with Former Executive, Pew Charitable Trusts, phone, Juneau, AK, October 7, 2015.
5. Interview with Manager, Pew Charitable Trusts, phone, Washington, DC, August 11, 2015.

References

ABARES. 2012. *Coral Sea Commonwealth Marine Reserve: Social and Economic Assessment of the Impacts on Commercial and Charter Fishing*. Canberra: Commonwealth of Australia.

Acharya, Amitav. 2004. "How Ideas Spread: Whose Norms Matter? Norm Localization and Institutional Change in Asian Regionalism." *International Organization* 58 (2): 239–75.

Acharya, Amitav. 2013. "The R2P and Norm Diffusion: Towards a Framework of Norm Circulation." *Global Responsibility to Protect* 5 (4): 466–79.

Adler, Emanuel. 1992. "The Emergence of Cooperation: National Epistemic Communities and the International Evolution of the Idea of Nuclear Arms Control." *International Organization* 46 (1): 101–45.

Adler, Emanuel. 1997. "Seizing the Middle Ground: Constructivism in World Politics." *European Journal of International Relations* 3 (3): 319–63.

AFMA. 2016. Eastern Tuna and Billfish Fishery. *Australian Fisheries Management Authority (AFMA)*.

Agardy, Tundi, Giuseppe Notarbartolo Di Sciara, and Patrick Christie. 2011. "Mind the Gap: Addressing the Shortcomings of Marine Protected Areas through Largescale Marine Spatial Planning." *Marine Policy* 35 (2): 226–32.

Akerlof, George A. 1980. "A Theory of Social Custom, of Which Unemployment May Be One Consequence." *The Quarterly Journal of Economics* 94 (4): 749–75.

Alger, Justin, and Peter Dauvergne. 2017a. "The Politics of Pacific Ocean Conservation: Lessons from the Pitcairn Islands Marine Reserve." *Pacific Affairs* 90 (1): 29–50.

Alger, Justin, and Peter Dauvergne. 2017b. "The Global Norm of Large Marine Protected Areas: Explaining Variable Adoption and Implementation." *Environmental Policy and Governance* 27 (4): 298–310.

Alger, Justin, and Peter Dauvergne. 2020. "The Translocal Politics of Environmental Norm Diffusion." *Environmental Communication* 14 (2): 155–67.

Allan, Jen Iris. 2019. "Dangerous Incrementalism of the Paris Agreement." *Global Environmental Politics* 19 (1): 4–11.

Allan, Jen Iris, and Jennifer Hadden. 2017. "Exploring the Framing Power of NGOs in Global Climate Politics." *Environmental Politics* 26 (4): 600–20.

Almany, G. R., S. R. Connolly, D. D. Heath, J. D. Hogan, G. P. Jones, L. J. McCook, M. Mills, R. L. Pressey, and D. H. Williamson. 2009. "Connectivity, Biodiversity Conservation and the Design of Marine Reserve Networks for Coral Reefs." *Coral Reefs* 28 (2): 339–51.

Alpine, J. E., and A. J. Hobday. 2007. "Area Requirements and Pelagic Protected Areas: Is Size an Impediment to Implementation?" *Marine and Freshwater Research* 58 (6): 558–69.

Altamirano-Jiménez, Isabel. 2013. *Indigenous Encounters with Neoliberalism: Place, Women, and the Environment in Canada and Mexico*. Vancouver: UBC Press.

Angel, Martin V. 1993. "Biodiversity of the Pelagic Ocean." *Conservation Biology* 7 (4): 760–72.

Annesley, Rhonda. 2015. "US Tuna Boats Kicked out of Fishing Grounds; Cannery Fish Supply in Jeopardy." *Samoa News*, June 19.

Arts, Bas, and Piet Verschuren. 1999. "Assessing Political Influence in Complex Decision-Making: An Instrument Based on Triangulation." *International Political Science Review* 20 (4): 411–24.

Asian Development Bank. 2016a. *Asian Development Outlook 2016: Asia's Potential Growth.* Asian Development Bank.

Asian Development Bank. 2016b. "Policies for Sustainable Growth Revisited: A Private Sector Assessment for Palau." Discussion Draft. Asian Development Bank.

Asian Development Bank. 2019. *Asian Development Outlook 2019: Strengthening Disaster Resilience.* Asian Development Bank.

Aswani, Shankar, and Richard Hamilton. 2004. "The Value of Many Small v. Few Large Marine Protected Areas in the Western Solomon Islands." *Traditional Marine Resource Management and Knowledge Information Bulletin* 16: 3–14.

Axelrod, Robert. 1986. "An Evolutionary Approach to Norms." *American Political Science Review* 80 (4): 1095–111.

Barham, Bradford L., and Oliver T. Coomes. 2005. "Sunk Costs, Resource Extractive Industries, and Development Outcomes." In *Nature, Raw Materials, and Political Economy*, edited by Paul Ciccantell, David A. Smith, and Gay Seidman, Vol. 10, Research in Rural Sociology and Development, 159–86. Bingley: Emerald Group Publishing Limited.

Barkham, Patrick. 2019. "Large Expansion to 'Blue Belt' of UK's Protected Marine Areas Announced." *The Guardian*, May 31.

Barkin, J. Samuel, and Elizabeth R. DeSombre. 2013. *Saving Global Fisheries: Reducing Fishing Capacity to Promote Sustainability.* Cambridge: MIT Press.

Barnett, Adam, Kátya G. Abrantes, Jamie Seymour, and Richard Fitzpatrick. 2012. "Residency and Spatial Use by Reef Sharks of an Isolated Seamount and Its Implications for Conservation." *PloS One* 7 (5). https://doi.org/10.1371/journal.pone.0036574.

Barnett, Michael N. 1997. "Bringing in the New World Order: Liberalism, Legitimacy, and the United Nations." *World Politics* 49 (4): 526–51.

Barnett, Michael N., and Martha Finnemore. 1999. "The Politics, Power, and Pathologies of International Organizations." *International Organization* 53 (4): 699–732.

Batliwala, Srilatha, and Lloyd David Brown. 2006. *Transnational Civil Society: An Introduction.* Bloomfield, CT: Kumarian Press.

Baum, Julia K., Ransom A. Myers, Daniel G. Kehler, Boris Worm, Shelton J. Harley, and Penny A. Doherty. 2003. "Collapse and Conservation of Shark Populations in the Northwest Atlantic." *Science* 299 (5605): 389–92.

Bebbington, Anthony, Leonith Hinojosa, Denise Humphreys Bebbington, Maria Luisa Burneo, and Ximena Warnaars. 2008. "Contention and Ambiguity: Mining and the Possibilities of Development." *Development and Change* 39 (6): 887–914.

Beldi, Lauren. 2018. "China's 'Tourist Ban' Leaves Palau Struggling to Fill Hotels and an Airline in Limbo." *ABC News*, August 25.

Bellwood, David R., Terry P. Hughes, C. Folke, and M. Nyström. 2004. "Confronting the Coral Reef Crisis." *Nature* 429 (6994): 827–33.

Bennett, Lance. 2004. "Social Movements beyond Borders: Understanding Two Eras of Transnational Activism." In *Transnational Protest and Global Activism*, edited by Donatella della Porta and Sidney Tarrow, Vol. 203, 203–26. Lanham: Rowman & Littlefield Publishers.

Bennett, Nathan James, Hugh Govan, and Terre Satterfield. 2015. "Ocean Grabbing." *Marine Policy* 57: 61–68.

Benson-Wahlén, Catherine. 2013. "The Anomalous Is Ubiquitous: Organizations and Individuals in Papua New Guinea's Conservation Efforts." The University of Michigan.

Bernstein, Steven. 2000. "Ideas, Social Structure and the Compromise of Liberal Environmentalism." *European Journal of International Relations* 6 (4): 464–512.

Bernstein, Steven. 2001. *The Compromise of Liberal Environmentalism.* New York: Columbia University Press.

Bernstein, Steven. 2002. "Liberal Environmentalism and Global Environmental Governance." *Global Environmental Politics* 2 (3): 1–16.

Betsill, Michele, and Elisabeth Corell. 2001. "NGO Influence in International Environmental Negotiations: A Framework for Analysis." *Global Environmental Politics* 1 (4): 65–85.

Betsill, Michele, and Elisabeth Corell. 2008. *NGO Diplomacy: The Influence of Nongovernmental Organizations in International Environmental Negotiations.* Cambridge: MIT Press.

Betts, Alexander, and Phil Orchard, eds. 2014. *Implementation and World Politics: How International Norms Change Practice.* Oxford: Oxford University Press.

Bloodgood, Elizabeth A. 2011. "The Interest Group Analogy: International Non-Governmental Advocacy Organisations in International Politics." *Review of International Studies* 37 (1): 93–120.

Bloodgood, Elizabeth A., Joannie Tremblay-Boire, and Aseem Prakash. 2013. "National Styles of NGO Regulation." *Nonprofit and Voluntary Sector Quarterly* 43 (4): 716–36.

Bob, Clifford. 2001. "Marketing Rebellion: Insurgent Groups, International Media, and NGO Support." *International Politics* 38 (3): 311–34.

Bob, Clifford. 2007. "'Dalit Rights Are Human Rights': Caste Discrimination, International Activism, and the Construction of a New Human Rights Issue." *Human Rights Quarterly* 29 (1): 167–93.

Böhmelt, Tobias, and Carola Betzold. 2013. "The Impact of Environmental Interest Groups in International Negotiations: Do ENGOs Induce Stronger Environmental Commitments?" *International Environmental Agreements: Politics, Law and Economics* 13 (2): 127–51.

Bowcott, Owen. 2019. "UN Court Rejects UK's Claim of Sovereignty over Chagos Islands." *The Guardian,* February 25.

Brady, Henry, and David Collier. 2010. *Rethinking Social Inquiry: Diverse Tools, Shared Standards.* Lanham: Rowman & Littlefield Publishers.

Buckle, Amanda. 2020. "Trump Removing Fishing Restrictions in the Northeast Canyons and Seamounts Marine National Monument." *Saving Seafood,* June 8.

Bull, Hedley. 1977. *The Anarchical Society: A Study of Order in World Politics.* Basingstoke: Palgrave Macmillan.

Bullard, Robert. 1990. *Dumping in Dixie: Race, Class, and Environmental Quality.* Boulder: Westview Press.

Bureau of Budget and Planning. 2014. "2014 Statistical Yearbook." Ministry of Finance, Republic of Palau.

Burke, Lauretta, Kathleen Reytar, Mark Spalding, and A. Perry. 2011. "Reefs at Risk." Washington: World Resources Institute.

Buxton, Colin, and Peter Cochrane. 2016. "Commonwealth Marine Reserves Review: Report of the Bioregional Advisory Panel." Canberra: Department of the Environment.

Buzan, Barry. 2004. *From International to World Society? English School Theory and the Social Structure of Globalisation*. New York: Cambridge University Press.

Campbell, Lisa M., Noella J. Gray, and Zoë A. Meletis. 2007. "Political Ecology Perspectives on Ecotourism to Parks and Protected Areas." In *Transforming Parks and Protected Areas: Policy and Governance in a Changing World*, edited by Kevin S. Hanna, Douglas A. Clark, and D. Scott Slocombe, 200–221. Abingdon: Routledge.

Campling, Liam, Elizabeth Havice, and Penny McCall Howard. 2012. "The Political Economy and Ecology of Capture Fisheries: Market Dynamics, Resource Access and Relations of Exploitation and Resistance." *Journal of Agrarian Change* 12 (2–3): 177–203.

Capie, David. 2008. "Localization as Resistance: The Contested Diffusion of Small Arms Norms in Southeast Asia." *Security Dialogue* 39 (6): 637–58.

Carpenter, Charli. 2005. "'Women, Children and Other Vulnerable Groups': Gender, Strategic Frames and the Protection of Civilians as a Transnational Issue." *International Studies Quarterly* 49 (2): 295–334.

Carpenter, Charli. 2007. "Setting the Advocacy Agenda: Theorizing Issue Emergence and Nonemergence in Transnational Advocacy Networks." *International Studies Quarterly* 51 (1): 99–120.

Cass, Loren R. 2012. *The Failures of American and European Climate Policy: International Norms, Domestic Politics, and Unachievable Commitments*. Albany: SUNY Press.

Caveen, Alex J., Tim S. Gray, Selina M. Stead, and Nicholas VC Polunin. 2013. "MPA Policy: What Lies behind the Science?" *Marine Policy* 37: 3–10.

Central Intelligence Agency. 2019a. "American Samoa—Economy." *The World Factbook*.

Central Intelligence Agency. 2019b. "Kiribati Economy." *The World Factbook*.

Chape, S., J. Harrison, M. Spalding, and I. Lysenko. 2005. "Measuring the Extent and Effectiveness of Protected Areas as an Indicator for Meeting Global Biodiversity Targets." *Philosophical Transactions of the Royal Society of London B: Biological Sciences* 360 (1454): 443–55.

Chayes, Abram, and Antonia Handler Chayes. 1993. "On Compliance." *International Organization* 47 (2): 175–205.

Checkel, Jeffrey T. 1997. "International Norms and Domestic Politics: Bridging the Rationalist–Constructivist Divide." *European Journal of International Relations* 3 (4): 473–95.

Checkel, Jeffrey T. 2001. "Why Comply? Social Learning and European Identity Change." *International Organization* 55 (3): 553–88.

Clapp, Jennifer. 2006. "Transnational Corporate Interests in International Biosafety Negotiations." In *The International Politics of Genetically Modified Food*, edited by Robert Falkner, 34–47. Berlin: Springer.

Clapp, Jennifer, and Doris A. Fuchs. 2009. *Corporate Power in Global Agrifood Governance*. Cambridge: MIT Press.

Clapp, Jennifer, and Linda Swanston. 2009. "Doing Away with Plastic Shopping Bags: International Patterns of Norm Emergence and Policy Implementation." *Environmental Politics* 18 (3): 315–32.

Clark, Ann Marie. 2010. *Diplomacy of Conscience: Amnesty International and Changing Human Rights Norms*. Princeton: Princeton University Press.

Claudet, Joachim (ed.). 2011. *Marine Protected Areas: A Multidisciplinary Approach*. Cambridge: Cambridge University Press.

Collier, David. 2011. "Understanding Process Tracing." *PS: Political Science and Politics* 44 (4): 823–30.

Collier, David, Henry Brady, and Jason Seawright. 2010. "Sources of Leverage in Causal Inference: Toward an Alternative View of Methodology." In *Rethinking Social Inquiry: Diverse Tools, Shared Standards*, edited by Henry Brady and David Collier, Second Edition, 161–200. Lanham: Rowman & Littlefield Publishers.

Collier, David, and Ruth Collier. 2002. *Shaping the Political Arena*. Notre Dame: University of Notre Dame Press.

Committee on Natural Resources. 2015. "The Potential Implications of Pending Marine National Monument Designations." Oversight Hearing before the Subcommittee on Water, Power and Oceans of the Committee on Natural Resources U.S. House of Representatives, One Hundred Fourteenth Congress, First Session, Serial No. 114-121. September 29. Washington, DC: Subcommittee on Water, Power and Oceans.

Commonwealth of Australia. 1999. *Environment Protection and Biodiversity Act*. C2004A00485 No. 91.

Cooley, Alexander, and James Ron. 2002. "The NGO Scramble: Organizational Insecurity and the Political Economy of Transnational Action." *International Security* 27 (1): 5–39.

Cortell, Andrew P., and James W. Davis. 2000. "Understanding the Domestic Impact of International Norms: A Research Agenda." *International Studies Review* 2 (1): 65–87.

Costello, Christopher, Daniel Ovando, Tyler Clavelle, C. Kent Strauss, Ray Hilborn, Michael C. Melnychuk, Trevor A. Branch, et al. 2016. "Global Fishery Prospects under Contrasting Management Regimes." *Proceedings of the National Academy of Sciences* 113 (18): 5125–29.

Cousteau, Jean-Michel. 2005. *Voyage to Kure*. PBS.

Cox, Robert. 1983. "Gramsci, Hegemony and International Relations: An Essay in Method." *Millennium: Journal of International Studies* 12 (2): 162–75.

Cutler, A. Claire, Virginia Haufler, and Tony Porter. 1999. *Private Authority and International Affairs*. Albany: SUNY Press.

Dacks, Rachel, Staci A. Lewis, Philip A. S. James, Lincy L. Marino, and Kirsten L. L. Oleson. 2020. "Documenting Baseline Value Chains of Palau's Nearshore and Offshore Fisheries Prior to Implementing a Large-Scale Marine Protected Area." *Marine Policy* 117. https://doi.org/10.1016/j.marpol.2019.103754.

Dashwood, Hevina S. 2012. *The Rise of Global Corporate Social Responsibility: Mining and the Spread of Global Norms*. New York: Cambridge University Press.

Dauvergne, Peter, and Genevieve LeBaron. 2014. *Protest Inc*. Cambridge: Polity Press.

Dauvergne, Peter, and Jane Lister. 2013. *Eco-Business: A Big-Brand Takeover of Sustainability*. Cambridge: MIT Press.

De Santo, Elizabeth M. 2013. "Missing Marine Protected Area (MPA) Targets: How the Push for Quantity over Quality Undermines Sustainability and Social Justice." *Journal of Environmental Management* 124: 137–46.

De Santo, Elizabeth M., Peter J. S. Jones, and A. M. M. Miller. 2011. "Fortress Conservation at Sea: A Commentary on the Chagos Marine Protected Area." *Marine Policy* 35 (2): 258–60.

De'ath, Glenn, Katharina E. Fabricius, Hugh Sweatman, and Marji Puotinen. 2012. "The 27-Year Decline of Coral Cover on the Great Barrier Reef and Its Causes." *Proceedings of the National Academy of Sciences* 109 (44): 17995–999.

della Porta, Donatella, and Sidney Tarrow. 2005. *Transnational Protest and Global Activism*. Lanham: Rowman & Littlefield Publishers.

Deloitte Access Economics. 2013. *Economic Contribution of the Great Barrier Reef*. Townsville: Great Barrier Reef Marine Park Authority.

DeMartini, Ee, Am Friedlander, Sa Sandin, and Enric Sala. 2008. "Differences in Fish-Assemblage Structure between Fished and Unfished Atolls in the Northern Line Islands, Central Pacific." *Marine Ecology Progress Series* 365: 199–215.

Department of Agriculture. 2015. *Australia's Seafood Trade*. Canberra: Department of Agriculture.

DeSombre, Elizabeth R. 2005. "Fishing under Flags of Convenience: Using Market Power to Increase Participation in International Regulation." *Global Environmental Politics* 5 (4): 73–94.

DeSombre, Elizabeth R., and J. Samuel Barkin. 2011. *Fish*. Cambridge: Polity.

Dimitrov, Radoslav S. 2005. "Hostage to Norms: States, Institutions and Global Forest Politics." *Global Environmental Politics* 5 (4): 1–24.

Donner, Simon D., and David Potere. 2007. "The Inequity of the Global Threat to Coral Reefs." *Bioscience* 57 (3): 214–15.

Donner, Simon D., William J. Skirving, Christopher M. Little, Michael Oppenheimer, and O. V. E. Hoegh-Guldberg. 2005. "Global Assessment of Coral Bleaching and Required Rates of Adaptation under Climate Change." *Global Change Biology* 11 (12): 2251–65.

Downs, George W., David M. Rocke, and Peter N. Barsoom. 1996. "Is the Good News about Compliance Good News about Cooperation?" *International Organization* 50: 379–406.

DuBois, Ellen Carol. 1994. "Woman Suffrage around the World: Three Phases of Suffragist Internationalism." In *Suffrage and Beyond: International Feminist Perspectives*, edited by Caroline Daley and Melanie Nolan, 252–74. New York: New York University Press.

Duffy, Rosaleen. 2006. "Global Environmental Governance and the Politics of Ecotourism in Madagascar." *Journal of Ecotourism* 5 (1–2): 128–44.

Duncan, Alan. 2016. "Foreign Office Minister Announces Significant Increase in UK Overseas Territory Marine Protected Area Coverage." Paper presented at the 2016 *Our Ocean* Conference, Washington, DC, September 15.

Edgar, Graham J., Rick D. Stuart-Smith, Trevor J. Willis, Stuart Kininmonth, Susan C. Baker, Stuart Banks, Neville S. Barrett, et al. 2014. "Global Conservation Outcomes Depend on Marine Protected Areas with Five Key Features." *Nature* 506: 216–20.

Elster, Jon. 1989. "Social Norms and Economic Theory." *The Journal of Economic Perspectives* 3 (4): 99–117.

Emslie, Michael J., Murray Logan, David H. Williamson, Anthony M. Ayling, M. Aaron MacNeil, Daniela Ceccarelli, Alistair J. Cheal, et al. 2015. "Expectations and Outcomes of Reserve Network Performance Following Re-Zoning of the Great Barrier Reef Marine Park." *Current Biology* 25 (8): 983–92.

Evenden, Matthew D. 2004. *Fish versus Power: An Environmental History of the Fraser River*. New York: Cambridge University Press.

Fabricius, Katharina E. 2005. "Effects of Terrestrial Runoff on the Ecology of Corals and Coral Reefs: Review and Synthesis." *Marine Pollution Bulletin* 50 (2): 125–46.

Falkner, Robert. 2008. *Business Power and Conflict in International Environmental Politics*. New York: Palgrave Macmillan.

Fearon, James. 1999. "What Is Identity (as We Now Use the Word)." Stanford: Stanford University.

Fearon, James, and David Laitin. 1996. "Explaining Interethnic Cooperation." *American Political Science Review* 90 (4): 715–35.

Fearon, James, and Alexander Wendt. 2002. "Rationalism v. Constructivism: A Skeptical View." In *Handbook of International Relations*, edited by Carl Carlsnaes, Thomas Risse, and Beth Simmons, 52–72. Thousand Oaks: SAGE.

Fennell, David A. 2014. *Ecotourism*. London: Routledge.

Ferguson, James. 2005. "Seeing like an Oil Company: Space, Security, and Global Capital in Neoliberal Africa." *American Anthropologist* 107 (3): 377–82.

Finnemore, Martha. 1993. "International Organizations as Teachers of Norms: The United Nations Educational, Scientific, and Cultural Organization and Science Policy." *International Organization* 47 (4): 565–97.

Finnemore, Martha. 1996a. *National Interests in International Society*. Ithaca: Cornell University Press.

Finnemore, Martha. 1996b. "Norms, Culture, and World Politics: Insights from Sociology's Institutionalism." *International Organization* 50 (2): 325–47.

Finnemore, Martha, and Kathryn Sikkink. 1998. "International Norm Dynamics and Political Change." *International Organization* 52 (4): 887–917.

Fischman, Robert L. 2005. "The Significance of National Wildlife Refuges in the Development of U.S. Conservation Policy." *Journal of Land Use & Environmental Law* 21 (1): 1–22.

Fox, Helen E., Carrie S. Soltanoff, Michael B. Mascia, Kelly M. Haisfield, Alfonso V. Lombana, Christopher R. Pyke, and Louisa Wood. 2012. "Explaining Global Patterns and Trends in Marine Protected Area (MPA) Development." *Marine Policy* 36 (5): 1131–38.

Freudenburg, William R. 1992. "Addictive Economies: Extractive Industries and Vulnerable Localities in a Changing World Economy." *Rural Sociology* 57 (3): 305–32.

Frieden, Jeffry A., and Ronald Rogowski. 1996. "The Impact of the International Economy on National Policies: An Analytical Overview." In *Internationalization and Domestic Politics*, edited by Robert O. Keohane and Helen V. Milner, 25–47. Cambridge: Cambridge University Press.

Friedlander, Alan, Yimnang Golbuu, Enric Ballesteros, Jennifer E. Caselle, Marine Gouezo, Dawnette Olsudong, and Enric Sala. 2017. "Size, Age, and Habitat Determine Effectiveness of Palau's Marine Protected Areas." *PLOS ONE* 12 (3).

Friedlander, Alan M., Jennifer E. Caselle, Enric Ballesteros, Eric K. Brown, Alan Turchik, and Enric Sala. 2014. "The Real Bounty: Marine Biodiversity in the Pitcairn Islands." *PloS One* 9 (6).

Fuchs, Doris A. 2007. *Business Power in Global Governance*. Boulder: Lynne Rienner Publishers.

Furnas, M. J. 2003. *Catchments and Corals: Terrestrial Runoff to the Great Barrier Reef*. Australian Institute of Marine Science & CRC Reef Research Centre.

Gaines, Steven D., Crow White, Mark H. Carr, and Stephen R. Palumbi. 2010. "Designing Marine Reserve Networks for Both Conservation and Fisheries Management." *Proceedings of the National Academy of Sciences* 107 (43): 18286–93.

Game, Edward T., Hedley S. Grantham, Alistair J. Hobday, Robert L. Pressey, Amanda T. Lombard, Lynnath E. Beckley, Kristina Gjerde, et al. 2009. "Pelagic Protected Areas: The Missing Dimension in Ocean Conservation." *Trends in Ecology & Evolution* 24 (7): 360–69.

Gamu, Jonathan, Philippe Le Billon, and Samuel Spiegel. 2015. "Extractive Industries and Poverty: A Review of Recent Findings and Linkage Mechanisms." *The Extractive Industries and Society* 2 (1): 162–76.

Gaymer, Carlos F., Angela V. Stadel, Natalie C. Ban, P. Cárcamo, Joseph Ierna, and Louise M. Lieberknecht. 2014. "Merging Top-Down and Bottom-Up Approaches in Marine Protected Areas Planning: Experiences from Around the Globe." *Aquatic Conservation: Marine and Freshwater Ecosystems* 24 (S2): 128–44.

Geddes, Barbara. 1990. "How the Cases You Choose Affect the Answers You Get: Selection Bias in Comparative Politics." *Political Analysis* 2: 131–50.

Goldstein, Judith, and Robert O. Keohane. 1993. "Ideas and Foreign Policy: An Analytical Framework." In *Ideas and Foreign Policy. Beliefs, Institutions, and Political Change*, edited by Judith Goldstein and Robert O. Keohane, 3–30. Ithaca: Cornell University Press.

Gourevitch, Peter Alexis, and James Shinn. 2005. *Political Power and Corporate Control: The New Global Politics of Corporate Governance*. Princeton: Princeton University Press.

Gray, John S. 1997. "Marine Biodiversity: Patterns, Threats and Conservation Needs." *Biodiversity & Conservation* 6 (1): 153–75.

Gruby, Rebecca L., and Xavier Basurto. 2013. "Multi-Level Governance for Large Marine Commons: Politics and Polycentricity in Palau's Protected Area Network." *Environmental Science & Policy* 33: 260–72.

Gruby, Rebecca L., Luke Fairbanks, Leslie Acton, Evan Artis, Lisa M. Campbell, Noella J. Gray, Lillian Mitchell, et al. 2017. "Conceptualizing Social Outcomes of Large Marine Protected Areas." *Coastal Management* 45 (6): 416–35.

Gulbrandsen, Lars H., and Steinar Andresen. 2004. "NGO Influence in the Implementation of the Kyoto Protocol: Compliance, Flexibility Mechanisms, and Sinks." *Global Environmental Politics* 4 (4): 54–75.

Halpern, Benjamin S. 2003. "The Impact of Marine Reserves: Do Reserves Work and Does Reserve Size Matter?" *Ecological Applications* 13 (sp1): 117–37.

Hartman, Brent J. 2011. "Extending the Scope of the Antiquities Act." *Public Land & Resources Law Review* 32: 192.

Haufler, Virginia. 2010. "Disclosure as Governance: The Extractive Industries Transparency Initiative and Resource Management in the Developing World." *Global Environmental Politics* 10 (3): 53–73.

Hazari, Bharat R. 1983. "On Factor Specificity, Trickle Down Effects and Regional Disparities in Income." *The Annals of Regional Science* 17 (2): 21–28.

Hilborn, Ray. 2015. "Marine Protected Areas Miss the Boat." *Science* 350 (6266): 1326.

Hilborn, Ray, and Daniel Ovando. 2014. "Reflections on the Success of Traditional Fisheries Management." *ICES Journal of Marine Science: Journal Du Conseil* 75 (5): 1040–46.

Hilborn, Ray, Kevin Stokes, Jean-Jacques Maguire, Tony Smith, Louis W Botsford, Marc Mangel, José Orensanz, et al. 2004. "When Can Marine Reserves Improve Fisheries Management?" *Ocean & Coastal Management* 47 (3–4): 197–205.

Hobday, Alistair J., Thomas A. Okey, Elvira S. Poloczanska, Thomas J. Kunz, and Anthony J. Richardson. 2006. *Impacts of Climate Change on Australian Marine Life*. Commonwealth of Australia.

Hocevar, John. 2016. "Ray Hilborn: Overfishing Denier." *Greenpeace*, May 12.

Hoegh-Guldberg, Ove, Peter J. Mumby, Anthony J. Hooten, Robert S. Steneck, Paul Greenfield, E. Gomez, C. Drew Harvell, et al. 2007. "Coral Reefs under Rapid Climate Change and Ocean Acidification." *Science* 318 (5857): 1737–42.

House of Representatives. 2013. *Parliamentary Debates: House of Representatives Official Hansard*, Forty-Third Parliament, First Session–Ninth Period, No. 7, June 4. Canberra: The Congress of the Commonwealth of Australia.

Howard, Brian Clark. 2014. "U.S. Creates Largest Protected Area in the World, 3X Larger than California." *National Geographic*, September 26.

Hughes, Terry P., Andrew H. Baird, David R. Bellwood, Margaret Card, Sean R. Connolly, Carl Folke, Richard Grosberg, et al. 2003. "Climate Change, Human Impacts, and the Resilience of Coral Reefs." *Science* 301 (5635): 929–33.

Humphreys, David. 2004. "Redefining the Issues: NGO Influence on International Forest Negotiations." *Global Environmental Politics* 4 (2): 51–74.

Hyde, Susan D. 2011. "Catch Us If You Can: Election Monitoring and International Norm Diffusion." *American Journal of Political Science* 55 (2): 356–69.

Jacques, Peter J. 2006. *Globalization and the World Ocean*. Lanham: AltaMira Press.

Jacques, Peter J., and Rafaella Lobo. 2018. "The Shifting Context of Sustainability: Growth and the World Ocean Regime." *Global Environmental Politics* 18 (4): 85–106.

Jameson, Stephen C, Mark H Tupper, and Jonathon M Ridley. 2002. "The Three Screen Doors: Can Marine 'Protected' Areas Be Effective?" *Marine Pollution Bulletin* 44 (11): 1177–83.

Jeffe-Bignoli, D., N. D. Burgress, H. Bingham, E. M. S. Belle, M. G. de Lima, M. Deguignet, B. Bertzky, et al. 2014. *Protected Planet Report 2014*. Cambridge: United Nations Environment Programme World Conservation Monitoring Centre.

Jentoft, Svein, Thijs C. van Son, and Maiken Bjørkan. 2007. "Marine Protected Areas: A Governance System Analysis." *Human Ecology* 35 (5): 611–22.

Johannes, Robert E. 1978. "Traditional Marine Conservation Methods in Oceania and Their Demise." *Annual Review of Ecology and Systematics* 9: 349–64.

Jones, Peter J. S., and Elizabeth M. De Santo. 2016. "Viewpoint–Is the Race for Remote, Very Large Marine Protected Areas (VLMPAs) Taking Us down the Wrong Track?" *Marine Policy* 73: 231–34.

Jones, Stephen R. G. 1984. *The Economics of Conformism*. Hoboken: Blackwell Publishing.

Jouffray, Jean-Baptiste, Robert Blasiak, Albert Norström, Henrik Österblom, and Magnus Nyström. 2020. "The Blue Acceleration: The Trajectory of Human Expansion into the Ocean." *One Earth* 2 (1): 43–54.

Kareiva, Peter. 2006. "Conservation Biology: Beyond Marine Protected Areas." *Current Biology* 16 (14): R533–R535.

Katzenstein, Peter J. 1996. *The Culture of National Security: Norms and Identity in World Politics*. New York: Columbia University Press.

Keck, Margaret E., and Kathryn Sikkink. 1998. *Activists beyond Borders: Advocacy Networks in International Politics*. Vol. 6. New York: Cambridge University Press.

Keck, Margaret E., and Kathryn Sikkink. 1999. "Transnational Advocacy Networks in International and Regional Politics." *International Social Science Journal* 51 (159): 89–101.

Kelley, Judith. 2008. "Assessing the Complex Evolution of Norms: The Rise of International Election Monitoring." *International Organization* 62 (2): 221–55.

Keohane, Robert O. 1990. "Empathy and International Regimes." In *Beyond Self-Interest*, edited by Jane J. Mansbridge, 227–36. Chicago: University of Chicago Press.

Keohane, Robert O. 2005. *After Hegemony: Cooperation and Discord in the World Political Economy*. Princeton: Princeton University Press.

Kerkhoff, Lorrae van, and Victoria Pilbeam. 2015. *Science, Culture and Community-Based Environmental Governance: A Pilot Study of Palau*. C2014/1285. Canberra: Australian Centre for International Agricultural Research.

Khagram, Sanjeev. 2004. *Dams and Development: Transnational Struggles for Water and Power*. Ithaca: Cornell University Press.

Khagram, Sanjeev, James V. Riker, and Kathryn Sikkink. 2002. *Restructuring World Politics: Transnational Social Movements, Networks, and Norms*. Minneapolis: University of Minnesota Press.

Klinsky, Sonja, Timmons Roberts, Saleemul Huq, Chukwumerije Okereke, Peter Newell, Peter Dauvergne, Karen O'Brien, et al. 2017. "Why Equity is Fundamental in Climate Change Policy Research." *Global Environmental Change* 44: 170–73.

Klotz, Audie. 1995. "Norms Reconstituting Interests: Global Racial Equality and US Sanctions against South Africa." *International Organization* 49 (3): 451–78.

Korauaba, Taberannang. 2015. "Protected Fisheries Area to Impact Kiribati's National Budget." *Island Business*, February 18.

Krook, Mona Lena, and Jacqui True. 2012. "Rethinking the Life Cycles of International Norms: The United Nations and the Global Promotion of Gender Equality." *European Journal of International Relations* 18 (1): 103–27.

Lamb, Joleah B., David H. Williamson, Garry R. Russ, and Bette L. Willis. 2015. "Protected Areas Mitigate Diseases of Reef-Building Corals by Reducing Damage from Fishing." *Ecology* 96 (9): 2555–67.

Le Billon, Philippe. 2013. "Resource Grabs." In *Corruption, Grabbing and Development: Real World Challenges*, edited by Tina Søreide and Aled Williams, 46–57. Northampton: Edward Elgar Publishing.

Leenhardt, Pierre, Bertrand Cazalet, Bernard Salvat, Joachim Claudet, and François Feral. 2013. "The Rise of Largescale Marine Protected Areas: Conservation or Geopolitics?" *Ocean & Coastal Management* 85: 112–18.

Lessig, Lawrence. 1995. "The Regulation of Social Meaning." *The University of Chicago Law Review* 62 (3): 943–1045.

Levy, David, and Peter Newell. 2005. "A Neo-Gramscian Approach to Business in International Environmental Politics: An Interdisciplinary, Multilevel Framework." In *The Business of Global Environmental Governance*, edited by David Levy and Peter Newell, 47–69. Cambridge: MIT Press.

Lewis, Jeffrey. 2003. "Institutional Environments and Everyday Decision Making: Rationalist or Constructivist?" *Comparative Political Studies* 36 (1–2): 97–124.

Liittschwager, David, and Susan Middleton. 2005. *Archipelago*. Washington, DC: National Geographic Society.

Lindblom, Charles E. 1982. "The Market as Prison." *The Journal of Politics* 44 (2): 323–36.

Lobo, Rafaella, and Peter J. Jacques. 2017. "SOFIA'S Choices: Discourses, Values, and Norms of the World Ocean Regime." *Marine Policy* 78: 26–33.

Lotze, Heike K., Hunter S. Lenihan, Bruce J. Bourque, Roger H. Bradbury, Richard G. Cooke, Matthew C. Kay, Susan M. Kidwell, et al. 2006. "Depletion, Degradation, and Recovery Potential of Estuaries and Coastal Seas." *Science* 312 (5781): 1806–09.

Lubchenco, Jane, Stephen R. Palumbi, Steven D. Gaines, and Sandy Andelman. 2003. "Plugging a Hole in the Ocean: The Emerging Science of Marine Reserves." *Ecological Applications* 13 (sp1): 3–7.

Lynham, John, Anton Nikolaev, Jennifer Raynor, Thaís Vilela, and Juan Carlos Villaseñor-Derbez. 2020. "Impact of Two of the World's Largest Protected Areas on Longline Fishery Catch Rates. *Nature Communications* 11 (979).

Magnuson, Warren, and Ted Stevens. 1976. *Fishery Conservation and Management Act of 1976. 16 U.S.C. 1801-1882; 90 Stat. 331.*

Mansbridge, Jane J. 1990. "Self-Interest in the Explanation of Political Life." In *Beyond Self Interest*, edited by Jane J. Mansbridge, 1–23. Chicago: University of Chicago Press.

March, James G., and Johan P. Olsen. 1983. "The New Institutionalism: Organizational Factors in Political Life." *American Political Science Review* 78 (3): 734–49.

March, James G., and Johan P. Olsen. 1998. "The Institutional Dynamics of International Political Orders." *International Organization* 52 (4): 943–69.

Marine Division. 2012. *Completing the Commonwealth Marine Reserves Network: Regulatory Impact Statement*. Canberra: Department of Sustainability, Environment, Water, Population and Communities.

McCook, Laurence J., Tony Ayling, Mike Cappo, J. Howard Choat, Richard D. Evans, Debora M. De Freitas, Michelle Heupel, et al. 2010. "Adaptive Management of the Great Barrier Reef: A Globally Significant Demonstration of the Benefits of Networks of Marine Reserves." *Proceedings of the National Academy of Sciences* 107 (43): 18278–85.

McLeod, Elizabeth, Rodney Salm, Alison Green, and Jeanine Almany. 2008. "Designing Marine Protected Area Networks to Address the Impacts of Climate Change." *Frontiers in Ecology and the Environment* 7 (7): 362–70.

Meder, Adrian. 2016. "'The Issue Was That Big, I Swear!': Evidence for the Real Impacts of Marine Protected Areas on Australian Recreational Fishing." In *Big, Bold and Blue: Lessons from Australia's Marine Protected Areas*, 349–62. Clayton: CSIRO Publishing.

Meyer, John W. 1979. *National Development and the World System: Educational, Economic, and Political Change; 1950-1970.* Chicago: University of Chicago Press.

Meyer, John W. 1980. "The World Polity and the Authority of the Nation-State." In *Studies of the Modern World-System*, edited by A. Bergesen, 109–58. New York: New York Academic Press.

Meyer, John W., John Boli, George M. Thomas, and Francisco O. Ramirez. 1997. "World Society and the Nation-State." *American Journal of Sociology* 103 (1): 144–81.

Meyer, John W., David John Frank, Ann Hironaka, Evan Schofer, and Nancy Brandon Tuma. 1997. "The Structuring of a World Environmental Regime, 1870–1990." *International Organization* 51 (4): 623–51.

Miller, Marian A. 1995. *The Third World in Global Environmental Politics*. Lanham: Lynne Rienner Publishers.

Milner, Helen V., and Robert O. Keohane. 1996. "Internationalization and Domestic Politics." In *Internationalization and Domestic Politics*, edited by Helen V. Milner and Robert O. Keohane, 1–22. New York: Cambridge University Press.

Morais, Gabriela Weber de, Achim Schlüter, and Marco Verweij. 2015. "Can Institutional Change Theories Contribute to the Understanding of Marine Protected Areas?" *Global Environmental Change* 31: 154–62.

Morato, Telmo, Simon D. Hoyle, Valerie Allain, and Simon J. Nicol. 2010. "Tuna Longline Fishing around West and Central Pacific Seamounts." *PLOS ONE* 5 (12).

Morgan, Lance. 2013. "Papahānaumokuākea Marine National Monument Case Study." Paper presented at the Argentina Oceanic MPA Workshop, Marine Conservation Institute, September 26.

Morrow, James D. 1994. "Modeling the Forms of International Cooperation: Distribution versus Information." *International Organization* 48 (3): 387–423.

Mullon, Christian, Pierre Fréon, and Philippe Cury. 2005. "The Dynamics of Collapse in World Fisheries." *Fish and Fisheries* 6 (2): 111–20.

Myers, Ransom A., and Boris Worm. 2003. "Rapid Worldwide Depletion of Predatory Fish Communities." *Nature* 423 (6937): 280–83.

Nadelmann, Ethan A. 1990. "Global Prohibition Regimes: The Evolution of Norms in International Society." *International Organization* 44 (4): 479–526.

Najam, Adil. 2005. "Why Environmental Politics Looks Different from the South." In *Handbook of Global Environmental Politics*, edited by Peter Dauvergne, 111–26. Northampton: Edward Elgar Publishing.

Newell, Peter. 2005. "Race, Class and the Global Politics of Environmental Inequality." *Global Environmental Politics* 5 (3): 70–94.

Newell, Peter. 2006. "Corporate Power and 'bounded Autonomy' in the Global Politics of Biotechnology." In *The International Politics of Genetically Modified Food*, edited by Robert Falkner, 67–84. Berlin: Springer.

Nielson, Daniel, Michael Tierney, and Catherine Weaver. 2006. "Bridging the Rationalist–Constructivist Divide: Re-Engineering the Culture of the World Bank." *Journal of International Relations and Development* 9 (2): 107–39.

Nixon, Rob. 2011. *Slow Violence and Environmentalism of the Poor*. Cambridge: Harvard University Press.

NOAA. 2015. "The MPA Inventory." *National Marine Protected Areas Center*. November 15.

NOAA. 2020. "The MPA Inventory." *National Marine Protected Areas Center*. June 10.

North, Douglass C. 1990. *Institutions, Institutional Change and Economic Performance*. New York: Cambridge University Press.

Nye, Joseph S., and Robert O. Keohane. 1971. "Transnational Relations and World Politics: An Introduction." *International Organization* 25 (3): 329–49.

Ocean Elders. 2014. "Letter to President Re: Pacific Remote Islands Marine National Monument | Ocean Elders." August 11.

Okereke, Chukwumerije. 2008. "Equity Norms in Global Environmental Governance." *Global Environmental Politics* 8 (3): 25–50.

Oracion, Enrique G., Marc L. Miller, and Patrick Christie. 2005. "Marine Protected Areas for Whom? Fisheries, Tourism, and Solidarity in a Philippine Community." *Ocean & Coastal Management* 48 (3): 393–410.

Pacific Islands Forum Fisheries Agency. 2014. Pacific Islands Forum Fisheries Agency 2013/14 Annual Report—Executive Summary. Honiara: Pacific Islands Forum Fisheries Agency.

Pala, Christopher. 2013. "Something's Fishy." *Earth Island Journal* 28 (3): 48.

Palau National Congress. 2003. *The Protected Areas Network Act. RPPL No. 6–39*.

Park, Susan, and Antje Vetterlein. 2010. *Owning Development: Creating Policy Norms in the IMF and the World Bank*. New York: Cambridge University Press.

Parks Australia. 2018. "Coral Sea Maps." Available at: https://parksaustralia.gov.au/marine/parks/coral-sea/maps/, last accessed 29 June 2019.

Pattberg, Philipp. 2006. "Private Governance and the South: Lessons from Global Forest Politics." *Third World Quarterly* 27 (4): 579–93.

Pauly, Daniel. 1995. "Anecdotes and the Shifting Baseline Syndrome of Fisheries." *Trends in Ecology & Evolution* 10 (10): 430.

Pauly, Daniel, Villy Christensen, Sylvie Guénette, Tony J. Pitcher, U. Rashid Sumaila, Carl J. Walters, Reg Watson, et al. 2002. "Towards Sustainability in World Fisheries." *Nature* 418 (6898): 689–95.

Pauly, Daniel, Reg Watson, and Jackie Alder. 2005. "Global Trends in World Fisheries: Impacts on Marine Ecosystems and Food Security." *Philosophical Transactions of the Royal Society B: Biological Sciences* 360 (1453): 5–12.

Pauly, Daniel, and Dirk Zeller, eds. 2016. *Global Atlas of Marine Fisheries: A Critical Appraisal of Catches and Ecosystem Impacts.* Washington: Island Press.

Payne, Rodger A. 2001. "Persuasion, Frames and Norm Construction." *European Journal of International Relations* 7 (1): 37–61.

Peluso, Nancy Lee. 1993. "Coercing Conservation?: The Politics of State Resource Control." *Global Environmental Change* 3 (2): 199–217.

Persha, Lauren, Harry Fischer, Ashwini Chhatre, Arun Agrawal, and Catherine Benson. 2010. "Biodiversity Conservation and Livelihoods in Human-Dominated Landscapes: Forest Commons in South Asia." *Biological Conservation* 143 (12): 2918–25.

Peterson, Angelie M., and Selina M. Stead. 2011. "Rule Breaking and Livelihood Options in Marine Protected Areas." *Environmental Conservation* 38 (3): 342–52.

Pierantozzi, Sandra S. 2000. "Palauans and Guest Workers: An Opinion Paper." *The Contemporary Pacific* 12 (2): 349–58.

PITI-VITI. 2020. Republic of Palau: Fiscal Year 2019: Statistical Appendices (Preliminary). Honolulu: Pacific Islands Training Initiative.

Pojas, Rhealyn. 2019. "Senate Says Palau Should Reciprocate Japan's Generosity by Allowing it to Fish After PMNS." *Island Times*, January 18.

Pomeroy, Robert S., John E. Parks, and Lani M. Watson. 2004. *How Is Your MPA Doing? A Guidebook of Natural and Social Indicators for Evaluating Marine Protected Area Management Effectiveness.* Gland: International Union for Conservation of Nature.

Prantl, Jochen, and Ryoko Nakano. 2011. "Global Norm Diffusion in East Asia How China and Japan Implement the Responsibility to Protect." *International Relations* 25 (2): 204–23.

Price, Richard. 1998. "Reversing the Gun Sights: Transnational Civil Society Targets Land Mines." *International Organization* 52 (3): 613–44.

Princen, Thomas. 1997. "The Shading and Distancing of Commerce: When Internalization is Not Enough." *Ecological Economics* 20 (3): 235–53.

Protected Planet. 2020. "Aichi 11 Target Dashboard." *UN Environment Programme* and *International Union for the Conservation of Nature.*

Reese, April. 2017. "Australian Government to Roll Back Marine Protections." *Science Magazine*, July 24.

Remengesau Jr., Tommy. 2016. David Helvarg interview with Tommy Remengesau Jr.

Revkin, Andrew C. 2016. "Obama's Expansion of Vast Pacific Reserve, Built on a Bush Foundation." *Dot Earth Blog.* https://dotearth.blogs.nytimes.com/2016/08/26/obamas-expansion-of-a-vast-pacific-reserve-built-on-a-bush-foundation/.

Rife, Alexis N., Brad Erisman, Alexandra Sanchez, and Octavio Aburto-Oropeza. 2013. "When Good Intentions Are Not Enough . . . Insights on Networks of 'Paper Park' Marine Protected Areas." *Conservation Letters* 6 (3): 200–12.

Risse, Thomas. 2016. *Domestic Politics and Norm Diffusion in International Relations: Ideas Do Not Float Freely.* Abingdon: Routledge.

Risse, Thomas, Stephen C. Ropp, and Kathryn Sikkink, eds. 1999. *The Power of Human Rights: International Norms and Domestic Change*. New York: Cambridge University Press.

Roberts, Callum M., Benjamin Halpern, Stephen R. Palumbi, and Robert R. Warner. 2001. "Designing Marine Reserve Networks Why Small, Isolated Protected Areas Are Not Enough." *Conservation in Practice* 2 (3): 10–17.

Rodrik, Dani. 1997. *Has Globalization Gone Too Far?* Washington, DC: Institute for International Economics.

Rodrik, Dani. 2011. *The Globalization Paradox: Democracy and the Future of the World Economy*. New York: W.W. Norton.

Roessig, J., C. Woodley, J. Cech, and L. Hansen. 2004. "Effects of Global Climate Change on Marine and Estuarine Fishes and Fisheries." *Reviews in Fish Biology and Fisheries* 14 (2): 251–75.

Rucht, Dieter, Hanspeter Kriesi, and Donatella della Porta. 1999. *Social Movements in a Globalizing World*. New York: St. Martin's Press.

Ruello, N. 2011. *A Study of the Composition, Value and Utilisation of Imported Seafood in Australia*. Canberra: Fisheries Research and Development Corporation.

Rutzick, Mark C. 2010. "Modern Remedies for Antiquated Laws: Challenging National Monument Designations under the 1906 Antiquities Act." *Engage* 11 (2): 29–36.

Sabatier, Paul A., and Christopher M. Weible. 2007. "The Advocacy Coalition Framework: Innovations and Clarifications." In *Theories of the Policy Process*, edited by Paul A. Sabatier, Second Edition, 189–217. Boulder, CO: Westview Press.

Sala, Enric, and Sylvaine Giakoumi. 2017. "No-Take Marine Reserves are the Most Effective Protected Areas in the Ocean." *ICES Journal of Marine Science* 75 (3): 1166–68.

Sala, Enric, and Sylvaine Giakoumi. 2018. "Counterpoint to Hilborn." *ICES Journal of Marine Science* 75 (3): 1163–64.

Sala, Enric, Lance Morgan, Elliott Norse, and Alan Friedlander. 2014. Expansion of the U.S. Pacific Remote Islands Marine National Monument. Washington, DC: Marine Conservation Institute.

Salant, Stephen W. 1976. "Exhaustible Resources and Industrial Structure: A Nash-Cournot Approach to the World Oil Market." *Journal of Political Economy* 84 (5): 1079–93.

Sandin, Stuart A., Jennifer E. Smith, Edward E. DeMartini, Elizabeth A. Dinsdale, Simon D. Donner, Alan M. Friedlander, Talina Konotchick, et al. 2008. "Baselines and Degradation of Coral Reefs in the Northern Line Islands." *PloS One* 3 (2).

Schlosberg, David. 2007. *Defining Environmental Justice: Theories, Movements, and Nature*. Oxford: Oxford University Press.

Schofer, Evan, and Ann Hironaka. 2005. "The Effects of World Society on Environmental Protection Outcomes." *Social Forces* 84 (1): 25–47.

Scott, W. Richard, and John W. Meyer. 1994. *Institutional Environments and Organizations: Structural Complexity and Individualism*. Thousand Oaks: SAGE.

Seawright, Jason, and John Gerring. 2008. "Case Selection Techniques in Case Study Research a Menu of Qualitative and Quantitative Options." *Political Research Quarterly* 61 (2): 294–308.

Seidman, Gay W. 2007. *Beyond the Boycott: Labor Rights, Human Rights, and Transnational Activism*. New York: Russell Sage Foundation.

Selig, Elizabeth R., and John F. Bruno. 2010. "A Global Analysis of the Effectiveness of Marine Protected Areas in Preventing Coral Loss." *PLoS One* 5 (2).

Sikkink, Kathryn. 1993. "Human Rights, Principled Issue-Networks, and Sovereignty in Latin America." *International Organization* 47 (3): 411–41.

Simmons, Beth, Frank Dobbin, and Geoffrey Garrett. 2008. "Introduction: The Diffusion of Liberalization." In *The Global Diffusion of Markets and Democracy*, edited by Beth Simmons, Frank Dobbin, and Geoffrey Garrett, 1–63. Cambridge: Cambridge University Press.

Smail, Stephanie. 2016. "Conservationists Criticise Plan to Reduce Coral Sea Marine Park Protection." *ABC News*, September 6.

Snow, David A., E. Burke Rochford, Steven K. Worden, and Robert D. Benford. 1986. "Frame Alignment Processes, Micromobilization, and Movement Participation." *American Sociological Review* 51 (4): 464–81.

Stalley, Phillip. 2018. "Norms from the Periphery: Tracing the Rise of the Common but Differentiated Principle in International Environmental Politics." *Cambridge Review of International Affairs* 31 (2): 141–61.

Steinberg, Paul F. 2001. *Environmental Leadership in Developing Countries: Transnational Relations and Biodiversity Policy in Costa Rica and Bolivia*. Cambridge: MIT Press.

Stoeckl, Natalie, Alastair Birtles, Marina Farr, Arnold Mangott, Matthew Curnock, and Peter Valentine. 2010. "Live-Aboard Dive Boats in the Great Barrier Reef: Regional Economic Impact and the Relative Values of Their Target Marine Species." *Tourism Economics* 16 (4): 995–1018.

Strang, David, and Patricia Mei Yin Chang. 1993. "The International Labor Organization and the Welfare State: Institutional Effects on National Welfare Spending, 1960–80." *International Organization* 47 (2): 235–62.

Stroup, Sarah S., and Amanda Murdie. 2012. "There's No Place like Home: Explaining International NGO Advocacy." *The Review of International Organizations* 7 (4): 425–48.

Studds, Gerry E. 1992. *National Marine Sanctuaries Reauthorization Act. P.L. 102–587*.

Sumaila, U. Rashid, Dirk Zeller, Reg Watson, Jackie Alder, and Daniel Pauly. 2007. "Potential Costs and Benefits of Marine Reserves in the High Seas." *Marine Ecology Progress Series* 345: 305–310.

Sunstein, Cass R. 1999. *Free Markets and Social Justice*. Oxford: Oxford University Press.

Sutton, S., and O. Li. 2008. "Attitudes of Recreational Fishers to the Rezoning of the Great Barrier Reef Marine Park." In *Proceedings of the 2008 Marine and Tropical Sciences Research Facility Annual Conference*, compiled by Robin Taylor and Suzaane Long, 96–101. Cairns: Reef and Rainforest Research Centre Limited.

Tallberg, Jonas, Lisa M. Dellmuth, Hans Agné, and Andreas Duit. 2018. "NGO Influence in International Organizations: Information, Access and Exchange." *British Journal of Political Science* 48 (1): 213–38.

Tarrow, Sidney. 2005. *The New Transnational Activism*. New York: Cambridge University Press.

Terrill, Eric, Seth Horstmeyer, Koebel Sakuma, Richard Douglass, and Ellen Kappel. 2015. *The Republic of Palau Exclusive Economic Zone Monitoring, Control, and Surveillance: The Next Five Years, 2016–2021*. Koror.

The Pew Charitable Trusts. 2014. *Expanded Protections for a U.S. Pacific Ocean Treasure*. The Pew Charitable Trusts.

The Pew Charitable Trusts. 2015. *Proposed Palau National Marine Sanctuary Map*. The Pew Charitable Trusts.

Tiberghien, Yves. 2007. *Entrepreneurial States: Reforming Corporate Governance in France, Japan, and Korea*. Ithaca: Cornell University Press.

Tilly, Charles. 2005. *Social Movements, 1768–2004*. Abingdon: Routledge.

Toonen, Robert J., T'Aulani Wilhelm, Sara M. Maxwell, Daniel Wagner, Brian W. Bowen, Charles RC Sheppard, Sue M. Taei, et al. 2013. "One Size Does Not Fit All: The Emerging Frontier in Largescale Marine Conservation." *Marine Pollution Bulletin* 77 (1): 7–10.

Udall, Tom, and Deb Haaland. 2019. *Antiquities Act of 2019, S.367, U.S.C.*

Ueki, Minoru, and Sarah M. Clayton. 1999. "Eco-Consciousness in Traditional Palauan Society." *Asian Geographer* 18 (1–2): 47–66.

UNGA (UN General Assembly). 2019. *A/CONF.232/2019/6.*

Urbina, Ian. 2016. "Palau vs. the Poachers." *The New York Times*, February 17.

US Department of Commerce. 2014. "Fisheries Economics of the United States 2012." NOAA Technical Memorandum NMFS-F/SPO-137. Silver Spring: National Oceanic and Atmospheric Administration.

Uyarra, Maria C., Andrew R. Watkinson, and Isabelle M. Cote. 2009. "Managing Dive Tourism for the Sustainable Use of Coral Reefs: Validating Diver Perceptions of Attractive Site Features." *Environmental Management* 43 (1): 1–16.

van der Pijl, Kees. 1989. "Ruling Classes, Hegemony, and the State System: Theoretical and Historical Considerations." *International Journal of Political Economy* 19 (3): 7–35.

Vernon, Raymond. 1980. "The Obsolescing Bargain: A Key Factor in Political Risk." *The International Essays for Business Decision Makers* 5: 281–86.

Vianna, G. M. S., M. G. Meekan, D. Pannell, S. Marsh, and J. J. Meeuwig. 2010. *Wanted Dead or Alive? The Relative Value of Reef Sharks as a Fishery and an Ecotourism Asset in Palau*. Perth: Australian Institute of Marine Science and University of Western Australia.

Walters, Carl, and Jean-Jacques Maguire. 1996. "Lessons for Stock Assessment from the Northern Cod Collapse." *Reviews in Fish Biology and Fisheries* 6 (2): 125–37.

Wapner, Paul. 1995. "Politics beyond the State: Environmental Activism and World Civic Politics." *World Politics* 47 (3): 311–40.

Wapner, Paul. 2002. "Horizontal Politics: Transnational Environmental Activism and Global Cultural Change." *Global Environmental Politics* 2 (2): 37–62.

Webster, D. G. 2009. *Adaptive Governance: The Dynamics of Atlantic Fisheries Management*. Cambridge: MIT Press.

Webster, D. G. 2015. *Beyond the Tragedy in Global Fisheries*. Cambridge: MIT Press.

Weeks, Rebecca, Garry R. Russ, Angel C. Alcala, and Alan T. White. 2010. "Effectiveness of Marine Protected Areas in the Philippines for Biodiversity Conservation." *Conservation Biology* 24 (2): 531–40.

Weible, Christopher M. 2007. "An Advocacy Coalition Framework Approach to Stakeholder Analysis: Understanding the Political Context of California Marine Protected Area Policy." *Journal of Public Administration Research and Theory* 17 (1): 95–117.

Wendt, Alexander. 1987. "The Agent–Structure Problem in International Relations Theory." *International Organization* 41 (3): 335–70.

West, Paige, and Dan Brockington. 2006. "An Anthropological Perspective on Some Unexpected Consequences of Protected Areas." *Conservation Biology* 20 (3): 609–16.

Western Pacific Regional Fishery Management Council. 2014. "An Ocean Legacy the US Pacific Island Way." Western Pacific Regional Fishery Management Council.

Whatmough, Sally, Ingrid Van Putten, and Andrew Chin. 2011. "From Hunters to Nature Observers: A Record of 53 Years of Diver Attitudes towards Sharks and Rays and Marine Protected Areas." *Marine and Freshwater Research* 62 (6): 755–63.

White, Cliff. 2019a. "South Pacific Tuna Corporation Executive Director Criticizes Global Tuna Trade." *SeafoodSource*, April 26.

White, Cliff. 2019b. "US Tuna Fleet Faces Tenuous Future." *SeafoodSource*, August 1.

White, Timothy D., Aaron B. Carlisle, David A Kroodsma, Barbara A. Block, Renato Casagrandi, Giulio A. De Leo, Marino Gatto, et al. 2017. "Assessing the Effectiveness of a Large Marine Protected Area for Reef Shark Conservation." *Biological Conservation* 207: 64–71.

Wilhelm, T'Aulani, Charles R. C. Sheppard, Anne L. S. Sheppard, Carlos F. Gaymer, John Parks, Daniel Wagner, and Nai Lewis. 2014. "Large Marine Protected Areas— Advantages and Challenges of Going Big." *Aquatic Conservation: Marine and Freshwater Ecosystems* 24 (S2): 24–30.

Williams, Marc. 2005. "The Third World and Global Environmental Negotiations: Interests, Institutions and Ideas." *Global Environmental Politics* 5 (3): 48–69.

Wood, Louisa J., Lucy Fish, Josh Laughren, and Daniel Pauly. 2008. "Assessing Progress towards Global Marine Protection Targets: Shortfalls in Information and Action." *Oryx* 42 (3): 340–51.

Worm, Boris. 2016. "Averting a Global Fisheries Disaster." *Proceedings of the National Academy of Sciences* 113 (18): 4895–897.

Zürn, Michael, and Jeffrey Checkel. 2005. "Getting Socialized to Build Bridges: Constructivism and Rationalism, Europe and the Nation-State." *International Organization* 59 (4): 1045–79.

Index

For the benefit of digital users, indexed terms that span two pages (e.g., 52–53) may, on occasion, appear on only one of those pages.

Tables and figures are indicated by *t* and *f* following the page number.